IMAGES OF THE OHIO VALLEY

THE ANDREW H. CLARK SERIES
IN THE HISTORICAL GEOGRAPHY OF NORTH AMERICA

Images of the Ohio Valley

A Historical Geography of Travel, 1740 to 1860

John A. Jakle

CARTOGRAPHER
Miklos Pinther

NEW YORK
OXFORD UNIVERSITY PRESS
1977

Copyright © 1977 by Oxford University Press, Inc.

Library of Congress Cataloging in Publication Data
Jakle, John A
  Images of the Ohio Valley.
  (The Andrew H. Clark series in historical geography
  of North America)
  Bibliography: p.
  Includes index.
    1. Ohio—Valley—Historical geography.   2. Ohio
  Valley—Description and travel.   I.   Title.
  F517.J28   977'.02   77-9570
  ISBN 0-19-502240-8
  ISBN 0-19-502241-6 pbk.

Printed in the United States of America

For Cindy

PREFACE

This book deals with the early Ohio Valley landscape, not so much as it was, but more as it was thought to be. Place images are my primary concern, specifically the place images recorded by travelers on their journeys in the Ohio Valley between 1740 and 1860. My region is that entire expanse of territory in North America encompassing the drainage of the Ohio River and its many tributaries. Conceptualized initially as a wilderness, this region was rid of its Indian inhabitants and converted to farms and cities. Changes manifested in the landscape were described by travelers, many themselves participants in the Indian conflicts, the establishment of agriculture, or the pursuit of commerce and industry. Others came strictly as tourists to see what had been accomplished in this first American "West."

In focusing on travelers' impressions, I ask the following questions: How was the Ohio Valley's early geography organized cognitively by those who traveled in the region? What did people think they saw? What did they think it meant? What satisfactions did they derive? I begin in Chapters 1 and 2 by exploring the travelers themselves. Who were they? How were they oriented to the landscape? Chapter 3 treats the "Wilder Images" of nature, the environment as relatively unspoiled by human activity. Chapters 4 and 5 concern the images of aboriginal life and military life as the Indians and the Americans enter an extended period of warfare. Chapter 6 treats "Pastoral Images," the impressions of the evolving agrarian landscape, and Chapter 7 treats "Urban Images," the view of the Ohio Valley's new towns and cities.

Since travelers' accounts constitute the raw material for this book, I allow the travelers to speak directly to the reader through numerous quotations. I hope that the reader will derive a greater feeling for the geographical past by experiencing past landscapes by way of the travelers' own words and not by my synthesis alone. Travel accounts are emphasized over other sources of information for two reasons. First, travelers of the eighteenth and the nineteenth century played peculiar roles relative to their geographical environments. They came with fresh eyes as strangers to new places. Most travelers had a heightened sense of environmental awareness. Second, it is my assumption that readers in the twentieth century will identify more readily with past geography through the idea of traveling. Travel carries a sense of adventure toward exploring new places. Let the reader closely identify with the travelers of the past to more readily appreciate the Ohio Valley's geographic past.

CONTENTS

FIGURES

*. . . the feel and the atmosphere, the layout and lingo,
of regions, of breeds of men, of customs and slogans, in
a manner and air not given in regular history.*

Carl Sandburg

IMAGES OF THE OHIO VALLEY

1 INTRODUCTION

When we cast our eyes on the map of any country, especially a new country, in which little else is seen than the situation of mountains, rivers, and plains, we are desirous to know what is the state of its soil and climate; what are the advantages its inhabitants may be expected to enjoy.

Gilbert Imlay, 1793

The Ohio Valley Concept

When English Americans in the mid-1700s looked west beyond the Blue Ridge Mountains, they imagined a vast territory sparsely populated and essentially available for the taking. Nomenclature used to identify this area varied from broad references to the "West" to specific concerns with locality as reflected in the names of the various land speculations fostered in anticipation of a second tier of English colonies beyond the mountains. Companies or intended colonies with such names as Ohio, Greenbrier, Pittsylvania, Indiana, Vandalia, Mississippi, Illinois, Wabash, and Transylvania were established between 1747 and 1774. Several names referred to the wilderness beyond the mountains; several referred to the American Indian. However, most names referred to western rivers, the most important landscape referents of the western traders, soldiers, and land speculators. The rivers and their associated valleys were important as prospective migration routes and promised future trade linkage to outside areas.

After the American Revolution no western river was as important as the Ohio River. Along with its tributaries (such as the Allegheny, the Kanawha, the Tennessee, the Cumberland, and the Wabash) it drained nearly three-quarters of the western land controlled by the new United States (Fig. 1-1). To the north lay the Great Lakes, dominated until the War of 1812 by the British fur trade; to the south were lands largely controlled by Spain until the establishment of Mississippi Territory in 1798. It is not surprising, therefore, that the Ohio Valley became synonymous with the West. The importance of the Ohio River in the nation's early fortunes was reflected by the names given the first territorial governments beyond the mountains. The "Territory North West of the Ohio" was established in 1787 and the "Territory South West of the Ohio" in 1790.

Although the name "Ohio" was attached early to the eastern portion of the Northwest Territory with the creation of the second Ohio Company in 1786, the broader term "Ohio Valley" was put to general use to describe the region centered on and drained by the Ohio River. The Ohio Valley remained an important regional conception through the mid-nineteenth century. This book concerns the evolution and decline of that conception as it explores the changing images associated with Ohio Valley regional stereotypes. Although most Americans in the late eighteenth and the early nineteenth century thought of the Ohio Valley as an integrated and highly uniform region, the specific images used to define the region varied between groups and through time. What was largely a wilderness in 1740 had by 1840 experienced the devastation of war, conversion by American settlers into an agrarian landscape, and the evolution of an urban civilization.

The creation of "free soil" states north of the Ohio River and the encouragement of slavery to the south eventually spelled the end of the Ohio Valley as a viable regional conception. By the 1830s most Americans had come to recognize a basic division between "North" and "South," with the Ohio River serving as a convenient boundary in the West between the two areas. With the rapid construction of the trunk line railroads in the 1850s the northern portion of the Ohio Valley was integrally linked with the Northeast. This area, midway between eastern centers of population and the new West of the Great Plains and Rockies, became a part of the "Middle West," specifically the "Lower Middle West." Similarly, the southern portion of the Ohio Valley came eventually to be known as the "Upper South."

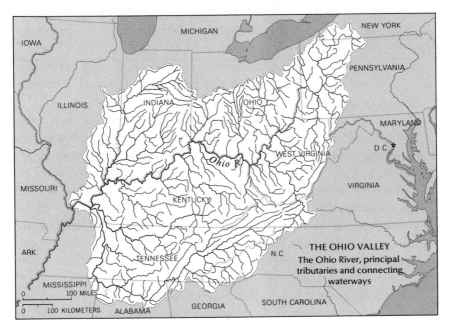

IOWA

MICHIGAN

NEW YORK

PENNSYLVANIA

ILLINOIS INDIANA OHIO

MARYLAND

D.C.

WEST VIRGINIA

Ohio R.

MISSOURI

VIRGINIA

KENTUCKY

ARK. N.C. **THE OHIO VALLEY**
The Ohio River, principal
tributaries and connecting
waterways

TENNESSEE

MISSISSIPPI
0   100 MILES
0   100 KILOMETERS ALABAMA GEORGIA SOUTH CAROLINA

Figure 1-1.

The Concept of Place

This book concerns the early Ohio Valley, but not the region as it really
was so much as the region it was thought to be. It concerns the impressions which travelers in the Ohio Valley recorded in their dairies, journals, and letters. The act of traveling in the eighteenth and the
nineteenth century usually involved a special relationship to one's
surroundings. Travelers in pursuing their routes usually tread new or
unfamiliar ground and read the landscape out of necessity in order to
ensure correct and proper passage. Traveling, being outside the daily
routine, imposed strain. Indeed, the word travel derived from the
French word "travail" meaning "trouble," "work," or "torment." Food
was often strange and available only at inopportune times; sleeping
arrangements were irregular. Primitive roads made traveling a true
adventure.

Beyond the logistics of travel were the opportunities to observe new
places and develop new insights. New places were sought out, experi-

enced, and, if possible, enjoyed. In doing so, travelers played special roles which served to relate them to their environments as strangers. The impressions which they recorded in their journals have special value. They reflect not the ordinary day-to-day awareness of people pursuing routine lives, but the heightened sensitivities of strangers deliberately encountering new places.

This book focuses on travelers' experiences recorded between 1740 and the Civil War. The 1740s marked the beginnings of English settlement in the Valley, and the Civil War marked the beginnings of rapid industrial change in the region. After 1860 few travelers bothered to record their experiences so easy had traveling become on the new railroads. Railroads had begun to tie the nation together and, as far as new construction in the landscape was concerned, rural and urban landscapes had begun to look increasingly alike. Distinctive differences between regions were muted, and there was little impetus to describe travel experiences which were increasingly common.

For travelers, the Ohio Valley concept was a hierarchy of related place images. Diagrammed is an example (Fig. 1-2). At a very general level most travelers' perceptions of the region involved stereotypes of natural and man-made environment. Many travelers were more concerned with nature and chose to focus on what I call the "wilder images." Man-made environments, in turn, were usually thought of as either rural or urban. Cities were usually categorized by size. Named places at various levels of a hierarchy (such as the Ohio Valley and the city of Cincinnati) were linked by general categories of place meaning (such as small town versus large city, urban versus rural, or natural versus man-made). Cincinnati, as the largest city in the region, contributed to most travelers' images of the Ohio Valley through ideas of urbanity and cultural landscape. Conversely, Cincinnati was known according to its regional setting.

The meaning given any city, town, rural neighborhood, or wilder area involved stereotyping its various behavioral settings. Usually private and public spaces were differentiated. Of the latter, travelers paid particular attention to taverns and to streets and highways, the settings travelers most frequented. Taverns, for example, were seen to constitute clusters of specific settings or situations for behavior. For most travelers barrooms differed from bedroom images, to beg an obvious example.

It is my intention to describe the most important images of the early

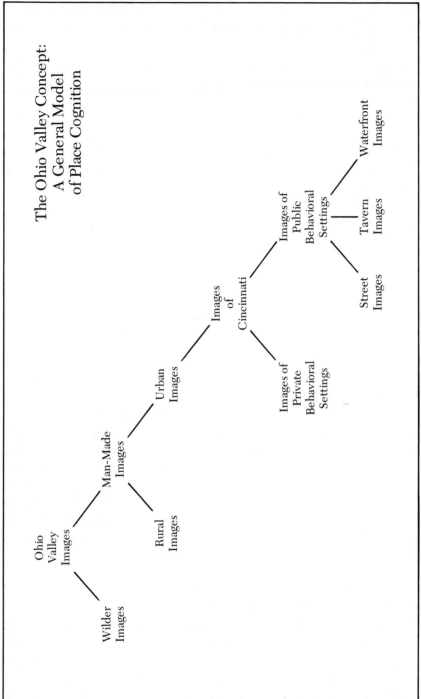

The Ohio Valley Concept:
A General Model
of Place Cognition

Ohio
Valley
Images

Wilder
Images

Man-Made
Images

Rural
Images

Urban
Images

Images
of
Cincinnati

Images of
Private
Behavioral
Settings

Images of
Public
Behavioral
Settings

Street
Images

Tavern
Images

Waterfront
Images

Figure 1-2.

Ohio Valley as recorded by travelers. I intend to show how specific places at various scales of definition were linked in a composite of imagery by general categories of place meaning. In this book I emphasize the images of (1) peacetime travel (routes and travel facilities), (2) wilder places (wilderness), (3) aboriginal life, (4) warfare (battlefields and forts), (5) pastoral places (farms and rural life), and (6) urban places (towns and urban life).

Places are given meaning on the basis of behavioral expectations. They are known by the people, the activities, and the objects commonly found in them. They are also known by their location relative to other places and the scheduling (opening and closing) of their activities. For example, at taverns in the early Ohio Valley males could obtain "spiritous liquor" and both men and women could obtain meals and overnight lodging. If a settlement contained a tavern it was appropriately considered a town, for taverns accommodated outsiders, a vital urban function. In "houses of private entertainment," as opposed to "public houses," services were more restricted and decorum more at the discretion of the host. Each type of tavern required different rituals of approach and different forms of conduct. Much of the difficulty and intrigue of traveling involved discovery and perfection of the idiosyncrasies of appropriate behavior as it varied from one setting and from one locality to another.

Each kind of place was symbolized differently in the landscape. Many images recorded by travelers derived from a persistent drive to identify landscape cues thus to orient properly to intended or expected social intercourse. Settings of a particular type were usually structured similarly, furnished and decorated in a similar manner, and often advertised using a highly standardized sign. Each of the most important types of settings in any community had their own peculiar look or signature. Residences, business buildings, churches, and government buildings were rarely mistaken one for another.

Value Orientations to Place

Once places were identified in a landscape, specific meanings were attached on the basis of past experience. Of most importance were the values people brought with them, rooted in their own personalities and the cultural heritage of their particular class or society. Thus the discussion of travelers' impressions that follows reflects as much on the backgrounds of the travelers themselves as it does on the reality of the past Ohio Valley landscape. Nonetheless, travelers shared certain impressions of their environment. In this book I pay particular attention to the following value systems: (1) utilitarian, (2) romantic, (3) picturesque, and (4) ecological values.

THE UTILITARIAN APPROACH

In its most severe form the utilitarian approach to landscape valued little that was not of immediate use to short-run profit-taking. This was, of course, the prevailing American view of environment. Landscapes were valued only in so far as they promised materialistic benefit. The British lecturer and writer James Buckingham remarked that Americans did not have strong perceptions of such a thing as beauty in landscape, for "they love their money too well."[1] Nature was unsentimentally regarded as a commodity. Where wealth could be extracted the natural environment was appreciated. Where nature threatened life or seemingly obstructed profit-taking it was treated with hostility. The same was true of man-made features. Landscape, in whatever form, was viewed primarily as possessing opportunity for personal gain.

Utilitarian landscapes reflected upon the people who inhabited them. One German traveler, Moritz Busch, declared in 1853 that Americans were "of a commercial spirit: cold, sober, cleverly calculating, intellectually ambitious, and a bit too hasty."[2] Almost everything that might have been considered romantic had been completely expunged from the land and the people. Only in the backward mountains of eastern Kentucky and western Virginia could romantic people be found, but even there "the chilling, sobering, leveling principle (disguised as merchants and preachers)" had pushed in from the North "on railroads and steamboats," he wrote.[3]

THE ROMANTIC APPROACH

Only where heroic events had occurred, where relics of the past remained on the landscape, or where nature survived pristine were romantic images likely. The young American James Hall summarized the influence that such places could have on the perceptive few. "Blame me not," he wrote, "for yielding, amid such scenes, to the influence of feeling, and giving up my whole soul to wild, and warm, and visionary fancies. It is a humiliating reflection that our sweetest hours are those

which are least connected with the realities of life."[4] Hall remarked of
western Pennsylvania that it was an endless task to point out all the
"fairy spots" which embellished that romantic country. The hills, valleys, and streams delighted the traveler not merely by their intrinsic
beauty, but also by evoking the heroic events of the pioneer past. "This
was one of the first points selected by those who commenced the work
of civilization in the western country," he wrote. "Here all the difficulties of a new settlement—the horrors of Indian warfare and the
bereavements of an isolated society . . . were encountered to the
fullest extent."[5]

Hall looked to the day when the poet and novelist would traverse
the region. One such novelist was Charles Dickens who, bored with
utilitarian scenes of primitive cabins and half-cleared fields, began to
fantasize. "Stumps of trees are a curious feature in American travelling," he wrote. "The very illusions they present to the unaccustomed
eye as it grows dark, are quite astonishing. . . . Now there is a Gre-
cian urn erected in the center of a lonely field; now there a woman
weeping at a tomb."[6] Deprived of "real" antiquity in the American
landscape, a European's quest for the romantic could strain the imagination. As Frances Trollope, the most controversial of all the English
visitors, put it, "Were there occasionally a ruined abbey or a feudal
castle, to mix the romance of real life with that of nature, the Ohio
would be perfect."[7]

Romantics sought emotional release in landscape. On crossing the
mountains on the National Road west of Cumberland in Maryland, one
traveler found himself deeply moved by the somber scene. "The still-
ness, the indefinite and mystic character of the forest, as if forming a
sort of infinite labyrinth; the stupendous rocks and precipices; the
moaning of waters as they rolled down the gullies . . . and then the
gradual appearance of night" formed a "general gloom" which produced "most melancholy sensations."[8] Another traveler was elated as
he stood where the National Road topped the bluff behind Wheeling.
"The Ohio is beneath your feet," he wrote. "The clear majestic tide,
the fertile islands . . . , the bold and towering heights opposite . . .
round which the river sweeps . . . present a splendid combination of
natural beauties: while the recollection of the wild border history of
this once frontier stream . . . throws a moral yet romantic charm upon
the memory: no man will ever forget his first view of the Ohio."[9] (See
Figure 1-3.)

Figure 1-3.
View of Wheeling, Virginia, c. 1840. Here travelers on the National Road caught their first glimpse of the Ohio River. (Charles A. Dana, *The United States Illustrated*, New York, n.d.)

THE PICTURESQUE APPROACH

Closely related to the romantic was the picturesque. Whereas the former might involve a quest for beauty in landscape, the latter always sought a particular kind of beauty: the view or scene whose perspective impressed the mind in an almost photographic manner. The picturesque approach to landscape was evolved by the English empiricists who placed emphasis on the senses as the source of what one knows. Vision was considered the most important of the senses, and those who pursued the picturesque sought to provide the mind with maximum visual stimulation. The English gentleman took pleasure in his surroundings. Many took to the wilder areas of the English Lake District and the Scottish Highlands in search of stimulating scenes that could be framed in the mind's eye. Many sought wilder images in North America and in so doing brought the idea of the picturesque across the Atlantic.

To the cultured Briton the American's lack of feeling for the picturesque was disturbing. James Buckingham, traveling the National Road
west from Wheeling, remarked on the lack of interest on the part of
American stage passengers in the passing scene:

> The constant succession of hill and valley in our route was complained
> of as an evil by most of our companions who had no perception of the
> beautiful landscape; indeed, this absence of taste for the . . . beauti-
> ful in nature appears to be a national characteristic.[10]

Another Englishman found that traveling among people who lacked
sympathy for beauty produced "languor and turpidity" of thought.[11]
Living in communities "so little alive to impressions of nature" caused
him to gradually fall into a "low estimate" of them himself. After a
while he regarded beauty as "little better than polished indolence."[12]

The word *sublime* was used to characterize the very unusual in the
picturesque; that which words were thought incapable of fully describing. The American Edmund Flagg revealed that sublimity was a result
not merely of "massive, extended, unmeasured greatness," but that
more often this feeling arose from the "combination of vast and powerful objects."[13] Thus the Ohio River "rolling its volumed floods through
half a continent" was sublime.[14] The word was easily overworked as
travelers used it as a kind of shorthand to describe scenes they really
did not care to detail. Properly used, however, it related to the visual
images that were capable of moving the emotions through the magnifi-
cence or power of the scene.

THE ECOLOGICAL APPROACH

Even among the earliest travelers to the Ohio Valley were men interested in natural history and science. After 1830 many women, particularly Europeans, also traveled for scientific edification, collecting specimens of plants and animals, visiting the learned men of the region, and
otherwise involving themselves in the objective study of nature. Few
were disappointed for, as one American boasted in the 1830s, the region contained the greatest variety of natural habitats from the
"mildest" to the "wildest, most rugged, abrupt, lofty, or depressed,
awful and sublime."[15] In the 1790s the naturalist Gilbert Imlay wrote
of the need to study the roots of human civilization in nature. To him
the Ohio Valley seemed an ideal laboratory. "When the unfolding covers of a new creation just bursting from the womb of nature, shall draw

men of science to trace and investigate the various phenomena which this country exhibits, I have no doubt," he wrote, "but the world will receive much pleasure and instruction."[16]

The approach of the natural historian embraced objectivity in the study of environment. Through the eighteenth and the nineteenth century, this primarily involved the discovery, naming, and cataloging of natural phenomena. For the few it embraced the posing and testing of general theories. Of course, the "grave sciences" did not excite everyone. James Hall, the would-be Romanticist, wrote that he would never be able to endure "the drudgery of travelling with an apparatus of microscopes, crucibles, thermometers, and quadrants" to say nothing of "maps, common-place books, and writing materials."[17]

The Travelers

Who were the travelers who recorded their impressions? Certainly they were a varied group, and yet they all had one important thing in common. They considered their journeys so beyond the ordinary that records of their impressions were kept. Whether these travelers differed substantially from those who did not keep travel diaries will never be known. I suspect that the journalists were something of a special breed, perhaps more aware of landscape and thus more observant of the passing scene. Certainly, the act of writing down impressions would have made them more observant. Meriwether Lewis, for one, realized this and practiced describing the Ohio River before launching his exploration of the Missouri River and the Pacific Northwest.[18]

THE ROUTES TRAVELED

Where people traveled obviously influenced what they saw. Thus I made an attempt to map all the travelers' routes, stopping places, and modes of travel for various periods. However, only 387 of the 468 available accounts of travel provided sufficient detail.[19] Aggregate travel patterns for the following periods are mapped: (A) 1740 to 1769; (B) 1770 to 1789; (C) 1790 to 1809; (D) 1810 to 1819; (E) 1820 to 1829; (F) 1830 to 1839; (G) 1840 to 1849; and (H) 1850 to 1860. Maps can be found in the Appendix.

The reader who compares the maps will reach several obvious conclusions. As might be expected, early travelers emphasized the eastern portions of the Valley, with later travelers gradually shifting their con-

cern westward. The Ohio River exerted considerable influence, particularly during the steamboat period of the 1830s and 1840s. After
1850, however, emphasis rapidly shifted northward toward the Great
Lakes with the building of the Middle West's railroad system. Relatively little emphasis was given the southern portion of the Ohio Valley. One can see in the later decades the growing split between North
and South clearly reflected in travelers' preferences of routes, destinations, and modes of travel.

TRAVEL RATIONALES

People traveled for a wide variety of reasons (Table 1-1). Between
1740 and 1809 the largest number of travelers were on military assignments. Most were field officers associated with military campaigns during or immediately preceding the French and Indian War (1757-1763),
Pontiac's Rebellion (1763-1765), Dunmore's War (1774), the American Revolution (1776-1783), the Indian Wars of the 1790s, and the
War of 1812 (1812-1815). After 1820 most military trips involved quar-
termaster duties or travel to new assignments. Closely related to military activities were trips undertaken by diplomatic envoys: for example, George Washington's trip in 1753 to Forts Venango and Le Boeuf
to request French withdrawal and assert English ownership of the
Upper Ohio Valley. Most of the merchants who traveled in the early
decades were suppliers of food and material to the army. Land survey
and land inspection brought various kinds of people to the region. Included were government agents marking out the Range and Township
system in the Northwest Territory, speculators looking for large tracts
of government land, and small farmers seeking new homes in the West.

   After 1810 most travelers were tourists. They came primarily to view
the region's landscape and meet its people. If they had other motives
for traveling, those reasons were subsidiary to the search for adventure: the deliberate seeking out of new circumstances. Included were
natural historians, such as Constantine Volney who was interested in
the climate and geology of the region, and English critics of the American scene, such as Basil Hall who depicted the American character in
rather negative terms.[20] Most Europeans were of the upper or upper-
middle classes and were engaged in the American equivalent of the
"Grand Tour." Most tourists were wealthy, for pleasure trips were still
very much a luxury. Most travel journalists were well educated.

   John Wright wrote in the preface of his journal that he had not trav-

Table 1-1. Travel Rationales

	Military Assignment	Diplomatic Envoy	Business	Land Survey & Inspection	On Tour	Migration	Church	Political	Visit to Relatives	Total
1740–69	11	6	2	2	1	0	0	0	0	27
1770–89	12	0	5	8	3	5	3	0	0	36
1790–1809	15	2	9	4	10	6	6	0	0	52
1810–19	5	0	3	3	22	7	4	1	0	45
1820–29	2	0	6	1	23	5	3	1	3	44
1830–39	1	0	3	3	58	5	12	0	2	84
1840–49	2	0	2	3	39	4	6	2	1	59
1850–60	0	0	1	0	39	1	3	1	0	45
	48	8	31	24	195	33	37	5	6	387

Source: Author.

eled for amusement seeking the "marvelous" nor had he invaded the "secret recesses of nature" in order to enrich the "cabinets of the curious" with "decayed bones and horned toads," but as a "plain practical farmer."[21] He traveled, he wrote:

> to inquire into the state and profits of agriculture and domestic manufactures; to find the present price of produce, and the prospects of a future market; to know the prices of necessary foreign articles [and to satisfy himself] respecting the salubriousness of the climate; the manners, customs, and moral character of the inhabitants; and the state and prospects of . . . literary and religious institutions.[22]

Wright traveled intending to write a book. Although many travelers who published their journals vigorously protested to the contrary, many actually undertook their trips anticipating fame and limited fortune from publishing a memoir. Wright's book was highly critical of the West in that he sought to convince Yankee farmers to stay in the Northeast.

Relatively few migrants or "movers," as they were called, kept journals. Lack of time and energy tended to preclude this activity. Not only were migrants confronted with new and difficult situations, but they had most of their household goods in tow as well as immediate responsibility for family and other dependents. Church-related trips saw missionaries traveling to the western Indians and ministers struggling to establish Christianity among the isolated frontier Americans. Many were Europeans come to visit affiliated American churches, usually in response to American requests for funds. Political trips involved members of Congress on their way to Washington, delegates traveling to political conventions, and political appointees journeying to new posts. Surprisingly, few of the travelers who wrote diaries traveled to visit relatives and friends.

THE ETHNICITY OF TRAVELERS

Where people came from greatly colored what they saw. Americans dominated the early decades of travel in the Ohio Valley, but after 1830 the majority were Europeans with a few Latin Americans. Whereas the Briton came more for pleasure, the German traveler was usually preoccupied with the emigration of other Germans. They visited the Europeans in Cincinnati and other places, reported on their progress, and sought advice for future emigrants. In total, nearly half of the travel accounts mapped for this study were written by foreigners. They are a particularly valuable source of environmental images. Foreigners tended to spend more time describing the details which Americans took for granted and ignored. Europeans had a heightened sense of being in a different environment and were less apt to dismiss the commonplace.

WOMEN AS TRAVELERS

Unfortunately, very few women wrote accounts of their travels in the early Ohio Valley. Most accompanied men (either fathers or husbands) on trips not of their own planning. Those who traveled alone or with female traveling companions, such as the British writer, Harriet Martineau, and the American writer, Anne Royall, were unusual for their day.[23] Women were largely limited to public conveyances. They did not have access to most places available to men, the barrooms, for example.

THE UNRECORDED TRAVELERS

Whole classes of people are unrepresented in the surviving travel literature. The experiences of black Americans are not recorded. Before 1860 most blacks entering the region came as illiterate slaves. A few, like William Brown who escaped at Cincinnati and made his way to Canada, learned to read and write and later recorded their travel experiences in book form.[24] The complete lack of American Indian travel accounts is most deplorable. The Ohio Valley, contested over by England and France and ultimately taken by Americans with force, was originally, of course, Indian territory. As only the Cherokees possessed a written language (and they only after 1821), distinctive Indian geographies were probably never written.

Writing Travel Accounts

The travelers wrote their accounts under varying circumstances. Many carried pocket notebooks in which brief phrases descriptive of the passing scene were written. At intervals (for some every evening and for others every few days) these notes were transcribed and elaborated in a more permanent diary or journal. For many, transcribing produced letters to friends or relatives who collected them, sometimes for publication. Those intending to publish usually stayed in hotels or private homes for extended periods in order to write and refine manuscripts.

This gave time to review other published works in order to give depth to observations. William Baxter thought the latter indispensable. Properly acquainted with places by means of books, he wrote, "the traveler knows what to look for, and does not fail to notice peculiarities which might otherwise escape him. He can thus more easily make comparisons, form true estimates, and hit upon the points of most general interest."[25] Of course, a traveler could be overly prepared. For a few travelers, travel became little more than a process for validating expectations. They moved through the landscape checking on what others had seen before them. The less original writers fell easy victim to plagiarizing and often copied verbatim the observations of others as their own.

Many biases entered. Travelers were often guilty of stereotyping from the basis of incomplete observation. The more objective writers were aware of their subjectivity and sought to control it. Elias Fordham noted how frequently he had begun a letter, put it in his traveling trunk, seen more, and found the impressions he had originally written down to be false.[26] Many travelers failed to verify their sources of information. Fordham continued that it was all too easy for a traveler to go to a tavern keeper and "pump from him for all he chooses to tell."[27] Nine times in ten, he thought, such information was incorrect. He suggested that no dependence could be placed on any representations, "but that of an intelligent, honest man, long resident in the country, and who is personally well disposed toward you."[28]

The act of writing, of describing the landscape in words, greatly influenced travelers' observational powers. Daniel Drake, the famous Cincinnati medical doctor, wrote in the 1830s that the astute observer suffers "nothing to pass without inspection" and from habit "connects all he sees with the memory of something seen before."[29] "He perceives new qualities, relations and functions, in the objects that lie along his path, and thus becomes original and inventive," he continued.[30] The act of writing aided such activity. Writing was as much an act of cognition as any other part of the travel experience.

One journalist, William Hall, conducted an experiment in writing and perception. Having just arrived on the edge of Little Prairie west of Albion, Illinois, in September of 1821, Hall spent a day wandering in the open air writing down impressions of his new environment. These impressions he sent to a friend in England as a measure of the new place to which he had come. He chose the autumnal equinox so that his friend could anchor the impressions in a meaningful time frame the more effectively to compare Illinois with England. The act of writing made his images more vivid, and many momentary and seemingly trivial impressions were captured and impressed upon Hall's memory that otherwise might have been lost. For example:

> Morning—Slight Frost, Sunrise, Perfect Stillness, save the tapping of the wood pecker. . . . The glistening of the various Flowers brilliant· with dew in the Sun . . . hops and Vines covering the tops of Fallen trees. . . . The leaves of the Sumac [*Rhus copallina*] beginning to turn red and those of the Sassafras [*Sassafras albidum*] changing to Yellow. . . . Air much colder when I got into the Prairie. Smoke arising from my neighbors chimney among the tall Trees: view of my own cabin from the opposite side of the Prairie . . .

> Noon—Cloudless sky. Gentle breeze nestling among the tops of the Trees, Hum of Bees and Insects. . . . noise and gaudy plumage of birds, shadow of the Turkey buzzards . . .

> Evening—Sky cloudless. Flights of Pigeons on the tops of oaks showering down Acorns to the Hogs below. Squirrels. Grotesque appearance of burnt stumps. Confusion of Fallen Trees. . . . wind still . . . setting sun.[31]

Such was the raw material out of which the travel journals were wrought.

It is my objective in this book to summarize those impressions of place significant to the travelers in the early Ohio Valley. Recognizing that the travelers were not a totally unbiased population of observers, I nonetheless think it important to attempt a verbal reconstruction of the Valley as they saw it. Whatever their biases, their records remain the best sources of information regarding early Ohio Valley impressions.

The use of travel journals as a point of departure is not novel. Historians researching the Ohio Valley and other sections of the United States have long made use of travel narratives.[32] Many important themes in American political, economic, and social history are rooted in the observations of such travelers as J. Hector St. Jean de Crèvecœur and Alexis de Tocqueville.[33] Although few have written on the Ohio Valley, historical geographers have gleaned from the travel journals descriptions of natural environment and settlement landscape.[34] It is in this latter tradition that this book is presented. Historians of the

Ohio Valley have tended to ignore the travel journals for what they really were: descriptions of place. Thus succeeding chapters in this book focus on various kinds of place experience beginning with the imagery of travel and nature and proceeding to the imagery of the farm, war and conquest, and urban life.

2 IMAGES OF TRAVEL

The American travels . . . in obedience to an innate need for motion and speculation. The Search for something better than already exists, accompanies and absorbs him constantly.

Marie Grandfort

The images that travelers obtained of the Ohio Valley were influenced by the conditions of travel. Basic to traveling were the daily concerns of moving from place to place, of eating, and of sleeping. Even in the earliest days when travelers moved by horse or canoe between the Indian towns, institutions in those towns catered to the travelers' needs. The Indians extended hospitality, providing food and lodging, travel information and guides, and companionship. The early European forts functioned as much as outfitting and supply points for travelers as they did for frontier defense. With American settlement came new institutions catering primarily to strangers. Taverns and hotels were a community's point of contact with the outside world. So also were the town's levee and, later still, its railroad depot. An infrastructure of the various modes of transportation and related service facilities could cocoon the unwary traveler. Landscape images were often based solely on the experiences of the route.

Travel journals gave emphasis to the places and conveyances which catered to the traveler's needs. This preoccupation with the images of travel did not necessarily detract from the visitor's ability to describe the Ohio Valley landscape, for traveling was very basic to that scene.

The United States was a nation of migrants; people moved and traveled frequently. The American viewpoint was one of impermanence and the anticipation of a better future in a new place. "There is certainly not any nation that can boast a greater disposition for travelling, than Brother Jonathan," one European wrote, using the pseudonym for the typical American.[1] John Woods, an English migrant to Albion, Illinois, remarked that most Americans in the area had resided at several places in at least three or four states.[2] One woman, the mother of twelve, had never had two children born in any one house and could not remember the number of places she had lived in since marrying.[3] Timothy Flint joked that Americans "like the Tartars" should "dwell in tents," for "everything shifts under the eye."[4] "The present occupants sell, pack up, depart," he wrote, "Strangers replace them. Before they have gained the confidence of their neighbors, they hear of a better place, pick up, and follow."[5] One Englishman noted that deep attachments to people in any given place did not exist and superficial relationships predominated. "Perhaps there is nothing more remarkable in the character of the Americans then the indifference with which they leave their old habitations, friends, and relatives," he wrote.[6]

Transportation

In the mid-eighteenth century movement was by foot, horse, and canoe. By the 1790s roads in the eastern portion of the Ohio Valley had been improved sufficiently to accommodate wagons, and stage service was regularly scheduled between such places as Pittsburgh and Philadelphia and Wheeling and Baltimore. On the rivers, flatboats and keelboats predominated. After 1820 steamboat and canal transportation evolved to be reinforced by the railroads after 1840. Each mode of transportation had its characteristic sights. Each oriented the traveler in a different way to the passing scene.

PEDESTRIAN TRAVEL

Perhaps no other form of movement placed the traveler as close to his environment as walking. To walk was to allow more time to see and to hear and otherwise imprint the images of the landscape on the memory. One could stop and linger to touch and to examine. Estwick Evans, a Welshman, took the art of walking to its height. Outfitted in a suit made of buffalo skin, he walked nearly 1,000 miles equipped with a rifle, a cooking pot, and minimal baggage stuffed into several large pockets. He wished, he said, to "acquire the simplicity, native feelings, and virtues of savage life."[7]

Most pedestrians seen on the road were simply too poor to travel in any other way. They carried a cloth knapsack or light leather valise hung over their backs.[8] Most could cover about forty miles a day on good roads if they were willing to spend thirteen or fourteen hours at their task. Sore feet was a constant complaint; cut and bleeding feet from ill-fitting shoes plagued many. Most Americans who could pay the fare preferred the exhilaration as well as the convenience of the faster speeds on stages and steamboats. Thomas Ashe, a Briton, complained, "An American has no conception of a person's being able to derive pleasure from a walk, or information from solitude: his sluggish faculties require palpable and active objects to give them exercise."[9]

TRAVEL BY HORSE

Traveling by horse also placed the traveler close to his environment. Charles Hoffman wrote of his ride across the Allegheny Mountains: "Nothing can be more exhilarating than a gallop over those heights on a bracing October day. The sudden breaks and turns of the mountain road open new views upon you at every moment; and the clear, pure atmosphere one breathes, with the motion of a spirited horse . . . [quickens the] pulse."[10] A rider could cover forty to fifty miles a day depending upon the terrain and the condition of the roads. Travelers with horses were burdened by the care of their animals. John James Audubon provided a description of the diligent horseman's daily routine.[11] At dawn the horse was cleaned and his back checked for sores from the previous day's ride. Off at a trot, stopping to water after the first hour, man and horse continued for fifteen or twenty miles before breakfast; the animal was then cleaned and fed on corn blades, cracked corn, or oats. At sunset the horse was watered, rubbed down, and his feet examined and cleaned. Fed on unthreshed oats in bundles of corn, a crushed pumpkin was added in season and always some hen's eggs when available. The horse's shoes were adjusted every third or fourth week. Blacksmiths were found in most towns.

Few taverns had stables, and animals generally spent the nights in the open even in winter. Many travelers carried bells which they attached to the horses for easier morning retrieval. Forage was unavailable in forested areas, and in the winter horses were often reduced to

chewing the bark of trees. Sprains, snakebites, and saddle sores were
common ailments. Epidemic diseases periodically swept the frontier.
In 1819 Richard Mason passed numerous dead and dying horses abandoned on the roadside between Maysville and Lexington in Kentucky.[12] A disease, locally called the "sore tongue," had affected every
stable within hundreds of miles.

Most horsemen traveled light. A coat, a saddle and blanket, a small
portmanteau or bag, and an umbrella constituted the visible equipment for most. One traveler itemized his clothing as a double suit of
clothes, a blue broadcloth cloak, shoes, socks, and a hat.[13] In 1817
Morris Birkbeck estimated the cost of traveling by horse at $1 per
day.[14] A good horse cost $100 to $150 or rented for $0.50 to $0.75 per
day.[15] Prices were low at Pittsburgh where travelers, taking to the
river, sold their horses bought in the East. Horses were sold by auction,
the auctioneer riding the animal through the streets calling for bids.[16]

TRAVEL BY WAGON AND CARRIAGE

Those who sought more comfort or carried large loads traveled by
wagon or carriage. Many preferred this mode to the stages with their
restrictions in scheduling, space, and privacy. Wagons were practical
only where roads were improved. But even improved roads could be
quite primitive. Many were simply tracks from which trees and brush
had been removed. Frequent stops to lift the wheels over the remaining tree stumps slowed travel. Roads were frequently a multiplicity
of tracks carved in an *ad hoc* fashion by travelers seeking to avoid various obstructions. Fallen trees, for example, were seldom cleared away;
they were simply bypassed. Roads in swampy areas were usually covered with "corduroy," small tree trunks split in half with the flat sides
facing down. The grooves which developed with use reduced the
shock of the wagon wheels slipping from log to log.

Great inconvenience was encountered at stream crossings. Fords predominated in the early stages of road development. Next came primitive bridges on the smaller creeks. Usually they consisted of two long
trees thrown over the stream about eight feet apart with split or round
pieces of timber laid across side by side.[17] Ferrying was necessary
across the larger rivers. In most instances, wagons were balanced on
two canoes or on small boats and taken across. The horses swam. Even
where roads were carefully constructed, repair was casual and infre-

quent. Road abuse was common. William Oliver passed a new log cabin near Martinsville in Illinois. A hole had been dug in the middle of the road and clay removed for the cabin's daubing.[18] Fences had been thrown across the highway in the vicinity.

Most wagons seen on the highways belonged either to "movers" or to teamsters. The former carried migrants and their baggage, and the latter carried freight. Migrants often walked beside their wagons to save the horses or oxen so vital to successful farming later on. This was especially true in the mountains where the animals climbed the steep slopes with difficulty. Few trusted the primitive hand brakes on the downslope runs; most passengers continued to walk.

The freight wagons were huge, standing ten to twelve feet high with canvas tops stretched on hoops. Usually drawn by either six horses or six oxen, the lead animals carried bells suspended in square frames to warn the unwary of a wagon's approach. The teamsters were considered by most travelers to be an unruly but picturesque lot. Most rode on their left shaft horse holding a multitude of reins and a whip. British travelers found the American wagons much larger than at home and were amused by the American's fashion of driving on the right side of the road.[19] Wagoners usually traveled in groups both for company and to assist one another in repairs. Freight wagons between Philadelphia and Pittsburgh averaged about twenty miles a day, requiring about three weeks for the trip.[20]

Only the wealthy could afford true carriages or "gigs." In Kentucky's Blue Grass, the planter's carriage, followed by several black slaves on horseback, was a common sight.[21] Most travelers who bought or rented vehicles chose the "rough and ready," described by one traveler as "a flat scaffolding raised on iron springs and four very slight wheels."[22] Four poles supported a leather awning and leather curtains. The vehicle was usually drawn by a pair of horses.

STAGECOACH TRAVEL

Stages provided scheduled service along the major roads. Of course, the uncertainties of the route made their schedules highly unreliable. The coaches had a distinctive look, being suspended on leather straps high above the axles. Compartments were rounded at the bottom to facilitate the fording of streams. Most stages carried ten passengers: nine sat on inside benches (with the middle bench having only a leather strap for a back) and one up top with the driver. Most coaches had leather curtains at the windows; a few had glass which was easily broken and seldom repaired.

In the winter, passengers saw little of the landscape when the curtains were closed. Passengers saw nothing at night. Most stage trips began at dusk from the originating town or city. Stages which stopped for an evening generally started again at two or three o'clock in the morning. Horses were usually changed every ten or fifteen miles giving passengers an opportunity to briefly warm themselves in the winter. On the main traveled roads the stages often moved in caravans. "Our long train of stages, with their brilliant lamps, reflected by the foliage was not devoid of interest and beauty," one British visitor wrote.[23]

Walt Whitman described the systematic procedure whereby passengers embarked from Cumberland, Maryland, on the National Road: "All the passengers' names were inscribed on a role (we purchased tickets in Philadelphia, at $13.00 a head, to go to Wheeling) and a clerk stands by and two or three negroes with a patent weighing machine. The clerk calls your name, your baggage is whipped on the machine, and if it weighs over fifty pounds, you have to pay extra. You are then put in the stage (literally put in, like a package, unless you move quickly) your baggage packed on behind and the next name called off."[24] When travelers chose to leave a stage they were often stranded for days when following stages proved unable to accommodate new passengers. Amelia Murray complained, "It is impossible to place any dependence upon the assurances of agents; when they have got your money, they will, without compunction, leave you in the lurch."[25]

Charles Dickens found the stage drivers all alike: "He is always dirty, sullen, and taciturn. He never speaks to you as you sit beside him on the box and if you speak to him, he answers . . . in monosyllables. He points out nothing on the road, and seldom looks at anything. He always chews and always spits."[26] Stage accidents were frequent. Godfrey Vigne's coach overturned in a Cincinnati street. "I was on the box, and expected to be kicked to pieces, as I fell close to the horses; but providentially they all four galloped off with the two front wheels," he wrote.[27] Charles Lyell encountered one man who claimed to have been overturned thirteen times in three years traveling between Cincinnati and Cleveland.[28] Stages moved at about four or five miles per hour.[29] The seventy-four-mile trip from Wheeling to Zanesville on the National Road in Ohio required twelve hours including stops for meals.[30] In 1817 William Harris estimated stage travel at ten cents per mile with another $1.25 per day for meals and lodging.[31]

TRAVEL BY BOAT

In the early days, travelers moved on the Ohio and other rivers by canoe. The largest, called "pirogues" by the French, carried upwards to four tons. Most were hollowed from logs. Paddled by four people, these vessels could make twenty to twenty-five miles a day upstream. Skiffs, called batteaux by the French, were small boats about twenty feet long. After 1780 their sterns were usually roofed with thin boards or canvas and their enclosure equipped with side curtains.[32] Some had a mast and sail, but most were propelled with oars. Skiffs were popular with travelers as late as the War of 1812. They were relatively cheap and offered great flexibility of action in river travel.

Flatboats were large flat-bottomed vessels with straight prows. They varied from ten to fifteen feet in width, being forty to 100 feet long. Called "Kentucky boats" and sometimes "family boats," it was, according to Timothy Flint, "no uncommon spectacle to see a large family, old and young, servants, cattle, hogs, horses, sheep, [and] fowls . . . bringing to recollection the cargo of the ancient ark."[33] Most were roofed except for a small portion of the foredeck where two or more men rowed; at the rear stood the steersman with his long oar.[34] Flatboats were estimated to cost $1 per foot in length at Pittsburgh in 1817 and to sell for one-quarter that price at Louisville or other ports downriver.[35]

The best time to descend the Ohio River was in the spring during flood. The inexperienced were advised to lash their boats together keeping to the main current and land as seldom as possible. Most travelers carried Zodak Cramer's *Navigator* which carefully described the river and made suggestions on its navigation.[36] The river was quite hazardous. Whereas crews could float with the current, a constant watch was necessary. A boat thrown on the head of an island refloated only with great difficulty. Other hazards included "planters," tree trunks rooted to the bottom, and "sawyers," trees less firmly rooted which rose and fell with the water level.[37] Cramer also described the towns and landings along the river's bank. The expectations of many travelers were based on the *Navigator,* and many copied verbatim Cramer's descriptions casting doubt on how much they themselves had

actually seen. During high water flatboats could run from Pittsburgh
to the mouth of the Ohio in fifteen days; ten days to Louisville was
considered a quick passage.[38] Under ideal circumstances flatboats averaged seventy to eighty miles a day.[39]

Flatboat travel prior to 1820 offered access to an unspoiled country.
Nature was relatively pristine along the river banks. Wilder images
were abundant. Settlers and settlement along the higher ground were
located at a distance and the vulgarity of the frontier less apparent
accordingly. Towns were few. The quiet boat provided few distrac-
tions. "There is something . . . in the gentle and almost imperceptible
motion, as you sit on the deck of the boat, and see the trees apparently
moving by you, and new groups of scenery still opening upon your
eye," Timothy Flint wrote in 1818.[40]

Sounds were amplified across the water. Many sounds came from the
boats themselves. William Harris observed: "We hail each other with
all the importance of merchantmen on the ocean. Who commands that
boat? Where are you from? Where bound? What's your cargo?"[41] Many
boats carried tin horns which "sent forth a wild music" in a minor
key.[42] These horns echoed from bluff to bluff in the fog, adding much
to the romance of the river. Other sounds included the turning of the
oars and the muffled sounds of laughter, song, and conversation. John
Audubon, among others, claimed that in the shallows along the bank
one could hear the rumbling noise of perch (*Perca flavescens*) and
other fish.[43] Sounds varied with the time of day and season. In summer
birds dominated in the early morning succeeded by the hum of the
locust and other insects. In the evening the frogs commenced with
dogs barking on through the night accompanied by the bells of the
cattle on the distant farms.[44]

Keelboats were built on keels, as the name implied, with pointed
prows to facilitate polling upstream. Twelve or fourteen crewmen
slowly walked the length of the boats on narrow walkways, their poles
set in the river bottom.[45] Most keelboats were ten feet wide and fifty
feet long with a low cabin usually divided into four parts: the steward's
quarters, a dining room, the "gentlemen's" quarters, and a ladies cabin.
The larger boats could carry upwards to 100 passengers. Boats could
attain three miles per hour upstream, but twenty miles in a day was an
exceptionally good run.[46] Crewmen on the keelboats, as on the commercial flatboats, were seen as a boisterous crowd. John Woods saw

them as "a rough set of men, much given to drinking whiskey, fighting, and gouging."[47] James Hall regarded them as "proverbially lawless and dissolute," for the arrival of several keelboats in a small town was the "certain forerunner of riot."[48]

CANAL TRAVEL

In the 1820s and 1830s canals were built in Ohio and Indiana to connect the Ohio River with Lake Erie (Fig. F). The Pennsylvania Canal and its connectors in western Pennsylvania were built in direct competition to New York's Erie Canal. The intention was to tie the Ohio Valley's evolving agriculture more directly to eastern markets giving western wheat, for example, an additional outlet to the southern market centered at New Orleans. As many travelers observed, the canals were shallow ditches three to six feet deep and fifteen to thirty feet wide. They were constructed from one river valley to another with locks providing the means of elevating boats from basin to basin. Adjacent rivers were dammed and water diverted to fill the canals. Canals were carried across creeks and rivers on covered aqueducts. Towns grew at regular intervals, their warehouses located along the wide turning basins which functioned as harbors.

The canal boats were very much like keelboats except that they were towed by mules attached by ropes. George Combe, a visitor from England, described the boats on the Pennsylvania Canal.[49] The gentlemen's cabin was forty-two feet long, fifteen broad, and seven high; the ladies' cabin twelve by thirteen feet, not including an attached dressing room six by seven feet. Toward the bow was a small barroom and kitchen. Light came from small windows along both sides of the boat and a small skylight in the roof. "Into this space were stowed thirty-five men, nineteen women, and ten children, seven of whom were at the breast," he wrote.[50] The beds were ranged in three tiers along the walls. Combe was particularly disturbed by the bedding. He reported: "During the day the beds, consisting of mattresses, sheets, pillows, and cotton quilts, were piled one above another. . . . The smell of animal effluvia, when they were unpacked, was truly horrid . . . they were saturated with the perspiration of every individual who had used them since the commencement of the season, or probably from the time when they were first taken on board."[51] Charles Dickens, who traveled the same canal three years later, complained of the washing facilities.[52]

There was a tin ladle chained to the deck and a tin basin filled with canal water set before a small mirror. Here hung the public comb and hairbrush.

Most travelers found canal travel monotonous, for the boats sat below the level of the towpaths and were almost everywhere surrounded by a profusion of vegetation. There was not much of a view. But Charles Dickens, for all the unfavorable impressions he held of the United States, found canal travel agreeable. He wrote:

> Even running up bare-necked, at five o'clock in the morning, from the tainted cabin to the dirty deck; scooping up the icy water, plunging one's head into it, and drawing it out, all fresh and flowing with cold, was a good thing. The fast, brisk walk upon the towing path, between that time and breakfast, when every vein and artery seemed to tingle with health; the exquisite beauty of the opening day, when light came gleaming off every thing; the lazy motion of the boat, when one lay idly on the deck, looking through, rather than at, the deep blue sky; the gliding on at night, so noiselessly, past frowning hills, sullen with dark trees . . . the shining out of the bright stars, undisturbed by noise of wheels or steam, or any other sound than the liquid rippling of the water as the boat went on: all these were pure delight.[53]

Canal travel was unpredictable. A heavy rain could rupture an embankment, leaving a canal dry for weeks. Boats frequently sank, and locks broke requiring repairs of several days. Under the best conditions canal boats averaged four miles per hour.[54] It required five days and nights to travel the 320 miles between Terre Haute, Indiana, and Toledo, Ohio, on the Wabash and Erie Canal.[55] On the Pennsylvania Canal the 286 miles between Harrisburg and Pittsburgh required three days and four nights including passage on the Portage Railroad near Hollidaysburg.[56] Here Allegheny Mountain imposed an impossible barrier to canal construction. Consequently, the boats were taken apart and hoisted over the mountain on a series of five incline planes. One traveler observed, "The boats are made, some in three, some in five compartments, and being merely forelocked together are easily carried across the hill."[57] The boats were raised and lowered by stationary engines; both horses and steam locomotives were used on the level, connecting stretches.[58]

Canals were surrounded by stagnant water almost everywhere, their construction having disrupted the original drainage. One traveler wrote of the Ohio and Erie Canal: "Carrion often floats on the surface [and] miasmata are generated, all which must render a residence near the bank unhealthy. It is in fact a nursery of fever and ague."[59] Another remarked that mosquitos made "murderous attack."[60] But no one had yet associated malarial fever with the mosquito carrier. Poorly drained places, as along the canals, were simply recognized as unhealthy.

STEAMBOAT TRAVEL

Steamboats represented a transportation revolution. No longer dependent upon human or animal muscle power, boats moved upstream at an average six miles per hour and downstream at speeds upwards to twelve miles per hour.[61] Keelboats required at least twenty-eight days between Cincinnati and New Orleans and ninety days for the return trip, but steamboats could manage the 1,400 miles down in twelve days returning in thirty-six.[62] With the new economies of scale, passenger fares were reduced. For example, first-class accommodations between Louisville and New Orleans cost only $15 in 1850.[63] This price included meals as well as transportation.

Most steamboats ranged in length from 70 to 150 feet. Built on a flat, narrow hull, a boat displaced only three or four feet of water, the various decks extending beyond the hull on every side. The steam engines were placed on the open lower deck, the boilers the most prominent attraction. Fredrika Bremer, the Swedish traveler, described one boat.[64] Beside each boiler stood a Negro, naked to the waist, flinging in firewood passed forward by other blacks. Behind the boilers a huge flywheel rose up through the various decks. The paddle wheels were enclosed in huge rounded boxes on either side of the vessel upon which the boat's name appeared in large letters.

The boat's second deck, supported by the framework of the paddle boxes and by posts placed at intervals around the bow and stern, contained the main salon and the ladies' cabin at the stern. The passengers' staterooms opened on to this large room which in most boats was painted white and gold with carpeting, sideboards, mirrors, lamps, and other elaborate furnishings. Stoves were placed at both ends of the room, but the one toward the bow was the favorite of the men. Here was the bar and several gambling tables. James Stuart found the outside balcony, which extended around the stern from paddle box to paddle box on his steamboat, a most agreeable walk except when the washing was hung out to dry.[65] John Beste observed slave women washing bed linen where water from the side wheels splashed upon the deck.[66]

A boat's third deck was called the "hurricane deck" since it was open to the wind. There the pilot's house was located, slightly elevated behind two giant chimneys. Here also were the escape pipes from which emitted loud jets of steam. It was impossible to be on this deck, Mrs. Houstoun complained, "without being covered with black sparks, or greased by some horrid invention in the neighborhood of the funnels."[67]

Meals were served in the grand salon. Henry Whipple wrote of the steamboat Goddess: "When the supper bell rang what a rush . . . and such a clatter of knives and forks and table ware, such screaming for waiters . . . such an exhibition of muscle and nerve."[68] A fellow passenger observed to him that it "looked for all the world like one great scrimage."[69] Most boats had two sittings for the paying passengers, the black servants eating at a third. Small toilet rooms were usually located against the paddle boxes. These rooms were provided with tin basins, towels, mirrors, a piece of soap, and a public hairbrush hanging on a cord. Deck passengers were without these amenities. Exposed to the elements on the lower level, they had to provide their own meals, many cooking on the deck. They were totally dependent upon the public privies which most towns maintained at or near their levees.

The steamboats stopped frequently to take on or put off freight and passengers and to refuel. Walt Whitman was amazed by the freight handling. He wrote:

> At one place . . . we shipped several hundred barrels of pork; ditto of lard; at another place, an uncounted (by me) lot of flour . . . besides . . . bags of coffee, rolls of leather, groceries, dry goods, hardware, all sorts of agricultural products, innumerable coops filled with live geese, turkeys, and fowls, that kept up a perpetual farmyard concert. To my eyes it was enormous; though people much used to such things didn't seem to consider it any wonder at all.[70]

On upriver trips fuelwood was loaded from scows lashed to the moving steamboats, the smaller vessels dropping back downstream once unloaded. Downriver trips required fuel stops four to six times a day. At each stop, vendors thronged the boats. Most were small boys selling apples, chestnuts, newspapers, and books.

Steamboat travel was not dependable during periods of low water. Descriptions of steamboats aground were numerous, containing some of the most vivid impressions of river travel recorded. William Baxter, riding in the pilot house of the steamboat Tishomingo, recorded the following scene as they approached two grounded boats near Paducah:

"that looks ay leetle billious, don't it?" "So I reckon," was the curt
reply; and the bell tolled for soundings. "Eight feet," sang out Jack
with the lead line, in slow recitative tones; "eight feet," echoed the
mate, on the hurricane deck, to the steerman above; "six feet large,"
was the next report, followed in ten seconds by "five feet scant". . . .
"three feet," rung in my ears; and the Tishomingo ran slap on the bar,
rolling the thumping as if her frail planks would part. "Go it again,
Massa," shouted a . . . negro.[71]

Steamboat travel involved a peculiar spectrum of sounds. The "snort,
snort, snort" of the high pressure steam engines, the shrill whistles, the
bells signalling the engineeers, the splash of the paddles, and the work
songs and chants of the black crewmen all combined to create a distinctive environment. Travelers also remarked on the noise of the grand
salon, the sounds of the cattle and the other animals, and the commo-
tion of children running loose on the outer decks. Steamboats were no-
toriously dangerous (Fig. 2-1). Carelessness caused many deaths. Many
officers and crews were poorly trained and little regulated by owners.
Captains overtaxed their engines, often in races with other boats.

Travelers reacted both negatively and positively to their steamboat
experiences. George Pierce found his trip on the Tennessee River monotonous, especially after the second day. He wrote: "Three meals a
day—reading a little, talking a little, walking a little, and all the while,
paddle, paddle, puff. The first step on solid ground brought a thrill of
pleasure."[72] But the Englishman James Robertson disagreed. "With
books, music, dancing, conversation, and other occupations . . . the
time passes rapidly, and a sort of subdued excitement is maintained,"
he observed.[73] The women read, did embroidery, or talked. But, irrespective of the mode of passing time, a new dimension had been added
to American travel. Travelers could move from place to place without
direct involvement in the logistics or mechanics of movement. They
could sit in their compartments or in the public spaces and be amused.
They could, if they pleased, move from place to place totally oblivious
to the passing scene. The traveler could be cocooned completely; a
protective, transportable environment encased him. Many travelers
knew the country not by what they saw, but by what they were told
in the comfort of the steamboat salons.

TRAVEL BY RAILROAD

What the steamboats provided in comfort, the railroads provided in
speed. In the 1830s and 1840s passenger trains on some lines exceeded

Arrowsmith's Panorama of Western Travel.

[DESIGNED FOR EXHIBITION IN ENGLAND.]

The Alleghany Mountains.—Railroad in distance.

Pittsburgh on a clear morning.

Western Steamboat, with full cargo.

Engineer on duty : two feet water on lower deck.

A Hot Boat.—Ten 56lbs. weights on safety-valve.

View of Cincinnati.—[Perfectly accurate.]

Running on a Bank.

Going over Falls of Ohio.—[Not exaggerated.]

twenty miles per hour, and by 1860 speeds had doubled on most rail-roads. Distances between towns seemed to shrink. By the beginning of the Civil War, Wheeling was only twenty-four hours from both Wash-ington and Baltimore and twenty hours from Cincinnati when trains kept their schedules.[74] The cars were thirty to forty feet in length with aisles down the middle and seats arranged along the sides. "The benches are like free seats in a church, with low backs, sometimes of padded velvet," one English visitor wrote.[75] The floors were usually carpeted or matted, and the windows generally had venetian blinds and shutters. Isabella Trotter found sleeping cars "ingeniously contrived to be like an ordinary car by day, but by means of cushions spread between the seats and a flat board let down half way from the ceiling, two tiers of very comfortable beds are made on each side of the car."[76]

Many, particularly Europeans used to private compartments, found railroad travel difficult in the United States. Charles MacKay com-plained of the Baltimore and Ohio Railroad:

> Without a proper place to stow away ones hat; with no convenience even to repose the head or back, except to the ordinary height of a chair; with a current of cold outer air continually streaming in, and . . . with the constant slamming of the doors at either end of the car . . . the passenger must, indeed, be "dead beat" who can sleep or even doze in a railway car in America.[77]

Henry Murray criticized

> the mixture of human and metallic heat, the chorus of infantile squal-lers—who kept responding to one another from all parts of the car, like so many dogs . . . and the intervals filled up by the hissing on the stove of the [tobacco] juice.[78]

Travelers looked on the speed of railroad travel with mixed emo-tions. Lillian Foster approved. "This almost telegraphic speed of rail-road traveling changes in a few hours the romance of childhood and the recitations of the school room into a vivid reality," she wrote.[79] Geo-graphic differences could be more readily appreciated, for "what used to cost a week's travel is now accomplished with pleasant ease in a sin-

---

Figure 2-1.
A Caricature of Western Travel. The dangers of steamboat travel elicited negative stereotypes among a spectrum of exaggerated travel images. (*Harper's New Monthly Magazine*, Dec. 1858)

gle day," she continued.[80] Many thought the motion of the speeding
trains exciting. "There is something very exhilarating in the act of being borne through a beautiful country at the rate of fifteen miles an
hour," one traveler wrote, crossing the mountains on the Pennsylvania
Railroad.[81] Scenes presented themselves in quick succession. His trip
was filled "with images as beautiful and varied as are brought to the
eye by every turn of a kaleidescope.[82]

Railroads could aid in the quest for the picturesque, but many
thought otherwise. "The lovers of the picturesque sustain a great loss
by means of the numerous lines of railroads that have recently come
into existence," James Fenimore Cooper wrote.[83] He continued:

> Everywhere a country presents its best face towards its thoroughfares.
> . . . All that has been done, therefore, in past ages . . . is being de-
> ranged and in some instances deformed. . . . Thus villages and towns
> are no longer entered by their finest passages, producing the best
> effects; but the traveler is apt to find his view limited by ranges of
> sheds, out-houses, and other deformities of that nature.[84]

Cooper decried that utilitarian spirit that was erasing interest from the
American scene.

Many cheered the railroads as the purveyors of progress. The minister James Dixon wrote:

> What music for the forest is a railroad train! How fine and perfect the
> harmony between . . . the leap of squirrels, the bounding of the
> hind, the stag, the deer, and all the other forms of life and motion
> peculiar to the wilderness. We dashed along through these forest
> scenes . . . intent only upon our mission of progress, though it should
> oblige us to cut down all the trees in the universe, disturb the repose of
> nature in her lair, and quench the lights of heaven by the smoke of our
> civilizing chimneys.[85]

The railroads cut across the landscape in straight lines and broad
sweeping curves, eating up the flat land along the rivers and generally
following paths of least topographic resistance. Travelers of the 1850s
crossed surveyors' stakes and new construction frequently. The journalist and landscape architect Frederick Law Olmsted wrote from
Asheville in North Carolina: "All this country is to be netted by railroads. . . . I have crossed engineer's stakes every day . . . and generally when I stop at night the farmer tells me that a railroad . . . is to
pass between his house and his corn crib, and that in consequence land
about him has lately become of great value."[86]

Europeans found American railroads lightly built. One Englishman wrote, "The American railroads are of the cheapest possible construction; the stations are mere sheds; the curves frequent and short; the gradients those of the surface of the ground . . . and the rails are only narrow slips of iron an inch thick, nailed down to horizontal sleepers."[87] Railroads were not fenced, as in Europe, and there were no crossing gates or crossing guards. Locomotives did not whistle continuously to warn of their approach.

The railroads initially served to define more substantially the hinterlands of river towns. They funneled agricultural produce and other freight to the levees and the steamboats. There the first passenger depots and freight houses were built. By 1854 Cincinnati's Union Station had a large arching roof covering over an acre of trackage and loading platforms. All was busy and chaotic. One traveler observed: "The engine whistles, the caterers for the city hotels, the porters, the hack-drivers, the agents of rival routes, all take part in the noise and bewilderment."[88] Trains stopped for meals and, although allowed half an hour, most travelers bolted their food and returned to the trains in a matter of minutes.[89]

Travel Information

Before the Civil War, a person's travel itinerary was usually an *ad hoc* creation. Specific destinations may have been known, but routes of access were usually chosen while traveling. Blocked canals, frozen rivers, and other hindrances diverted travelers, as did the opening of new stage lines and the completion of new railroads. Travel guides kept updated only by anticipating new transport connections, many of these expected services never materializing. By necessity the traveler always inquired locally as to the actual existence of routes and their condition.

People who traveled by horse or wagon often had great difficulty keeping their route once chosen. There were few road signs and, where new paths had been opened around obstructions, travelers encountered regular labyrinths. Travelers were wise to ask directions constantly, particularly of one another. Locals were often misleading, both intentionally and unintentionally. William Faux thought that Americans knew nothing of the time and distance separating places. The phrase, "But a little bit through," was a term applied to any distance, he wrote.[90] Often directions contained too much detail. William Oliver wrote, "Not the slightest peculiarity in the surface of the ground, not an old log, or singular looking tree, is omitted, the patience of the narrator seems to be inexhaustible."[91] Where roads were simply blazed trails, a traveler might be told to "Keep the three-notched road."[92] Unfortunately, it often required an experienced woodsman to read the notches, such a diversity of notching identified so many roads in any one area. On the frontier few locals used the roads and often could not give adequate directions. Johann Schoepf observed of western Pennsylvania in 1783 that locals traveled overland. "Guided by the sun, the course of streams, the appearance of the trees, they travel straight to the place they are going and seldom lose their way," he wrote.[93]

Foreign travelers were surprised to find most Americans reasonably well acquainted with the geography of the United States. This undoubtedly reflected that the population was highly mobile and that most people had lived in several places often thousands of miles apart. "You will scarcely meet [anyone] who cannot tell you that Pittsburgh is full of coal and smoke; that in New Orleans the people play cards on Sunday; that living is dear in Washington City; and cod-fish cheap at Boston," James Hall wrote.[94] Only the black slaves seemed ignorant of places. Frederick Law Olmsted quizzed some slaves along his route in Tennessee. He wrote: "Their notions of geography were amusing. They asked about Indiana, and said that I must have passed through it coming from Texas, confusing it, probably, with Louisiana; and they asked if New York were not the country the Yankees came from—'the people that used to come peddling.' "[95] People on the frontier regularly inflated the value of their own locales. Morris Birkbeck, a migrant to Illinois whose journals were widely read, observed that "people generally speak favourably of their own country, and exaggerate every objection or evil; when speaking of those to which we are going."[96]

Meals and Lodging

The traveler on the early frontier was dependent upon the tavern. There he found food and rest for himself, and if necessary, for his horse. Substantial hotels appeared in the larger towns as the Ohio Valley matured. Perhaps the fanciest hotels were the spas that catered to special breeds of traveler: the tourist and the vacationer. In the taverns and hotels, travelers achieved their principal interface with the local society and culture. The view was often distorted, but highly representative of what local communities presented to the world by way of image. Travelers met a cross section of the local population in the bars and other public rooms. There they discovered local food preferences and otherwise sampled the essence of the locale.

TAVERNS

Frontier taverns were of two types: the public tavern and the "house of private entertainment." The former were built and operated especially as taverns. Usually large log, frame, or brick buildings, they frequently had wooden piazzas or porches in front. On a post, twenty-five or thirty feet high, hung the tavern sign. "Private houses" were residences which took overnight guests. Most were marked by hand-painted signs reading "Movers' Accommodation," "Movers taken in here," or, simply, "Entertainment."[97] In the late eighteenth and the early nineteenth century, practically every house along a principal road boarded travelers as an important source of income. Thus farmland along a highway was usually inflated in value given this extra earning power.[98] Farmers in isolated areas had little choice but to accept travelers at night and, accordingly, many operated taverns in self defense with established rates and procedures.

Many a traveler found himself at a "Preacher Biram's" or a "Widow Moore's," often putting up for the night by sharing the beds of the family. "[I] felt a little embarrassment [sic] in undressing and getting into the same bed with husbands and wives," one traveler wrote.[99] More often than not, travelers were simply offered the floor for the night. Richard Mason shared a small cabin with twenty-four people and two calves; ten of the company were travelers sleeping before the fire.[100] Although "private houses" offered few amenities, they were generally more orderly, for locals were not allowed to drink on the premises.

Public taverns thrived where regularly scheduled stages ran and where a local neighborhood could support a public drinking place. They were clearly identified by their large signs, the outlines usually visible up to a quarter of a mile. On most signs in the early 1800s a picture was painted with the name of the proprietor given below, one or two letters at the end of the name being put over the others in a reduced size.[101] The picture usually gave its name to the establishment. David Jarrett, who traveled from Pittsburgh to Indianapolis through Columbus and Cincinnati in 1834, listed the names of the taverns where he stayed. Included were the signs of the Wheat Sheaf, the

Wagon, the Spread Eagle, the Goddess of Liberty, the Rising Sun, and General Washington.[102]

As a local drinking place, taverns usually sported a group of loafers seated before the door or sprawled across the porch. François Michaux wrote of Kentucky: "If a traveler happens to pass by, his horse is appreciated; if he stops, he is presented with a glass of whiskey, and then asked a thousand questions, such as, where do you come from? Where are you going? What is your name? Where do you live? What profession? Were there any fevers in the . . . country you came through?"[103] This curiosity, Michaux concluded, was "natural to people who live isolated in the woods, and seldom see a stranger."[104] Idlers were more apparent in the slave states where blacks performed the hard labor and whites emulated a landed gentry. "Today I have observed hundreds of idlers . . . sitting in the public places lounging in the bar-rooms of taverns and coffee houses, collected in squads at the corners of streets, lolling on benches in front of the houses, or balancing, Yankee fashion, on two legs of a chair—all apparently at a loss how to get rid of time," Frederick Hall wrote at Lexington, Kentucky, in 1837.[105]

Taverns varied in cleanliness and order, although the dirty and otherwise unsatisfactory places elicited the most comment. "Stages rattled up to the inn-door, at the most unseemly hours of the night, and we heard the whoops and halloos of the passengers," Mrs. Houstoun wrote at one tavern.[106] "Every one of the window-frames in the room were broken [and] we lost no time in stuffing into the apertures some towels, and tattered remnants of carpets and finally succeeded in keeping out the . . . noise and . . . unwholesome night air," she continued.[107] Bedbugs were a real problem being "constantly carried in the cloaths [sic], luggage, etc., from one house to another until many a bug," Adlard Welby quipped, "has been as great a traveler as Mr. Birkbeck himself." Few private rooms were available, and guests were required to share beds with strangers when need arose. "American travelers hardly ever talk to each other, but they make no objection to sleeping in the same bed," a French traveler wrote.[108]

The arrival of a traveler at a "private house" often set in motion the preparation of his meal. Perhaps, the children were set to chasing down a chicken. Otherwise, the traveler ate the regular family fare. "Supped on pumpkins, cabbages, rye coffee without sugar, bones of venison, salted pickles, etc.—all in the midst of crying children, dirt, filth, and misery," wrote Richard Mason from a tavern at Hindostan in southern Indiana.[109] Public taverns had regularly scheduled meals announced by the ringing of a dinner bell. The food was that of the locale. The food, John Wright wrote from Ohio, was "extremely unpleasant to an eastern stomach," being chiefly "hog, hominy, and hoe cake."[110] "I am reduced to a mere traveling mummy," he later complained by letter to a friend.[111] One English traveler observed that "A profusion of animal food is placed on the table, and the quantity increases in proportion to want of refinement in the people of the district."[112] As an area matured, greater variety was introduced to the tables of local taverns. One visitor observed in western Pennsylvania in 1848:

> The middle of the table is covered with perhaps a dozen plates, which are poked on without any order whatever, and containing the most promiscuous collection of eatables you can imagine . . . stewed peaches, salt fish, honey in the comb, fried potatoes, butter, preserved plums, frizzled pork, apples in molasses, cucumbers in vinegar . . . tomato jelly, biscuits, coffee, corncakes, and musk.[113]

The bar was usually located in one corner of the dining room or in an adjacent room. Here the barkeeper poured the drinks or sold jugs of liquor and otherwise ran the tavern, registering guests and tending to their wishes when it suited. In these large public rooms the traveler not only encountered the food of the locality, but the gossip and the music as well. Jew's harps, banjoes, and other instruments provided the background for many a rollicking barroom scene. The doors and walls were often covered with advertisements, particularly ads for sheriffs' sales.

HOTELS

In the larger towns and cities, hotels siphoned off the first-class trade, eventually replacing the smaller, less efficient taverns. Hotels, such as the Burnet House in Cincinnati and the Galt House in Louisville, amazed even the European travelers. The French traveler Marie Grandfort wrote in 1853, "Owing to their instincts of locomotion, the Americans have naturally paid the most attention to all that appertains to life on the road. Thus their hotels are incomparable for size, luxury, and style of management."[114] The American hotel was kept in constant activity. Locals came to learn the latest news and to visit with friends in the public rooms. "If motion be life," continued Grandfort, "there is no central point in the world where more vital energy is consumed in twenty-four hours than in the hotels of the United States."[115] John Richard Beste wrote of Cincinnati's Burnet House:

> [I] could not but admire the arrangement and architecture of the building, which was more like a church on the outside, and a London club house within than like a hotel according to European notions. A broad flight of steps, in the middle of a lofty basement, surrounded with a stone balustrate, led up to a large building . . . five stories high . . . surmounted by a dome and lantern, from which rose a flag-staff bearing a wide banner.[116]

Robert Playfair found himself "bewildered by numerous long galleries and the existence of four staircases all alike."[117] The Burnet House contained over 300 rooms and 1,000 beds.

Most hotels included a large reception area with registration desk, a bar, a reading room where newspapers were kept, a general lounge, a ladies' lounge, bathing rooms, and a dining room. Guests assembled for meals with the ringing of bells carried by "bell boys" through the corridors. John Richard Beste stayed with his family for over a month at Terre Haute's Prairie House during the summer of 1854. His diary details the workings of this small hotel. The typical breakfast included hot and cold breads of different kinds, pancakes and fritters, milk, butter buried in large lumps of ice, molasses, blackberry preserves and syrup, steaks, roast, boiled chickens, and tea, coffee, and chocolate.[118] "As waiters," he wrote, "there were six or seven boys . . . from eight to twelve years old, who all ran about the room barefooted, but who were, otherwise, neatly dressed in white jackets and aprons."[119] A black steward had charge. Dinner at noon usually comprised roast beef, steaks, chicken and veal pie, roast lamb, veal and mutton, boiled ham, pigeons, and roast pork. Vegetables included peas and beans, hominy, potatoes, squash, "and always boiled ears of green Indian corn."[120] Sweets included cherry, squash, and apple pies and sometimes stewed pears and roasted apples. Then followed cheese and dessert consisting of "large bowls of iced cream and water melons."[121] Guests sat at long tables, and the food was passed on plates. Blacks, both travelers and servants, ate at a separate table. Overhead fans were installed in many hotel dining rooms manipulated by black servants. Houseflies were a constant menace everywhere.

Bedrooms were often dirty and little cared for. Linen was changed infrequently, and often guests found it necessary to clean a room before settling in. Mrs. Houstoun found her hotel at Pittsburgh to be a "great wide-spreading, open mouthed building, lighted from top to bottom with most unpleasantly smelling gas and noisy with bustling waiters and flippant chambermaids."[122] Cockroaches were nearly everywhere. She found the rooms gloomy and dingy, the red curtains and carpets covered with accumulated coal dust. The hotel looked centuries old and, accordingly, it was difficult for her to imagine Pittsburgh as a new city. At Cincinnati's Jefferson Hotel, Moritz Busch found "spider webs in the corners of the [bed] canopy, broken window panes, an unlockable door, a washstand without a basin, and a barroom full of ragged, unkempt Irishmen."[123] Hotel rates varied from $2 to $5 per night depending upon the accommodations.[124]

SPAS

Spas or health resorts developed at many of the larger springs in the Ohio Valley. Most were located in the mountainous eastern section where cool summer temperatures at higher altitudes, the scenery, and the spring water combined to attract vacationers and tourists. The spas were the most popular resorts of early nineteenth-century America. The largest, such as White Sulphur Springs in present-day West Virginia, attracted the most fashionable elements of southern planter society, and many from the urban upper class of the Northeast and West as well. A visit to a spa was actually a social event, although the supposed medicinal effects of the spring waters provided the primary excuse to congregate.

Many planters along with their families made the rounds each summer going from spa to spa. James Buckingham saw this as important therapy for southern gentry women. With slaves performing all the labor "home becomes wearisome, tedious, and montonous; and anything which offers the relief of change is acceptable," he wrote.[125] The requisites for a successful resort, another traveler wrote, were a ballroom, a water cure, and a cook, for spas were intended "for a world that employs the summer . . . to flirt, freshen, and fatten."[126]

Frederick Marryat described White Sulphur Springs in 1838. The resort was situated in a narrow valley, the cleared area estimated at about twenty acres. He wrote:

> At one end of the valley is the hotel, with the large dining room for all the visitors. Close to the hotel, but in another building is the ball-room, and a little below the hotel on the other side, is the spring itself; but

. . . the great charm of this watering place is the way in which . . . the hills . . . are covered with little cottages, log houses, and other picturesque buildings, sometimes in rows and ornamented with verandahs.[127]

The cabins consisted of one, two, or more rooms, each containing a bed, a table, a mirror, and two or three chairs.

Each day had its routine. "In the morning they all turn out from their little burrows, meet in the public walks, and go down to the spring before breakfast . . . after dinner they ride out or pay visits, and then end the day, either at the ball-room, or in little societies among one another," Marryat observed.[128] At night hundreds of people crowded the ballroom. The room was well lit by scores of lamps reflected in mirrors. Black musicians constituted the orchestra, and black servants crowded the windows to watch the dancing. James Buckingham observed most of the guests to be "genteel in dress, appearance, and manners"; but there were many "extravagant specimens of American dandies" who were coarse and vulgar.[129] He was amused at the excess to which many females pushed the prevailing dress styles. "Extremely compressed waists, very low bodices, greatly exposed back, and perfectly naked shoulders, hugely protruding bustles, and artificially projecting busts, added to the most beseeching coquetry of attitude and manner," he wrote.[130]

Health and Personal Comfort

Although hotels, spas, and other places of convenience catered to travelers and although steamboats and railroads greatly reduced the difficulties of moving from place to place, travel was still very fatiguing even in the 1850s. Rarely was there enough time or adequate facility for bathing and tending to housekeeping chores. Rarely could the traveler achieve adequate privacy. Mixed with a varied population in drafty stages and railroad cars and in dirty hotel rooms and confronted with strange and often poorly prepared food, the traveler was more vulnerable to disease. Most Ohio Valley travelers felt the effect of prolonged illness during their trips.

Bathing was a rare pleasure. Adlard Welby complained: "Where or when an American uses water for the purpose of washing more than his face and fingers, does not appear, for no water ever goes up stairs at a tavern . . . [rather] under the shed of the house, water and tin basins are placed in the morning, and each one on coming down rubs his face and hands."[131] A few bathed in the rivers and creeks. Only in the larger cities were bathing houses available; portable bathtubs were rare even in private homes.[132] James Buckingham, the British traveler and lecturer, observed, "The men seemed as if they did not shave more than once a month, or wash more than once a year; the women looked as though a comb never went through their hair, or soap and water over their skins."[133]

Many travelers found it difficult to keep clothes in order. Even the fastidious James Buckingham confided, "I change my shirt, when it is convenient, twice a week, and sometimes take my clothes off when I go to bed."[134] An unkempt appearance, however, was not necessarily undesirable. The Englishman Patrick Shirreff thought his threadbare clothes brought him more in contact with the lower classes, enabling him "to see them in their real character."[135] Nicholas Cresswell's experience vividly illustrated the importance of dress on the frontier. A member of the English gentry class, he came to the Ohio Valley in 1775 to survey land in Kentucky for a consortium of investors. On the outward trip, when he dressed immaculately in silver buckles and fine suits, the frontier element maintained its distance, but on his return, robbed of his fine clothes, without shoes, and literally destitute, his relations with frontier settlers were totally changed. For the first time mention of sex enters his journal. "Last night Miss Grimes came. A fine blooming Irish girl. The flesh overcame the spirit," he confided.[136] Given employment by an Indian trader and thus dressed in hunter's garb for a second trip west, Cresswell found still another world of social experience. Of a young Indian girl he noted, "She was young, handsome, and healthy, fine regular features and fine eyes, had she not painted them red before she came to bed."[137] The next morning he wrote, "My bed fellow is very fond of me this morning and wants to go with me. I find I must often meet with such encounters . . . if I do not take a squaw to myself."[138]

Sex was a subject little mentioned in the travel journals. Yet there was a degree of latent preoccupation, particularly on the part of the bachelor males. Such a comment as "there is . . . far more female loveliness in Nashville, than . . . in any other city in the Union," was typical.[139] Prostitution was everywhere, but only an unusual event brought it to print. Friedrich von Wrede wrote from Cincinnati: "A jealous party not being tenderly and quickly received into a house oc-

cupied by questionable females, soaked the house with water from a
fire engine and so disorganized the place that, midst the monstrous ex-
ultation of the multitude, the unchaste residents of the house hurriedly
took to flight."[140] Pornography was readily available, hawked on the
steamboats by small boys.[141] One traveler reported from Ohio that "the
barbershops and the coffee-houses are filled with the same indecent
prints and engravings, chiefly of French manufacture, that are to be
seen stuck on the walls to gratify the perverted taste of the Kentuckians
and Virginians."[142] On one steamboat, James Logan saw men "looking
up through some holes cut in the flooring above, and by laughter ex-
pressing their gratification."[143] He learned from the crewmen that it
was common on steamboats for the women in the ladies' cabins to be
so exposed.

Travelers contracted the spectrum of diseases which plagued the
early Ohio Valley. Included were the very serious illnesses like cholera
and smallpox as well as the less serious like ague and the "milk sick."
Ague was so common that many people considered it a part of normal
life. Work schedules, court dockets, and other events were adjusted to
allow for a sufferer's recurring attacks. An attack began with yawning
and stretching and a tired feeling. Cold sensations increased until the
victim's teeth chattered. After an hour or so, warmth returned increasing to a high fever with severe back pains. Profuse sweating ended
each attack. Cholera struck as quickly. One traveler wrote of his experience aboard the steamboat Scotland: "I did not think cholera was
contagious and so I often rubbed ill persons when they were taken
with cramps. They suffered terribly and at times screamed fright-
fully. . . . An hour after the attack a victim would be so changed
one would scarcely know him. His eyes sunk into his head and the
whole body shriveled. Very few recovered."[144] He was amazed at the
lack of concern of many passengers: "While one was lying fighting in
death, others would sit nearby drinking and playing cards. As soon as
one died, the ship was stopped, a shallow grave was dug, and the body
was thrown in without any coffin. The grave was covered with sand
and the journey was resumed."[145]

The Influence of Travel

The taverns, hotels, stages, steamboats, and railroads sheltered the
traveler. In so doing the institutions of travel helped to smooth the dif-

ferences from place to place, to facilitate the transition from one area to another. But travel, as a way of life, purveyed the whole of America. One English visitor observed that certain classes made "a business of traveling" in Europe, but in America there were very few who did not travel frequently over long distances.[146] Travel was an American obsession. Nowhere was this truer than in the West where migrants sought out new opportunities and tourists followed to see what they were accomplishing.

The traveler in the Ohio Valley could think of himself more as a participant and less as an observer. Much of the region's culture hinged on constant mobility. The traveler was as much a "mover" as any other. He was not only a seeker of information, but a source of information to others in the districts through which he passed. His evaluations of place could potentially turn to his own monetary or other advantage, even though his objective in travel might be otherwise directed. His action, as a traveler, was close to America's cultural mainstream.

What a traveler saw was influenced by the conditions under which he traveled. Those who moved slowly through the landscape on foot, by horse, or by carriage had greater opportunities to observe places close at hand. Those who moved quickly by railroad or who obscured themselves in steamboats saw less. The mode of transport and type of accommodation influenced whom one met and what one learned indirectly of a locality.

Travel was (and is) primarily a process of validating expectations. Expectations regarding routes and accommodations, being more immediate to a traveler's well-being, did, through association, easily influence his view of the other aspects of place. One traveler stranded at an isolated railroad station on the Illinois prairie found no interest or beauty in the place solely on the basis of poor travel connections.[147] Comfort, whether in motion or in one's lodging, colored landscape interpretations both as initially conceived and as evaluated and reformed during the journal-writing process. Comfort seemed to invite more of the romantic and encourage the search for the picturesque. Discomfort invited more practical, utilitarian reactions to landscape. Severe discomfort, as in illness, could destroy observation altogether. Josiah Espy, who had traveled to Ohio to find a new farm, admitted: "The nature of the country between Chillicothe and New Lancaster, I find very indistinct, the fever and ague during the ride had almost destroyed my curiosity for observation."[148]

3 WILDER IMAGES

We went out with no other preparation than our parasols . . . determined upon having a day's enjoyment of the wildest scenery we could find.

Frances Trollope

To most Americans of the eighteenth and the nineteenth century, nature was something to be conquered, to be humanized through the forces of European culture. A wilderness, as the Ohio Valley was initially thought to be, was viewed by many as a savage and dangerous place, alien to civilized life. Such feelings rationalized the often blind destruction of the natural environment. Nature was to be tamed at any cost. A few romanticized the wilder places, for the human spirit, despoiled by civilized society, could find renewal in simpler, primitive circumstances. One traveler wrote, "There is a certain tranquility and balm in the forest that heals and calms the fevered spirit and quickens the languid pulses of the weary and disheartened with the breath of hope."[1] European views of nature were alien to most of the Indians living in the Ohio Valley. They viewed their lives as dependent upon nature and, ideally, the environment was to be respected and not abused. Nonetheless, few Indian communities were capable of subsisting without European or American items of trade which could be obtained only by destroying the region's fur resource and by selling large tracts of land for white settlement.

When the first white travelers entered the Ohio Valley it was al-

ready a zone in transition: a frontier of European culture. Like the settlers, most travelers valued nature for its potential for development.
Attention focused on the weather and climate, the topography, and the
species of plants and animals found. What was the environment of
Ohio Valley like? Was its climate similar to eastern areas? Was the
land mountainous or flat? Was the soil fertile? What flora and fauna
could be found? Was it a proper place for settlement?

In the later years, after the land had been cleared for farms and
towns, the traveler's concern for nature continued. Many sought wilder
places in the remaining forests, particularly in the Appalachian Mountains. Many natural curiosities in the region, particularly the mineral
springs and the caves, were packaged as tourist attractions. Mammoth
Cave was among the more notorious of these places. Here visitors clam-
bered along the subterranean passages in a truly alien world where the
romantic and picturesque aspects of place were glorified.

Talking about the Weather

Nearly every traveler commented on the weather. Roads blocked by
rain-choked rivers, drought and the lack of water for horses, and un-
timely storms were among the inconveniences of travel. However, most
travelers looked beyond the day-to-day weather to generalize about the
Ohio Valley's climate. Were summers longer than in the East? Were
winters shorter? Many sought to relate climate to other aspects of the
natural environment. For example, how was climate reflected in vegetation? Above all, was the climate of the Ohio Valley comfortable and
healthy? Travelers sought to identify both geographical and temporal
patterns. Was the season as advanced in the mountains as in the lowlands? When did the various seasons begin and what were they like?
Much attention was given to describing the extremes of weather. Some
formulated laws to describe what they had seen. A few were concerned
to perfect techniques for measuring meteorological and other environmental conditions.

A first concern was to compare the Ohio Valley with adjacent areas.
Opinions were based on actual observations and the general concensus
of residents in areas visited. In 1784 John Filson wrote of Kentucky:
"This country is more temperate and healthy than the other settled
parts of America. In summer it has not the sandy heats of which Virginia and Carolina experience, and receives a fine air from its rivers. In

winter, which at most only lasts three months . . . the people are safe in bad houses. . . . Snow seldom falls deep or lies long."[2] The naturalist Constantine Volney reported that trees and plants "which require a warm climate" are found "three degrees further north on the west of the Alleghanies than to the east on the Atlantic coast."[3] Most saw the Appalachian Mountains as a beneficial block to arrest "those chilling, blighting, furious, and sometimes tremendous eastwardly storms."[4] Most Easterners, particularly New Englanders, were conditioned to feel that the climate back home was more severe.

Early observers relied more on local folklore, and when promoting an area, as John Filson did in Kentucky, their pronouncements were rarely more than wishful thinking. By the 1840s scientists, such as Dr. Daniel Drake at Cincinnati, had developed a system of correspondents (usually doctors at military posts) who regularly recorded weather information with standardized instruments. When Drake reported that temperatures ranged approximately six degrees higher west of the Mississippi River in comparison to the eastern Ohio Valley, his observations were somewhat better founded in fact.[5] Of course, Drake was well aware of the limitations of his data. He had an insufficient number of places reporting, observations were not always standardized as to time of day and condition of site, instruments were inaccurate, and, finally, army doctors were constantly being shifted from post to post with gaps in data resulting.

Climatic differences could be observed in various ways. Climate obviously varied between high and low elevations. Drake assumed a reduction in mean annual temperature of one degree Fahrenheit for each 200 feet of elevation.[6] Temperature differences were most apparent in the spring when vegetation in the lowlands was observed to be more advanced than in the mountains. Vegetation was thus a key clue to climate. Many claimed to see climatic differences in peoples' faces. For example, Mrs. Basil Hall, accompanying her husband northward from New Orleans, observed that "the northern climate shows itself in the increased brilliancy of complexion in place of the sallow faces we have of late been in the habit of seeing."[7]

The nature of the seasons held profound interest. When did each season begin? What was it like and how long did it last? William Oliver wrote of his new farm near Albion, Illinois, that winter did not begin in earnest until mid-January.[8] Then came northwest winds sweeping the prairie "with a chilling blast that made the bones of one's face ache."[9] Most agreed that spring was very short with the hot weather of summer arriving soon after the spring equinox. The French naturalist Constantine Volney wrote of the "sudden transition from severe cold to violent heat" when vegetation "burst forth, its progress . . . extremely rapid."[10] Most Europeans found the summer heat and humidity of the Ohio Valley quite oppressive. An Englishman wrote at Louisville: "The thermometer rose this day to 100° and the heat and perspiration were intolerable. I was compelled to relieve myself of my upper garments; to throw myself on a naked mattress; and with the windows open and remaining perfectly still, the perspiration rose on my skin in globes, collected in my hair, and coursed down my face and hands."[11]

Most travelers agreed that autumn was the most pleasant season in the Ohio Valley. One reason was the unusual condition of the atmosphere during "Indian Summer" which Drake described as "an apparent smokiness through which the sun and moon, when near the horizon, and especially in the evening, appear of a crimson hue."[12] Drake attributed the effect to the widespread forest and prairie fires.

Weather was constantly changing with seemingly as much variation within seasons as between seasons. Volney reported that the winds were "perpetually varying from one quarter of the compass to its opposite" and that alterations in the temperature were "as great as they are sudden."[13] Drake saw the shifts as an interplay of air masses, although he did not use that term. In the nation's "climatic geography" there were four regions in which the air "differed widely," he wrote.[14] They were in order of importance for the Ohio Valley: the Gulf of Mexico, the continental interior west of the Mississippi River, the Great Lakes, and the Arctic. "It cannot be doubted that nearly all the rain which falls in the Interior Valley is brought from the Gulf of Mexico by our southerly winds," he wrote. "When they reach the middle latitudes, a cooler atmosphere condenses a portion of their vapor into rain or snow; and they often meet with northwest currents which greatly increase the condensation."[15] Drake's interest in climate was primarily medical. He found the "sudden vicissitudes" in the weather "trying to the constitution," especially in the late autumn when summer clothing was not yet laid aside and in the early spring when it was prematurely put on.[16] He thought climatic inconsistency produced relapses of ague and fever, accelerated the development of tuberculosis, and gave rise to rheumatism and croup.

Did the clearing of the Ohio Valley forests appreciably change the region's climate? Testimonies collected by Constantine Volney during his travels convinced him that summers were longer and winters shorter with less precipitation in cleared areas.[17] Volney explained that forests on hill and ridge tops intercepted the clouds and encouraged precipitation, and hills stripped of vegetation made for drier conditions. Gilbert Imlay thought that cleared land was more thoroughly warmed by the sun; the land, in turn, warmed the atmosphere.[18] Such thinking probably prevailed in the nineteenth century. Only a few, like Daniel Drake, argued that these conclusions were premature, for the facts were simply not available.[19]

Travelers tended to emphasize extremes. Exceptionally high or low temperatures or prolonged drought or heavy rain were always topics of ready conversation wherever travelers went. Violent weather received more consideration than normal or average conditions. It was a rare individual who could ignore the power of a thunderstorm. Harriet Martineau, traveling by steamboat on the Ohio River, described the surreal qualities of one violent storm:

> I saw the squall coming in a dark line, straight across the river. Our boat was hurried under the bank to await it. The burst was furious; a roaring gust, and a flood of rain. . . . All was nearly dark as night. . . . Lightning was all abroad. . . . One splendid violet coloured shaft shot straight down into the forest; I saw a tall tree first blaze and then smoulder at the touch. A horse floated by, dead and swollen.[20]

One minister, after experiencing such a storm, exclaimed: "Oh it was grand! God's own voice in God's own temple!"[21]

Tornados were even more impressive. John Audubon was traveling by horse eastward from Shawneetown, Illinois, when he observed to the southwest a yellowish oval spot where he had seen a thunderstorm brewing.[22] Within minutes the wind had put the whole forest in "fearful motion." Trees creaked as they bent and then began to disintegrate: first the limbs and then the upper trunks as a cloud of dust and foliage enveloped the scene. A quarter-mile wide swath of destruction was left in the storm's wake. Twigs and small branches could be seen following the funnel. The sky assumed a "greenish lurid hue," and a noxious smell of sulphur filled the air. Although few tornados were actually seen, the paths of destruction, or "fallen timbers," which remained were visible to travelers for decades.

Travelers expended considerable effort simply describing the sky. It

took no profound interest in the atmosphere to enjoy a sunset or to recognize an unusual cloud condition. Early morning and evening skies
were emphasized. The start and finish of each day seemed to require
a checking of the heavens. For some it was a curiosity to know what
the weather would be. For others it was a habit of esthetic appreciation. "The early morning air was loaded with that dull, still closeness
which foretells a day of sweltering heat," one traveler wrote.[23] "The
still, cold frosty mornings gave a vigour and boldness of outline to the
mountain scenery that extended its limbs and heightened its effect,"
wrote another.[24]

Sunrise was a magic time of day. The most startling effects were experienced on the rivers. The fog lifted slowly to hang suspended, sometimes for hours, above the river valleys. Viewed from a high elevation
the sight could be most novel. One traveler wrote of "the thick mists
of the night" that "lay on all the valleys like a sea of sleeping waters."[25]
Not all were content simply to admire the morning scene. In September of 1810, John Melish conducted a series of experiments at Louisville.[26] Fog occurred, he found, when the air temperature fell at night
below the temperature of the water: the greater the difference, the
thicker the fog. When the air and water temperatures equalized, the
fog began to dissipate.

The Contrast of Forest and Prairie

Nothing was more conspicuous in the landscape than vegetation. Trees
were noted for their size, beauty, and potential use, and they were
used to judge the quality of soil. Vegetation communities were seen to
vary from place to place according to the drainage, the elevation, and
the latitude. Many travelers noted the effects of forest succession on
abandoned farmland. Those who traveled far enough to the west were
amazed with the prairies, as a very different kind of environment.
Vegetation epitomized nature. Nature was a forest or wild-prairie thing.

"Every region presents you with its favorite species," one traveler
wrote.[27] Observed changes in vegetation increased one's sense of place,
for vegetation was indicative of other environmental aspects. Daniel
Drake considered vegetation "the most unerring indication of climate,"
but realized that such factors as topography and drainage, parent rock
and soil, and the "art and enterprise of man" also influenced vegetation

distribution.[28] The species most noted throughout the region included several kinds of oaks (*Quercus*), ashes (*Fraxinus*), walnuts (*Juglans*), hickories (*Carya*), hackberries (*Celtis*), maples (*Acer*), beeches (*Fagus*), and elms (*Ulmus*). Yellow-poplar or tulip tree (*Liriodendron tulipifera*), the Kentucky coffee tree (*Gymnocladus dioicus*), honey locust (*Gleditsia texana*), red bud (*Cercis canadensis*), sassafras (*Sassafras albidum*), persimmon (*Diospyros virginiana*), dogwood (*Cornus florida*), and sumac (*Rhus copallina*) were also frequently mentioned. Noted primarily in the lowlands were willows (*Salix*), cottonwoods (*Populus deltoides*), and sycamores (*Platanus occidentalis*). The Appalachian Mountains were distinctive for their pines (*Pinus*), birches (*Betula*), hemlock (*Tsuga canadensis*), and, especially, mountain laurel (*Kalmia latifolia*). In the lower Ohio Valley, particularly in poorly-drained areas, the distinctive bald cyprus (*Taxodium distichum*) and red cedar (*Juniperus virginiana*) were found. Toward the north were junipers (*Juniperus communis*) and buckeyes (*Aesculus glabra*); toward the south were chestnuts (*Castanea dentata*), black locust (*Robina pseudoacacia*), and magnolia (*Magnolia tripetala*). To the west on the prairies was the bur oak (*Quercus macrocarpa*).

Beauty in the forest was observed in many forms. In the oak, hickory, and chestnut communities travelers marvelled at the openness of the forest floor and its almost park-like appearance, with giant trees widely spaced with little undergrowth. The great size of the trees fascinated, and most travelers who descended the Ohio River by flatboat managed at some point along the way to measure a giant tree. From George Washington's journal one learns of a large sycamore of forty-five foot circumference at the mouth of the Kanawha River; nearby was another thirty-one feet around.[29] Many of the giant sycamores were hollow and could accommodate a man on horseback.[30] Almost as impressive as the trees themselves were the various species of hanging vines, particularly where sunlight penetrated as along the banks of the rivers.

Fires provided the most spectacular forest scenes. Fires burned out of control each fall charring hundreds of thousands of square miles. Most were set by hunters who sought to flush game and thin the undergrowth. Crossing the mountains in autumn provided nighttime spectacles. In 1803 at Laurel Hill west of Bedford, Pennsylvania, one traveler found the ridges of the various mountains ablaze; over a distance of fifty miles the flames reflected on the clouds of smoke.[31] Another traveler on the Ohio River reported the smoke so thick that during an

entire day of traveling he could not see from one bank of the river
to the other.[32]

Utilitarian orientations to the forest were many. Picking up on local
lore or applying back-home wisdom, travelers translated stands of
chestnuts, yellow poplars, and other trees into fence posts and the
equivalents of log cabins. But the most widespread form of resource
evaluation concerned the soil.

The most fertile soil sported combinations of locust, walnut, buckeye,
maple, elm, beech, and pawpaw (*Asimina triloba*). "Middle rate" land
consisted of oaks combined with hickories, dogwood, and maples. "Indifferent land" contained mostly black and white oak with some hickory. François Michaux, traveling in Kentucky, wrote, "They appreciate
the fertility of the land by the different species of trees that grow
there; thus when they announce the sale of an estate, they take care
to specify the particular species of trees peculiar to its various parts,
which is sufficient index for the purchaser."[33] Travelers as early as the
1820s found vast acreages of farmland abandoned to the forest. In
Kentucky locust trees appeared in abandoned pastures, but walnut
trees grew first on previously cultivated ground. Red cedars claimed
the poorest land and stood to symbolize agricultural failure and the
triumph of nature over man. This linking of trees with soil fertility continued in the travel literature until the 1840s.

The prairies initially symbolized infertility and were often called
"barrens" accordingly. The first grasslands, called "glades," were encountered in western Pennsylvania. Initially used by settlers for pas-
turage they were considered "naturally free" of timber, although burning by the Indians was probably responsible. Early opinion was that
the thick grass prevented the seeds of trees from reaching the soil. Although the Pennsylvania glades had been converted to cultivation by
1790, many settlers on encountering grasslands farther west persisted
in considering them infertile. Soil that did not grow trees might not
grow crops.

The real reasons for shunning the prairies probably had little to do
with suspected infertility. The light plows used in cultivating forest
soils could not tackle thick prairie sod. On the wet prairies poor drainage was an additional problem. Timber for buildings, fences, and fuel
had to be obtained elsewhere at prohibitive costs. Western prairies
were usually avoided by the earliest settlers and thus survived as "natural" environments well into the 1850s and 1860s. Travelers following

a road through a populated country would suddenly break out onto a grassland and find themselves alone sometimes for hours until the forest was regained.

The first view of a large prairie was often quite startling. "The view of that noble expanse was like the opening of bright day upon the gloom of night, to us who had been so long buried in deep forests. To travel day after day, among trees of a hundred feet high, without a glimpse of the surrounding country, is oppressive," Morris Birkbeck wrote of English Prairie in Illinois.[34] In the forest, the horizon extended no more than a few hundred yards, but in the prairies vistas of ten miles or more were common.

Many compared the prairies to the ocean. In the summer the tall grass, sometimes as tall as a man on horseback, rippled in the wind like waves. In the distance the edges of the forest seemed like seacoasts. The British traveler Simon Ferrall wrote, "Before us lay a rich green undulating meadow, and on either side, clusters of trees, interspersed through this vast plain in beautiful irregularity . . . the waving of the high grass and the distant groves rearing their heads just above the horizontal line, like the first glimpse of land to the weary navigator."[35] Basil Hall, himself a sea captain, had thought descriptions of the prairies exaggerated only to discover that the "appearance of the distant insulated trees, as they gradually rose above the horizon or receded from our view, was so exactly like strange sails heaving in sight."[36] Ferrall found the scene "sublime," for "ideas expand and the imagination is carried far beyond the limits of the eye."[37]

The prairies, given the general flatness and lack of trees, could become monotonous. After riding all day across the Grand Prairie of Illinois more than one traveler imagined himself exactly where he had started in the morning. One wrote that the eye soon became "satiated with the spreading fields of grass" and that a "feeling of desolation" derived from traveling across "unvaried plains."[38] In the depressions or "slues" where it was perpetually marshy, a traveler's horse might sink to its chest in the mire. Insects, particularly mosquitos, were a chronic problem. During the dry season the hot glare of the sun and dust raised by the horses brought discomfort. After the initial pleasure of discovery, most travelers were glad to put the prairies behind them.

British travelers likened the prairies to English parklands, for interspersed across them were small groves of trees, particularly bur oak. These trees with their thick bark withstood the fires which each fall and spring scorched the prairies. Set by hunters, these fires destroyed most other tree saplings, leaving the ground covered in grass and small woody plants. Where the fire had been withheld the forests encroached on the prairies. Prairie fires were as spectacular as forest fires. William Hall found one blaze on Little Prairie "a most sublime spectacle."[39] Towards evening thick clouds of smoke obscured the horizon. With darkness the flames could be seen moving in a bright irregular line of several miles extant "ranging towards you with increased fury, roaring, crackling, and thundering up the slope" and into the forest.[40] Sometimes four or five separate fires could be seen at once.

On the Lookout for Wildlife

Nearly every traveler commented on the animal life of the region. Those who early descended the Ohio River by canoe or rode or walked overland into present-day Kentucky and Ohio were amazed both by the variety of animals and by their large numbers. In the early years attention was focused on the larger exotic species rare or unknown in the East. Animals were described not only as curiosities, but, more importantly, as food sources, for the earliest travelers were dependent upon wild game for sustenance. George Croghan wrote in 1765 from the mouth of the Kanawha River that "here buffaloes [*Bison bison americanus*], bears [*Euarctos americanus*], turkeys [*Meleagris gallopavo*], with all kind of wild game are extremely plenty. A good hunter, without much fatigue to himself could here supply daily 100 men with meat."[41] After 1810 attention shifted. The larger game animals, such as the bison, elk (*Cervus canadensis*), deer (*Odocoileus virginianus*), and bear had disappeared before the hunter's gun. Travelers glimpsed small animals from the decks of the steamboats in their eagerness to see wilder images. The more exotic species were so rare after 1830 that travelers interested in viewing specimens were reduced to visiting museums in the larger cities.

Two animals attracted maximum attention: the bison and the gray squirrel (*Sciuridae carolinensis*). Although the bison were never numerous in the forested portions of the Ohio Valley (herds rarely numbered more than a few hundred), their seasonal migrations eastward to the salt springs of Kentucky, Tennessee, and western Virginia created an extensive system of game trails or "buffalo traces." Not only were the bison the largest animals in North America, but they had produced "avenues" in the wilderness which greatly facilitated the movement of white settlers into the region. Kentucky's Wilderness Road through

Cumberland Gap to Louisville followed a series of buffalo traces as did the road from Louisville to Vincennes across southern Indiana. Indeed, travelers in the nineteenth century leaving the Big Lick near present-day Roanoke, Virginia, could travel over a thousand miles to the Grand Prairie of Illinois without leaving roads originally derived from buffalo traces.

Buffalo traces were well inscribed in the landscape where they crossed major rivers and where they approached the major salt springs or "licks." The trace which led from Maysville, Kentucky, on the Ohio River across the Blue Grass Basin to Louisville crossed the Kentucky River at present-day Frankfort. Here in 1784 the early historian and promoter of Kentucky, John Filson, found "a great road large enough for wagons . . . sloping with an easy descent from the top to the bottom of a very large steep hill."[42] Filson also described the licks.

> To these the cattle repair and reduce high hills rather to valleys than plains. The amazing herds of buffaloes which resort thither, by their size and number, fill the traveler with amazement and terror, especially when he beholds the prodigious roads they have made from all quarters, as if leading to some populous city; the vast space of land around these springs desolated as if by a ravaging enemy. . . . These are truly curiosities and the eye can scarcely be satisfied with admiring them.[43]

Animals had been coming to the licks in search of salt for thousands of years. The remains of prehistoric bison, mastadon, and mammoth were found at Big Bone Lick southwest of Cincinnati.

Squirrels attracted attention for their migrations. Traveling in the fall of 1783, Johann Schoepf was amazed by the large numbers of gray squirrels migrating eastward over Allegheny Mountain.[44] The failure of nuts and acorns was said by locals to be the cause, and all predicted a hard winter. Squirrel was served at every meal at every tavern along the road to Pittsburgh. Most impressive were the migrations across the Ohio River when squirrels by the tens of thousands would halt passing steamboats sometimes for hours.

A few travelers sought to detect the ranges of certain common species. One traveler observed six species of squirrels between New Orleans and Louisville, "but always one kind in any given locality."[45] The ranges of various birds, particularly the exotic species such as the passenger pigeon (*Ectopistes migratorins*) and the parrot (*Psittacus carolinensis*), were most easily discernible. Both were common to the southwestern portion of the Ohio Valley and were first seen below

Louisville by steamboat passengers bound down the Ohio River. The parrots, called parroquets or parakeets by most, were common around the salt springs and were hunted for their colorful green plumage. The passenger pigeons lasted longer, but only due to their vast numbers. Their flocks, numbering tens and even hundreds of thousands of birds, could darken a morning sky. The passage of a single flock could take hours. The pigeon roosts were equally as impressive, provided one could stand the dirt, stench, and noise. Acres of timber, stripped bare of leaf, awaited the return of the flocks at night.

Birdlife held special fascination probably because birds were so easily seen in flight, especially from the decks of steamboats on the rivers. Most enthusiasts were excited by the soaring eagle (*Haliaeetus leucocephailus*) or turkey buzzard (*Cathartes aura*). Carrion birds brought special interest as they added to the sense of danger in wilder places. One hunter wrote: "The turkey buzzards were seen hovering in the air, and, after wet weather, were often observed sitting in the sun-shine, with outspread wings, on the highest trees."[46] The birds added a dimension of sound to the otherwise quiet scene except at night when the howl of the wolves (*Canis lupus*) and the scream of the wildcats (*Lynx rufus*) dominated in the winter, and the noise of insects in the summer.

New Englanders seemed especially interested in the fish of the Ohio and other rivers. Before 1800 the fish caught at Marietta, Cincinnati, and other places made phenomenal stories for friends and relatives back home. Thomas Hutchins, the geographer and surveyor, reported carp (*Cyprinus carpio*), sturgeon (*Acipenser sturio*), perch (*Perc flavescens*), and catfish (*Ictalurus iacustris*) of "uncommon size," the catfish weighing from fifty to 100 pounds.[47] Another saw a catfish four feet long, and still another traveler saw one which measured six inches between the eyes.[48]

Scenic Curiosities

Nothing was more popular than to ascend a mountain to take the view (Fig. 3-1). If not mountain scenery, then the roll of hill and valley was clearly preferred to the monotony of the flat plains. The Alleghenies provided much excitement. In the eighteenth century the Alleghenies were called the "Endless Mountains" because of the seemingly endless repetition of parallel valleys and ridges.

Figure 3-1.
Celebrating the View over Virginia's Great Valley. (*Harper's New Monthly Magazine*, Jan. 1856)

Most Europeans thought the range, with its low, heavily wooded ridges, contrasted poorly with the Alps, Pyrennes, and other European mountains. Volney noted that the highest ridge, Allegheny Mountain, was approached by a series of gentle and gradual ascents . . . scarcely noticed."[49] But to Americans of the seaboard, inexperienced in European landscapes, the Alleghenies were impressive. One traveler stopped on Allegheny Mountain to write of "high ridges, deep valleys, and steep precipices. . . . One of the most sublime and beautiful scenes . . . [for] as far as human sight could reach, in every direction . . . [were] chains of mountains."[50] Another traveler wrote of mountains "piled upon each other in masses which blend at last with the clouds above."[51] "At one point," he continued, "they lie in confused heaps together; at another they lap each other with outlines as distinct as if the crest of each were of chiselled stone . . . some swelling more gradually from the vales below, show in the blue distance like waves."[52] As the travelers continued west the mountain landscape gave way to hills and ultimately to the flat glacial till plains of Ohio, Indiana, and Illinois, broken only by the valleys of major rivers. South of the Ohio River on the Cumberland Plateau the topography was more varied and broken.

Travelers sought scenic curiosities in keeping with the romantic and picturesque traditions. As often as not, these were unusual landforms such as the Hawk's Nest in present-day West Virginia. Passengers traveling by stagecoach along the New River Valley of present-day West Virginia were treated to a special stop. Alighting from the coach and walking about 200 feet they found themselves on the flat top of a rock jutting out above the river valley below. One visitor wrote: "We laid hold for safety on the bare boughs of a . . . cedar on the edge of the precipice and willingly gave ourselves up to the silent contemplation of one of the most magnificent prospects to be found in North America. The river . . . is here seen winding its course . . . along an open plain at the foot of a glorious chain of mountains. . . . This is a spot where nature may fairly be said to bid defiance to the pencil."[53] The Englishman James Matheson was impressed with the scene, for it conveyed "the idea of perfect solitude," but was disgusted with his fellow passengers whose "employ was to throw stones across the river and their astonishment was to find that no stone they could cast would reach it."[54]

Those of subtle mind could find similar inspiration even among Ohio's low hills and plains to the northwest. Elizabeth Willson, elderly and crippled from a stroke, was taken by her daughters to the small ravine of Allum Creek near present-day Delaware, Ohio. The walls of the ravine were nearly perpendicular to the clear water below and "not only beautiful but sublimely grand."[55] She wrote:

> Oh, how I love the unformed scene
> Where naught but God's own finger's been;
> For naught of human power or skill
> Could e'er have framed this beauteous hill;
> These smooth high walls of alumed slate
> Display a power supremely great.[56]

No other place excited the romantic mind as much as Mammoth Cave. So different was this subterranean world that a walking trip of a few hours might elicit a fuller spectrum of impressions than several weeks of surface travel. Equipped with oil lamps and lunches, the men outfitted in flannel jackets and miner's boots and the women in special gowns and sometimes pantaloons, visitors descended through a large depression littered with broken bottles, oyster shells, and other rubbish. The sensations on entering the cave were many. More than one visitor wavered back and forth testing the air with both arms extended, one hand warm and the other cold. The air in the cave remained remarkably steady throughout the year at 59° F which contrasted sharply with the hot temperatures of most Kentucky summer days. Visitors made their way "after the manner of a mole" first bending as the guide shouted, "the Valley of Humiliation," and then scrambling up a slope of loose rock at the "Hill of Difficulty" only to squeeze through "Fat Man's Misery."[57] Harriet Martineau wrote: "We were obliged not only to go on hands and knees, but to crawl lying flat. It is a sensation worth knowing, to feel oneself imprisoned in the very heart of a mountain, miles from the sunlight. . . . Never was there a more magnificent prison or sepulchre."[58]

Sense perception was heightened by the strange environment and the difficulties of moving around. The feeling of confinement, strange sound effects, unusual odors, the feel of the floor and walls, and strange visual impressions all entered in. Lady Stuart-Wortley felt "a strange oppression and a longing for the sun and the free fresh air."[59] She viewed the excursion as a "sort of temporary burial."[60] The darkness, on the other hand, reminded Harriet Martineau of childhood nightmares, especially "the sense of infinite distance."[61] Stimulating was "the gloom, the echo of the footsteps, the hollow sound of voices, the startling effect of lights seen unexpectedly in a recess in a crevice, or high overhead," she wrote.[62] She called it "a chaos of darkness and rocks with wandering and inexplicable sounds and motions," for everything appeared alive.[63] "The slowly growing stalactites, the water ever dropping to the plashing pool, the whispering airs" seemed to have a consciousness all their own.[64]

Such an alien environment had to be humanized. Derived from the romantic impulse, each portion of the cave was named, landmarks identified, and, thereby, special meanings attached. The sequence of travel

from the "Great Vestibule" led along "Audubon Avenue" to the so-
called "Kentucky Cliffs" and the "church." There followed the Gothic
Avenue" and ultimately the "Dead Sea" and the "River Styx" by way of
the "Giant's Coffin," the "Elephant's Head," and the "Fairy's Orchard."
As stated in one well-known guide book, the cave was said to contain
"226 avenues, 47 domes, numerous rivers, 8 cataracts, and 23 pits, some
of which [possessed] so great a degree of grandeur as completely to
beggar description."[65] All was "so architectural" to one visitor.[66] The
different shapes and forms by which space was structured were
"strangely unexpected," and the various combinations of light and form
"flooded, satiated, and staggered the craving sense of the love of the
wonderful," he wrote.[67]

Not everyone was pleased with the cave. One traveler found the
stone dull, uniform, and only "sublime" (pun intended).[68] Another
likened the cave to a gigantic drain, "regular, smooth, and plastered
looking."[69] Signs of human desecration were everywhere. At the far-
thest end where the visitors turned back towards the entrance, the
walls were covered with advertisements, and here many visitors lifted
their lamps to smoke their initials on the cavern's ceiling and walls.

Besides enjoying unusual landforms, a few sought to explain the region's geology. One traveler at Chattanooga on the Tennessee River
wrote:

> I strolled out to look at the rocks. . . . I found the anticlinal structure
> occasionally well marked, the beds not observing the steady horizontal
> position [as] at Tuscumbia and Decatur. I was not surprised at this,
> always expecting that the nearer I approached . . . the Allegheny
> Mountains, the more I should find the beds influenced by the great
> movement which has modified the surface . . . into their ridges
> and valleys.[70]

Charles Lyell, the famous British geologist, observed carefully the terraces along the Ohio River to write, "The materials of the great terrace
of loam and gravel became more and more coarse as we approach
nearer the mountains between Wheeling and Pittsburgh and at the
same time the terrace itself is more and more elevated above the level
of the river."[71] He could only theorize that the amount of subsidence as
well as subsequent upward movement, which followed the period of
glaciation, had been greater inland or farther north than in the South

or nearer the Gulf of Mexico. Men like Lyell sought out the leading geologists of the Ohio Valley: people like William Maclure and David Dale Owen of New Harmony in Indiana whose work would ultimately lead to the founding of the U.S. Geological Survey. Their traveling with American colleagues in the field, inspecting rock and fossil collections, and discussing the local geology did much to enhance scientific geology in the United States.

A few travelers sought to regionalize the Ohio Valley according to its underlying geology and to contrast these regions and the Valley as a whole with other areas. Constantine Volney saw the Ohio Valley divided into four geologic areas: (1) the "Granite Region" of the Blue Ridge Mountains, (2) the "Regions of Sandstone" comprising all the Alleghenies west from the Blue Ridge, (3) the "Calcareous Region" including "all the western or back country" underlain by limestone, and (4) the "Region of Sea-sand" referring to glacial till plains of the Northwest which Volney associated with sea deposition and not continental glaciation.[72] Nothing attracted more attention than the karst topography of Kentucky and Tennessee of which Mammoth Cave was a part. As the limestone easily dissolved, much of the drainage was underground. Volney was surprised by the large number of sinkholes which "swallowed up" creeks which "suddenly disappear from the view of the astonished traveler, sinking into the ground amid thickets."[73] Volney also observed that most of the rivers of Kentucky and Tennessee were "enclosed in grooves between two perpendicular banks."[74] The Kentucky River was particularly noted for its gorge.

Few Ohio Valley travelers experienced an earthquake, but those who did retained vivid memories. Earthquakes, particularly the "New Madrid earthquake" of 1811, provided many a story to entertain later travelers in tavern barrooms and on steamboats. Audubon was crossing the Kentucky Barrens when the New Madrid earthquake struck. His horse suddenly stopped and placed its feet "as if walking on a smooth sheet of ice."[75] Then suddenly "all the shrubs and trees began to move from their very roots," he wrote, "and the ground rose and fell in successive furrows."[76] At Vincennes, Lydia Bacon and her husband were awakened by the shaking of their house. Their first impression was that the Indians were trying to break in. Earthquakes, she thought, served to "shew us the fallibility of earthly enjoyments and the necessity of religion."[77]

The Use of Nature

In the late eighteenth century the Ohio Valley was relatively unspoiled by the civilization of the eastern seaboard. Yet, for all of its pristine beauty and its scenic curiosities, most Americans viewed the region as a vast untapped resource base which held the nation's economic future. As we will see, the Ohio Valley's wilder images were celebrated for the promise which tomorrow held. The climate and soil promised rich harvests when the forests were cleared and the wilderness reduced to a garden. And the forests of the Ohio Valley promised farms for untold millions. Frances Trollope caught the spirit of the hour when she wrote in the rough draft of her travel book: "I used to think when hearing of the 'eternal' forests of A[merica] that people spoke as looking backward to the eternity of time [that] they had endured, but I now began to suspect that it was in looking forward to the eternity of [the] space they covered."[78]

Nature in America was big. America's future would be great. One British traveler remarked that the great difference between American and European scenery was that "here all is on much larger a scale."[79] He continued, "nature is here wrought out with so much more boldness, that it seems everywhere to have a sort of large-featured sublimity; and when you turn your mind from it to Europe, it seems like reversing the telescope and reducing creation to miniature."[80] Another wrote: "In America there seems a tendency in nature to do everything by wholesale. There are regions of plains, then regions of hill; instead of the less imposing . . . hill and dale."[81] Mrs. Trollope added, "Everything seems colossal on this great continent; if it thunders, it is all done fortissimo."[82] Edward Dicey, another Briton, thought the "single grand feature" about American scenery was its vastness.[83] The grand scale of nature, he thought, affected the American mind and invited grand schemes. "Sheer size and simple greatness possess an attraction which we in the old world can hardly realize," he wrote.[84]

The Americans came forward and conquered the western wilderness. The land was subdued. Yet, as shown, travelers continued to seek the wilder images even after the farms, towns, and cities came to dominate the landscape. Many sought reminders of what it had been like. Some sought to describe the few unspoiled forests and prairies which survived. Daniel Drake declared in the 1830s, "We should transmit to posterity a graphic description of the Great Valley, as it appeared in primitive loveliness to the eyes of the pioneers."[85] Others decried, as Harriet Martineau, the inability to fully learn from nature before nature was destroyed in the name of progress. She wrote:

> The primitive glories of nature have, almost always since the world began, been dispensed to savages; to men who . . . have no power of bringing into contrast with it the mind of man, as enriched and stimulated by cultivated society. Busy colonists, pressed by bodily wants, are the next class. . . . The next are those who would make haste to be rich. . . . Not to such alone should the primitive glories of nature be dispensed; glories which can never be restored. The philosopher should come, before they are effaced, and find combinations and proportions of life and truth which are not to be found elsewhere.[86]

The uses which travelers saw in nature shifted dramatically during the period. Early travelers saw utility in a nature relatively unspoiled. Later travelers faced with landscapes vastly altered by farms and towns sought esthetic appreciation in the residuals of nature. The more spectacular or unusual aspects of nature always attracted the most attention; but by the mid-nineteenth century many of these scenic wonders had been developed specifically for the tourist. The "wilder" images of nature were being packaged within an evolving tourist industry.

4 IMAGES OF ABORIGINAL LIFE

Sell a country! Why not sell the air, the clouds and the great sea, as well as the earth? Did not the Great Spirit make them all for the use of his children?

Tecumseh

The Indians who lived in the Ohio Valley only nominally controlled the region. The Shawnee, having lived along the Cumberland River in the early eighteenth century, had split into two groups, one group migrating as far south as Florida, but all reassembling along the Upper Ohio River by 1740 under the authority of the Iroquois Confederacy. The Delaware Indians, invited to the Susquehanna Valley by William Penn, vacated those lands for homes along the Allegheny River with, again, the Iroquois of New York as overlords. During preceding generations the Iroquois had systematically cleared the Ohio Valley of its population, people probably descended from the early mound builders. When lands in present-day Pennsylvania and West Virginia were ceded by the Iroquois in 1768 white settlers began to migrate into the Ohio Valley.

The Delaware and Shawnee resented the Iroquois cession of their hunting grounds and from the basis of that resentment became easy pawns in the struggle for empire between France and Britain. Later, when Britain and the United States competed for control of the western Ohio Valley and Great Lakes areas, the Miami, Wyandots, Pottawotami, Wea, and Piankishaw were also drawn into bloody conflict. Never did the Indians of the Ohio Valley act in concert for more than short periods. By the late eighteenth century most tribes hardly functioned as political units. Most had broken into squabbling groups rarely as large as a few hundred persons who moved seasonally to hunt and trap and who were completely dependent upon the European fur trade for many of the necessities of life. Occasionally, powerful leaders rallied the Indians to purify themselves of European ways or counter the invasion of a white army, but, by and large, Indian government was *ad hoc* and ineffectual. This latter situation greatly contributed to the instability of Indian culture and economy.

When travelers saw the mounds and earthworks now identified with prehistoric Adena, Hopewell, and Mississippian cultures, they could not believe that the Indians were responsible for their construction, so disorganized had Indian society become. The Indians were viewed by most white settlers as hostile savages. The traders, particularly the French who intermarried with the Indians in the Wabash settlements, maintained good relations. Of course, the traders who supplied rum, brandy, and corn whiskey did much to undermine Indian self-sufficiency. Alcoholism affected large numbers in every tribe, creating unstable personalities and abject poverty. Where a large mixed Indian and white population evolved, as among the Cherokees in present-day Tennessee and northern Georgia, the work of the missionaries brought a high level of civilization equal to if not exceeding that of most frontier whites. White prejudice ruled, however, and the Cherokees along with the other tribes were ultimately removed to reservations beyond the Mississippi River.

The Indian Mounds

Travelers sought out the Indian mounds as one of the region's outstanding curiosities. Mounds were noted as early as 1750 by Thomas Walker who saw near the head of the Cumberland River in Kentucky "a round hill made by art about twenty feet high and sixty over the top."[1] Most impressive were the large clusters of mounds and earthworks. Grave Creek at present-day Moundsville, West Virginia, was a popular stopping place for travelers descending the Ohio River. In 1775 Nicholas Cresswell described the largest mound as "a round hill something like a sugar loaf about 300 feet in circumference at bottom, 100 feet high, and about 60 feet in diameter at top where it forms a sort of ir-

Figure 4-1.
The Great Mound at Marietta, Ohio. This area was preserved as the town's cemetery. (E. G. Squier and E. H. Davis, *Ancient Monuments of the Mississippi Valley*, Washington, D.C., 1848)

regular basin."[2] Around the base ran a ditch sixty feet in width. Near the summit stood a huge white oak estimated by Meriwether Lewis in 1805 to be at least 300 years old.[3] The mound was completely covered with maples, hickories, oaks, and other trees, their trunks covered by the initials of visitors.[4]

The mounds and earthworks at Marietta, Ohio, also received considerable attention (Fig. 4-1). Marietta was established by the second Ohio Company and became the capital of the Northwest Territory. The initial settlers, most from New England, found an irregular square enclosure of about forty acres which contained four truncated pyramids about ten feet in height. Nearby was a truncated mound about thirty feet high surrounded by a circular wall. Connecting the larger enclosure with the Muskingum River was an excavated path called the *Sacra Via* by the settlers. In 1788 the Ohio Company passed a resolution reserving the two large enclosures and the mound as a public garden; shade trees were to be planted once the wild forest was stripped away. Badly eroded, the mounds and embankments were rescued in the 1830s by Marietta citizens who established a fund to restore, fence, and maintain them. This was probably the first instance of historic preservation in the region.

What had the mounds and earthworks been used for? At Marietta, white settlers saw ceremonial ways and ritual centers, perhaps platforms for temples. Military minds, like that of William Henry Harrison, saw fortifications. Several mounds were located high along the bluffs on the Harrison farm at North Bend, Ohio. Harrison imagined that here "a feeble band was collected . . . to make a last effort for the country of their birth, the ashes of their ancestors, and the altars of their gods."[5] But the mounds were primarily burial places, particularly the Hopewell mounds of which there were probably over 10,000 in Ohio alone.

Who built the mounds? This was one of the great philosophical questions of the nineteenth century. Initially, white racism provided most of the answers. Clearly, some vanished race of "mound builders" was responsible. Commentators sought to establish ties with old world civilizations. Perhaps a lost tribe of Israelites or Tartars, Greeks, Persians, Romans, Vikings, Hindus, or Phoenicians had been responsible, their civilization ultimately destroyed by the modern savages. As Filson speculated, the mounds proved that the region was "formerly inhabited by a nation farther advanced in the arts of life than the Indians."[6] The mounds, he continued, "are usually attributed to the Welsh, who are supposed to have formerly inhabited here; but having been expelled by the natives, were forced to take refuge near the sources of the Missouri."[7]

Most travelers thought the mounds could not have been built by the Indians who were obviously incapable of undertaking large engineering projects in the European manner. But most mounds were built piecemeal by small groups. Indeed, the process was observed by the French at Natchez in the early eighteenth century. There the Indians still followed the old practice of setting a circle of stakes in the ground around a funeral bier and heaping dirt within to form a small mound.

Most travelers were saddened by the thoughtless destruction of the earthworks. Farmers leveled the smaller mounds with their plows. In towns, streets were surveyed through rather than around the larger earthworks. Thomas Ashe reported that Cincinnati's principal street was cut through one mound exposing "its strata and remains to every person passing by."[8] "Children often amuse themselves in undermining the banks . . . and often find arrow points, beads, and many other curiosities," he continued.[9] A few of the mounds at Cincinnati were systematically excavated by Daniel Drake in 1815, but most were destroyed without investigation. One traveler, the lecturer James Buckingham, reported that "so indifferent were those who superintended and those who executed the labour, that they were rather astonished at [his] inquiries as to whether anything of interest had been found."[10]

The mounds, most located on or near fertile floodplains, had been built over a long period of Indian history beginning about 500 B.C. The cultures most identified with the construction of burial mounds were the Adena (500 B.C.-200 A.D.) and the Hopewell (200 B.C.-400 A.D.), both named after the locations in Ohio at which characteristic artifacts were first identified. The temple mounds were associated with Mississippian culture (900 A.D.-1400 A.D.) brought by migrants from the lower Mississippi Valley. The big mound at Grave Creek was of Adena origin, while the earthworks and most of the mounds at Marietta were of Hopewell origin. Mississippian temple mounds were found near present-day Evansville and at other points along the lower Ohio River. The mounds signified periods of relative peace and stability when large populations supported by agriculture lived in large village complexes or towns.

Observing Indian Life

The American's knowledge of the Indian derived from a variety of sources. The news and gossip of a largely illiterate pioneer settler population provided most of the innuendo and prejudice. This group left few written records. The traders who went seasonally into the Indian towns or who lived there permanently were evidently also too absorbed in everyday affairs to record experiences. Missionaries, to the contrary, were diligent in recording their observations, although most depicted Indian life with strong biases. Few missionaries appreciated Indian culture, and they sought to replace Indian ways with their own culture. Military personnel also had a first-hand look, but meeting the Indian on the battlefield or at treaty negotiation obviously involved adversary roles. Travelers were greatly conditioned by what other whites believed, and their reports must be treated carefully.

Many whites captured during wartime wrote diaries or later dictated depositions describing their hardships. Some, particularly those who ultimately remained with Indian families, looked favorably on Indian life, but most clearly wrote to express negative associations. The captives' accounts did much to solidify white prejudice. Accounts were used as propaganda against the Indians in the mid- and late nineteenth century. Even illustrated materials appeared, as in the 1859 *Harper's Magazine* account of the capture of Daniel Boone in 1775 (Fig. 4-2).

CAPTURED BY THE INDIANS

Most narratives of Indian captivity contained five elements, each reflecting a stage in the captivity episode. First came the capture itself and the forced march to an Indian town usually located at a far distance. Second, the individual was adopted into a tribe after a ritual hazing. Unlucky prisoners were tortured and killed, the description of this grisly business representing the third element in the stories of those who survived. Next, most narratives described life as a member of an Indian family or as a slave. Here emphasis was usually placed on the unique aspects of Indian culture and the manner in which Indian life was different. Finally, most narratives described the escape or release sequence, including the forced return of many whites who preferred to remain with Indian families.

Capture was often accomplished by ambush. James Smith, a soldier working on Braddock's Road during the abortive British advance on Fort Duquesne in 1755, was surprised by Indians concealed in a "blind of bushes."[11] His companion, who tried to escape, was shot and scalped. Flatboats on the Ohio River were decoyed by calls of help and then set upon and scalps and captives taken. Many whites, particularly women and children, were captured in raids on isolated frontier cabins. Mary Jemison, who later bore seven children by two Indian husbands, was captured in 1755 as a child of thirteen. Her father was killed during the attack on the family cabin. Pursued by revengeful whites, the Indians later killed her mother, brothers, and sisters, their scalps displayed on hoops hung on poles. She wrote: "Those scalps I knew [were] taken from our family, by the color of the hair. My mother's hair was red; I could easily distinguish my father's and the children from each other."[12]

Captives were led to Indian towns by long marches of hundreds of miles. Prisoners were usually tied with buffalo hide at night which

Figure 4-2.
Daniel Boone's Capture near Lower Blue Lick in 1778. (Benson J. Lossing, "Daniel Boone." *Harper's New Monthly Magazine*, Oct. 1859)

sometimes cut off the circulation in arms and feet so that they could hardly stand the next morning. The Indians built long fires often fifty feet or more in length and slept in two rows on either side. When breaking camp the Indians dispersed in all directions to confuse trackers as to their true direction. A column, once re-formed, trotted or ran; those prisoners who could not keep pace were killed.

James Smith was led to an Indian camp at Fort Duquesne where, as the warriors approached the fort, they gave the "scalp halloo" signifying success over their enemy. This was answered by the firing of muskets and cannon at the fort. With this ritual of approach, the women, children, and men of the camp rushed forward to greet the advancing party forming a "gauntlet" through which the captives were forced to run to the safety of a chief's lodge. Pelted on the head, neck, back, and legs, Smith was badly injured and required a crutch for several weeks to walk. For those who could not reach the end of the gauntlet, death came by tomahawk.

Smith witnessed the celebration of Braddock's defeat. Late in the afternoon of July 9, 1755, the French regulars and the Indians returned from the battle scene some ten miles away. Smith observed that "they had a great many bloody scalps, grenadiers' caps, British canteens, bayonets, etc., with them."[13] For hours they kept up a constant firing of small arms and cannon. About sunset a dozen prisoners, "stripped naked, with their hands tied behind their backs and their faces and part of their bodies blacked," were burned to death beside the Allegheny River.[14] The slaughter of captives continued for weeks. Mary Jemison saw at the large Shawnee town at the confluence of the Scioto and Ohio rivers the "heads, arms, legs, and other fragments of the bodies of some white people who had just been burned." It was like "pork . . . hanging on a pole."[15]

_____The butchery and depravity of the Indians increased through time. In part this reflected the general breakdown of the Indian's social fabric. More and more the acts of violence were actions of individuals unsanctioned by tribal and intertribal councils. But it also reflected what white settlers and soldiers were doing. Whites were hardly immune from committing atrocities. In 1779 Henry Hamilton, the British commander under attack at Vincennes, witnessed the work of George Rogers Clark and his men. Fort Sackville, although surrounded by Clark's small army, flew a flag of truce when Indians allied to the British cause approached. Seized by the Americans they were lined up before the fort and executed. Hamilton wrote, "foreseeing their fate [they] began to sing their death song and were butchered in succession. . . . A young chief of the Ottawa . . . having received the fatal stroke of a tomahawk in the head, took it out and gave it again unto the hands of the executioner who repeated the stroke.[16] Hamilton's shock at the incident probably hastened his decision to surrender Vincennes. Americans accused Hamilton of instigating the British purchase of American scalps at Detroit, calling him the "hair buyer." He was, perhaps as much as any other, responsible for the inhumanity displayed in the West during the American Revolution.

Before the American Revolution prisoners who survived were usually adopted into an Indian family, often to replace a recently deceased member. After the Revolution prisoners were usually attached to Indians as slaves. Those who were adopted were expected to become Indians in appearance and action. James Smith described his physical transformation.[17] His hair was pulled out except for a three- to four-inch square on the crown. This was fixed in three braids "stuck full" of silver broaches. His nose and ears were pierced and fixed with ear rings and "nose jewels." His clothes were taken, and he was given a "breech clout," and his head, face, and body painted in various colors. A ruffled shirt, a pair of leggings and some moccasins and garters dressed with beads, porcupine quills, and red hair completed his basic outfit. Feathers were tied in one of the braids. With a pipe, tomahawk, and "pole cat skin pouch" he became the well-equipped Indian.

Male prisoners were expected to participate in the hunt, clear land, and pursue other male occupations. If adopted into the family, they functioned as an equal among equals, but, if a slave, life could be harsh. Mathew Bunn, captured near Fort Hamilton in Ohio in 1791 had to build "huts" for five families, cut and haul wood, and dress deerskins during his short captivity.[18] Females were given to household chores and to agriculture. Most were married to Indian husbands and some, like Mary Jemison, were remarried when widowed. Most captured whites became thoroughly acculturated within a few years unless, of course, they escaped or were released. David Jones noted in 1772 that whites living among the Delawares in Ohio had "the very actions of the Indians and speak broken English."[19] "Might we not infer," he wrote, "that if Indians were educated as we are, they would be like us?"[20]

Relatively few prisoners escaped, since the Indian tradition of killing all who attempted escape discouraged prisoners from trying. Mathew Bunn tried nonetheless. Held as a slave in a Miami Indian town near Fort Wayne, Bunn, without shoes and coat, slipped away one winter's night walking to the Maumee River. He wrote: "Having nothing on my feet or legs, the crust of the snow being almost hard enough to bear me up, but breaking through nearly every step. . . . My feet and legs looked as if they had been cut and hacked with sickles and crosscut saws, the blood pressing forth from each . . . wound."[21]

Stealing a canoe the next night at another town, he floated with the current down the Maumee River only to be captured by other Indians, escape again, and finally, helped by an English trader, reach Detroit by boat. During the Indian War of the 1790s the British repatriated numerous Americans, conveying them east to Niagara for release.

INDIAN STEREOTYPES

Almost all white visitors to the Indian country attempted to describe the appearance, dress, and mannerisms of the Indians. Although there were differences from tribe to tribe with various changes through time, relatively permanent stereotypes emerged. Most observed that Indian males were well formed, athletic, and healthy; the females were more often heavyset. One saw few crippled and unhealthy people, probably because those with severe disabilities did not survive long the rigorous, highly mobile life. Disease and epidemics, most of European origin, regularly decimated the Indian towns, leaving a fit population by white standards. Most travelers noted the peculiar copper skin color of the males, achieved by the regular application of grease and the juices of various plants.

Even the earliest visitors found the Ohio Valley Indians greatly influenced by European dress. Henry Timberlake, a British envoy to the Cherokees in 1761, observed that the Indian men wore shirts "of the English make" and mantles or match coats of European style thrown over their shoulders.[22] The Cherokee women wore long European-style dresses or skirts, with their hair sometimes "reaching to the middle of [their] legs and sometimes to the ground, club'd and ornamented with ribbons of various colours." Of course, the men of all tribes stripped to their loincloths and covered themselves with paint in going into battle. Those who were attacked by Indians could speak correctly of "naked savages." After the War of 1812 most Indians came to dress almost exactly like whites except on feast days or other special celebrations.

Although most whites found it difficult to distinguish between the members of various tribes, the Indians themselves made very subtle distinctions. Constantine Volney, visiting at Vincennes in 1795, quoted the Miami chief Little Tortoise: "We can distinguish every nation . . . at first sight: the face, the complexion, the shape, the knees, the legs, the feet, are to us certain marks of distinction: by the print of the foot we can distinguish not only men, women, and children, but also tribes."[23] Whites, Little Tortoise said, turned out their toes while Indians "carried them straight before."[24] When the chief had visited Philadelphia. he had been overwhelmed by the variety of different types of people seen in the streets. To him whites were an anonymous mass for their diversity.

Drunken Indians were observed by most travelers. Alcoholism was a considerable problem. The various tribes continually requested the French, English, and American governments to restrict the availability of alcohol, but so important was it to the fur trade that little was ever done. Apparently, Indians were more vulnerable to alcohol's effects. As their traditional high protein diet of corn and beans was converted with very high efficiency into glucose, foods high in carbohydrate, such as sugar and alcohol, had led to obesity and alcoholism. Indians rarely drank alone but usually drank in small groups where the tradition of reciprocal gift-giving encouraged the complete consumption of whatever alcohol was available. An Indian's status in a reciprocal feast was a function of the amount he could give and consume. The circle of Indian drinkers passing a common cup or dipper of brandy, rum, or whiskey was a frequent sight.[25]

INDIAN POPULATION AND SETTLEMENT

The Indian population of the Ohio Valley was never large. In the late eighteenth century it probably numbered no more than 6,000 persons scattered between the Allegheny and Wabash Rivers in the north and along the Tennessee River and its tributaries in the south (Table 4-1).[26] There was little overt evidence of Indian influence on the Ohio Valley landscape and little evidence of Indian presence even along the most traveled routes. Whites on the Ohio River in the 1760s often traveled for days without seeing any signs of Indian life. John Jennings on a three-week, 1,000 mile trip from Fort Pitt to the mouth of the Ohio River passed only one inhabited Indian town, one abandoned town, and three large encampments (Table 4-2).[27] Hunter's cabins were seen on six of the days. These cabins, most of log, served the hunting and war parties where the major trails crossed the Ohio River.

Indian towns were often quite large. Many were fortified. In 1750 Christopher Gist, agent for the first Ohio Company, described the lower Shawnee town on the Ohio River at the mouth of the Scioto River as containing "forty houses on the south side . . . and 100 on the north, with a kind of state-house of about ninety feet long, with a

Table 4-1. Gilbert Imlay's 1797 Estimate of the Ohio Valley Indian Population

Tribe	Location	Number
Cherokees	Between the Great Bend of the Tennessee River and the Appalachian Mountains	2,500
Chickasaws	Between the Cumberland River and the Choctaw Nation	500
Lezars	Between the Mouth of the Ohio River and the Wabash River	300
Piankashaws, Vermilions, Mascoutins, and Weas	Between the Wabash River at Quiatanon and the Illinois River	1,330
Miamis	Between Fort Wayne and the Miami River	400
Mingoes	Lower Scioto River	50
Mohicans	Between the Scioto and Muskingum Rivers	40
Shawnees	Upper Scioto River	250
Delawares	Between the Tuscarora River and Lake Erie	450
Senecas	Allegheny River	140
Total		5,960

Source: Gilbert Imlay, *A Topographical Description of the Western Territory of North America* (London, 1793), p. 290.

light cover of bark in which they hold their councils."[28] Gist estimated the town's population at about 300 people.[29] Chillicothe town, also a Shawnee town, was fortified much like the larger frontier stations of Kentucky.[30]

Usually towns were irregularly laid out. Houses were placed where convenient, families and clans often living together. There were no streets as such. Wigwams dominated in the early years. Light, conical-shaped frames of bent saplings were used on summer houses; sturdier timber structures with gabled roofs on winter houses. Smoke rose through holes in the ceilings. Inside, bearskins were usually spread on the ground about the fires. Walls were usually hung with bones, corn-stalks, dried venison, implements, tools, and weapons.[31] Log cabins dominated most towns after 1790. Where white influence was great towns were regularly laid out in a grid of streets. In the Moravian mission town of New Schoenbrunn in present-day Ohio, Nicholas Cress-well observed "sixty houses . . . built of logs and covered with clap-boards . . . regularly laid out in three spacious streets which met in the center, where there is a large meeting house built of logs sixty

Table 4-2. Indians in the Landscape: John Jennings's Observations from Fort Pitt
to the Mouth of the Ohio River, March 8 to 28, 1766

Date	Location	Indication of Indian Population
March 8	Fort Pitt	
9		Passed Seneca Town
10		Saw Indian women
11		
12		Passed Indian encampment
13	Big Sandy River	Passed Indian encampment
14	Scioto River	Passed abandoned Shawnee Town
15		Saw hunters' cabins
16		Saw fortified hunter's cabin; passed large encampment
17	Big Bone Lick	
18		Saw hunters' cabins
19	Kentucky River	Saw hunters' cabins
20		Saw hunters' cabins
21		Heard sun fire (assumed it to be from Indian hunting party); passed hunter's cabin
22		
23		"Saw a smoke at a great distance" (assumed it to be caused by Indian hunters)
24	Green River	
25		
26	Tennessee River	
27	Fort Massac Ruins	
28	Mouth of the Ohio	

Source: John Jennings, "Journal From Fort Pitt to Fort Chartres in the Illinois
Country, March-April, 1766," *Pennsylvania Magazine of History and Biography*,
31 (1907), 145.

foot square covered with shingles, glass in the windows, and a bell."[32]
From the look of their towns, John Filson was moved to remark, "The
Indians are not so ignorant as some suppose them, but are . . . quick
of apprehension, sudden in execution, subtle in business, exquisite in
invention, and industrious in action."[33]

After 1820 travelers encountered more and more Indians living on
individual farmsteads; many operated taverns in their houses. This
was particularly true in the Cherokee and Chickasaw areas of Tennessee and the northern portions of Georgia, Alabama, and Mississippi.
The more affluent Indian families owned black slaves and grew cotton

or ran livestock farms. One traveler found a "half breed" Choctaw and his Chickasaw wife farming just off the Natchez Trace.[34] Together they owned 60 horses and over 200 cattle. The couple spoke English and considered themselves progressive. They admitted that "many have talked of resuming their old customs, which the whites have gradually undermined; but are unable, from the loss of their traditions."[35] The husband suggested that the Indian heritage "might be recovered from distant tribes over the Mississippi," but that the Choctaws were "acting more wisely in seeking civilization."[36] The porch of their house was "hung with saddles and bridles, side-saddles with smart scarlet housings, rifles, shot pouches, powder horns, and deer, buffalo, and bearskins. Several dogs were lying about. The farm was worked by black slaves.

Acculturation

Many forces operated to undermine traditional Indian life-ways and to encourage the Indian's adoption of American culture. The most important factors were economic. As tribe after tribe encountered the European trading system they all voluntarily adopted a cash economy for the purchase of luxuries and then, increasingly, for the purchase of necessities. Traditional dependence on hunting and Indian agriculture was lost to be slowly replaced by American agriculture once the fur trade died. The transition was slow and painful and not fully complete when the tribes were forced from their residual lands in the 1830s. Throughout the early nineteenth century most Indians were in a "middle state," as Henry Schoolcraft called it. They had "lost all the more noble and redeeming traits of the savage character, without having arrived at the possession of any one striking and important characteristic of the civil state."[37] In exchanging "their primitive manners and simple customs for those which have been superinduced by a resort to trading stations and a dependence on foreign supplies" they had not yet "imbibed a taste for agriculture calculated to compensate for the loss."[38]

   The missionaries sought to speed the acculturation process. Tolerated by most tribes in relation to their willingness to teach the new technologies of agriculture and industry, the missionaries came seeking Christian converts. They were more successful, however, in diffusing technology, the practical arts needed by the more progressive Indians to establish farms, mills, and businesses of various kinds. In the early years most religious conversions were deathbed conversions. Many travelers, particularly the ministers, sought out the missions to witness the acculturation process first-hand. Many were representatives of the missionary societies that funded the schools.

At various periods counterforces operated to retard acculturation. Espousing a return to traditional ways, charismatic leaders like Tecumseh and his brother, The Prophet, not only sought to establish military alliances between the tribes to defend Indian territory, but encouraged the complete rejection of white culture. The most rabid followers of Tecumseh and his brother were teenagers and young men who used acts of terror to coerce the majority of the Delaware and Shawnee adults to follow their leadership. But leaders like Tecumseh could not have risen to power had the Indians not had legitimate grievances against the whites. The Shawnee and Delaware had never been adequately compensated for the loss of hunting grounds. Even those tribes that did receive satisfaction at the treaty negotiations found, more often than not, that the various colonial governments and later the American government did not abide by agreements and/or continually demanded more concessions. A Delaware chief who resisted the missionary David Macelner's request to establish a mission on the Muskingum River in 1772, exclaimed that "it was not their interest to appear so friendly to the white people who had already crowded too fast upon their land and drove them from their hunting ground; that all [the English] were after was to get their lands and bring them to slavery, that the English Religion would bring them off from their knowledge and love of war, and then they should be an easy prey to their enemies."[39]

Conclusion

By the time white settlers began to pour into the Ohio Valley the Indian had largely acculturated to European ways. Long dependent upon the fur trade for luxuries, most Indian tribes had come to depend upon the whites for such necessities as salt and gunpowder. Their basic tools for hunting and trapping and the weaponry they used to defend their land were of European manufacture. After 1800 many Indians lived in log cabins. Many lived in towns, which were very much like American frontier settlements, and after the War of 1812 most Indians even dressed like Americans. Indian leaders actively sought to educate their tribes in the skills of American agriculture.

The travelers' view of the Indian was usually one of disdain. The Indians' abandonment of their own culture left them dependent upon the whites. Indians functioned as suppliers of furs and other resources and were totally at the mercy of the trading establishment. Yet the Indians had not adopted enough of the white man's technology to stand as an equal in most travelers' eyes. Indian culture was seen as marginal and definitely inferior. Of course few of the travelers' observations were made first hand. Of those who had direct experience, particularly the traders, few left diaries or journals. The most vivid accounts were provided by escaped or freed captives, and their accounts were usually biased.

After 1840 only a few hundred Indians remained in the Ohio Valley. Most were of mixed blood. Most lived on private land granted to them for governmental service or purchased outright from the federal government. A few attempted to adhere to tribal government, as did the relic band of Cherokees who returned to western North Carolina from Oklahoma; but most remaining Indians lived as private citizens ultimately to be absorbed into white and black populations.

5 IMAGES OF MILITARY LIFE

300 houses and wigwams were burnt. There were several orchards . . . girdled or cut down, and, at least, 20,000 bushels of corn in the ear was collected and destroyed.

Thomas Irwin, 1790

War was a way of life in the Ohio Valley for three generations after 1750. While France and Britain and later the United States competed for control of the region's resources, the Indians fought to maintain control of their territory. Perhaps the outcome was inevitable. The superior population and technology of the American nation prevailed, but not before a unique chapter of military conflict had been written in Ohio Valley history. War in all its brutality reduced people to savagery and left a residue of racial hatred only compounded later in the Indian wars of the Far West.

War in the Ohio Valley was usually a three-sided affair: two white nations scrambling for control of the fur trade, land, or both and the Indians, allied with one or the other, hoping to retain territorial and other rights. Not always were the Indians united in their efforts, as different tribes often fought on different sides. In interpreting the period's military affairs, many have presumed little more than overt French and British and, later, British and American military confrontation. But the Indians were more than pawns. The Indians carried the brunt of the military campaigning for the French in the French and Indian War and for the British in the American Revolution, the war-

fare of the 1790s, and the War of 1812. This involvement was for Indian objectives: to prevent white settlers from further encroaching
on Indian lands.

Military Campaigning

Military campaigns played an important role in the history of the
region. Unfortunately, surviving records depict the various conflicts
solely from the white viewpoint. For the British and Americans who
participated, the long marches through the wilderness were adventures.
They provided an exciting change from daily routines, particularly for
militia troops only temporarily removed from home. For some, military
campaigns provided opportunities to seek glory; others sought opportunities to avenge the losses of previous fighting. Military campaigns had
a cycle: the assembly of the troops, their training (if any), their movement to the attack, a battle, and either retreat or removal to a point of
safety where the army was disbanded. Usually the entire sequence required no more than three or four months. Mapped are the principal
campaigns between 1750 and 1813 (Figs. 5-1 to 5-4).

Troops for a campaign were usually assembled at an established
military post. Fort Niagara served the French as, for example, during
Céloron de Blainville's 1749 expedition down the Allegheny and Ohio
rivers. The French treated these two rivers as a single river calling
them "La Belle Rivière." Blainville's attempt to demonstrate by force
French ownership of the Ohio Valley was much ridiculed by the In-
dians who outnumbered his expedition at every point along the way.
The French commander was forced to bury at the mouths of selected
rivers his bronze plaques declaring French sovereignty over the region.
Later the French fortified the Allegheny corridor southward from Lake
Erie with forts at Presqu'Isle, Le Boeuf Creek, Venango, and Duquesne
(Fig. 5-1).

For the English, Fort Cumberland served the abortive campaigns of
Washington (1754) and Braddock (1755) which attempted to dis-
lodge the French at the "Forks of the Ohio." Forts Loudon and Littleton, east of the mountains, were important staging points prior to Britain's actual seizure of Fort Duquesne under General Forbes and his
field commander Colonel Bouquet. The actual fall of Duquesne reflected as much the British victory at Niagara in 1759 as the approach
of Forbes's army. With Niagara fallen Duquesne could not be supplied

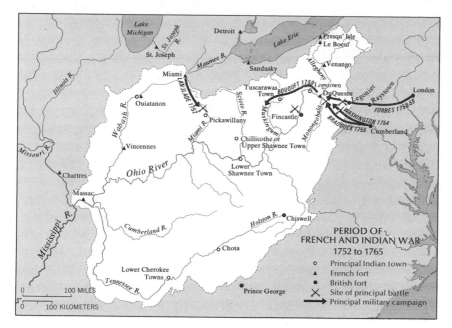

Figure 5-1.

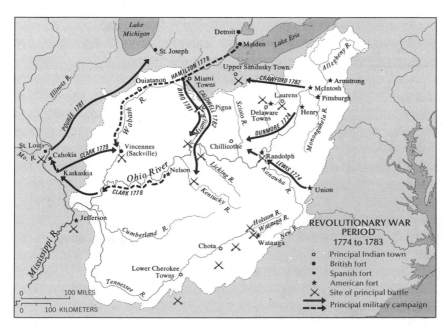

Figure 5-2.

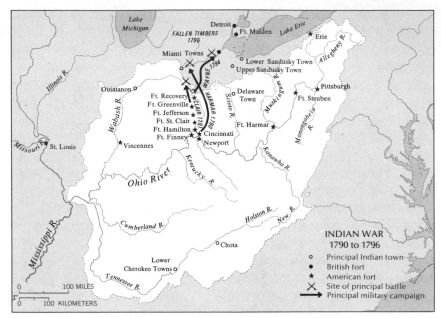

Figure 5-3.

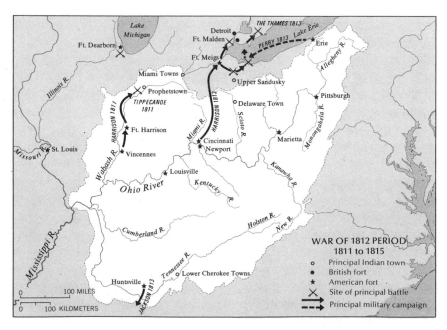

Figure 5-4.

and was, therefore, abandoned by the French. Fort Duquesne, renamed Fort Pitt, later became the principal staging place for subsequent American campaigns against the British-allied Indians during the Revolution. By the 1790s the arsenal at Newport, Kentucky, served a principal staging function as did the string of forts built northward from Cincinnati into the heart of the Indian country (Fig. 5-3).

The troops gathered were usually a mixture of regular army and militia units. Both varieties of soldier often came untrained and poorly equipped. An important exception was the campaign of Anthony Wayne in 1793 and 1794. Wayne built a special training base called Legionville near the site of the abandoned Indian town of Logstown near Pittsburgh. There the army was prepared for Indian fighting before its move to Cincinnati, from which it marched northward to Wayne's decisive victory at the Battle of Fallen Timbers. Wayne succeeded with his disciplined force where Generals Josiah Harmar and Arthur St. Clair had failed in 1790 and 1791 respectively. With Wayne's victory the Indians lost all claim to the Ohio River as a boundary between white and Indian settlement. The armies which operated in the Ohio Valley during the eighteenth and the nineteenth century varied from a few hundred men, as served under Clark in his attack on Vincennes in 1778, to larger forces numbering over 7,000 as served with Forbes in 1758.

The movement of large armies required roads to accommodate wagons and artillery. Many of these roads later became important migration and commercial routes. Braddock's Road from Cumberland, Maryland, to the Monongahela River near Pittsburgh and Forbes' Road from Forts Legonier and Littleton to the forks of the Ohio River were the most important (Fig. 5-2). Braddock's Road was constructed as the army moved, but Forbes' Road was constructed well in advance of the army.

A particular order of march was maintained once an army was underway. St. Clair's army marched north to its defeat in two columns about 200 yards apart with artillery pieces both leading the way and bringing up the rear. Horses and cattle were kept in the interval between the two advancing lines.[1] Wayne's army seemed disorganized to one junior officer. From his diary we read:

> During the March this day [we] passed over much close brushy ground and many old Indian settlements now grown up in weeds, briars, and

shrubs almost impervious—these combined with the meander of the river and the heights which here and there jutted in not only threw us beyond the reach of signals from the centre, but I do verily believe separated the wings of the army more than a mile on opposite banks of a river in many places unfordable—and of consequence had the enemy attacked the conflict must have been determined.[2]

An army moved between three and six miles a day. St. Clair's army moved four miles a day on the average and required about a month to move north to the battle site from Fort Jefferson.[3] The same distance was covered in less than two days as the army, splintered into remnants after its defeat, retreated in complete disorder.

All commanders sent out reconnaissance parties, but despite the best of information armies were often lost relative to their intended objectives. St. Clair thought he was on a branch of the Maumee River, but was, in fact, on the headwaters of the Wabash River over thirty-five miles to the west. No commander was more poorly informed than Major James Grant who commanded over 1,000 Highlanders and several hundred Virginians assembled on the heights above Fort Duquesne in 1758. Grant was in advance of Forbes's main army. Reconnaissance had earlier reported the fort to be a poorly-made wall of wood and clay about nine feet high. Scouting parties had seen no tents nor Indian encampments, but reported smoke and the sounds of Indian dancers to the north along the Allegheny River. There hidden on an island were over 1,000 Indian warriors. Grant, convinced that he held the superior force, acted brashly. "To convince our men they had no reason to be afraid, I gave directions to our drums to beat the reveille," he wrote.[4] Obscured by a heavy fog, a large Indian force hit the camp's left flank. The battle was soon decided with Grant's force killed or captured almost in its entirety.

Most marches involved real hardship, particularly for the soldiers on foot. Perhaps no army overcame more difficulty than Clark's small group. Wading sometimes to their necks in swollen rivers with their rifles and powder held over their heads, the men suffered terribly in the cold February weather. Clark worked hard to keep the spirits of his men high. "I suffered them to shoot game . . . and feast on it like Indian war dancers—each company, by turn, inviting the others to their feasts. . . . This was greatly encouraging and they really began to think themselves superior to other men, and that neither the rivers nor the season could stop their progress," he wrote.[5]

Several armies allowed women to accompany the troops. Most came as prostitutes. Over 250 women accompanied St. Clair's army of 1,400 men to the crossing of the Miami River. Beyond that point only two or three women were to be allowed to each company, but many disregarded the order and "when the men commenced crossing the river they also plunged into the stream. . . . Many of them got . . . on to the artillery carriages and rode astride of the cannon."[6] Fifty-six women were killed in the ensuing battle along with over 600 soldiers.[7]

Many campaigns involved the building of light fortifications along the route of march. The British army built a string of fortified camps along Forbes' Road in 1758 and 1759. One, Fort Legonier immediately west of Allegheny Mountain, withstood a large Indian and French assault after Grant's defeat. The several campaigns of Harmar, St. Clair, and Wayne north from Cincinnati produced a string of forts in the Miami, Auglaize, and Maumee River Valleys (Fig. 5-3). From St. Clair's letter to the Secretary of War we read: "Outlines of a fort were laid out and the work was commenced . . . the houses were all covered, the platforms laid in the bastions . . . with four good bastions, one on each corner . . . constructed of large hewed timber laid horizontally, the curtains of the work forming the outer walls of the barracks."[8] Two cannon were installed, a salute was fired, and the structure was named Fort Jefferson.

Supply was a persistent problem. Most armies moved by horsepower, and forage and feed for the horses was of prime concern. The men had to be fed. Necessary also were implements for building roads and forts and, of course, the munitions and arms for battle. It is surprising how ill-prepared most armies were. With slow communications and the problem of moving across unoccupied territory, the armies rarely marched with more than a week's supply of food. Equipment and livestock often proved inadequate. "A trifle can stop an army," Bouquet advised in 1758.[9] "The rogue who made our saddles did not fill them enough, and almost all the horses have arrived so saddle sore that they will be unfit for service for three weeks. . . . If we open a new route we shall not have enough axes because they very often break."[10] Many suppliers cheated, and some were overly diligent in spending government monies. "We received 300 [cattle] yesterday from Virginia, small, lean and as poor as they could be. This cursed avarice of these narrow minds makes them hunt for bargains, without a thought of the consequences."[11] If such problems bothered the commanders, the real suffering fell to the common soldiers who, placed on reduced rations and inadequately clothed, jeopardized their lives in battle with faulty equipment.

Not only did the soldiers suffer physically from the lack of adequate supplies, but they suffered from inept leadership. Commanders did not adequately prepare their armies, as they were not adequately prepared themselves. In 1755 the pompous Edward Braddock committed over 1,900 men to ambush in anticipation of a European-style battle. With drums and bag-pipes sounding, the men marched in the best eighteenth-century style to their deaths. Only 500 survived. Commanding officers were often ill, too ill to effectively control their armies. During 1758 and 1759 General Forbes was confined to bed, first at Harrisburg and then at Carlisle, and never did accompany his army to the Ohio Valley. Arthur St. Clair, by his own words, was "worn down with illness and suffering under a painful disease, unable to either mount or dismount a horse without assistance."[12]

BATTLEFIELD IMAGES

Once in battle it was very much a fight for self-preservation, particularly where group order dissolved as it so frequently did into hand-to-hand combat. Yet the real images of battle were so easily forgotten, the heroics of individuals so readily subsumed under the names of their commanders. Even the outcome of a battle could be turned around and distorted beyond recognition. In 1811 William Henry Harrison left the Tippecanoe battlefield convinced that he had suffered a disastrous defeat. Only later was it discovered that the Indians had disbanded nearby Prophetstown and the objective of Harrison's campaign had thus been achieved. What seemed a defeat loomed as a victory and later, greatly romanticized, it carried Harrison to the presidency of the United States, and John Tyler, too.

What was seen on the battlefields? The dominant images seem to have been the advancing enemy, their dress and decorum, mutilation and death, the winning and surrender of ground, and the remnants of battle, the dead and the wounded. St. Clair's defeat serves as an example. Reveille had just sounded and the camp was breaking into its morning routine when Indians struck the advance line of militia which immediately gave way in panic and rushed into the main camp. Checked by the first line of regulars, the Indians refocused their attack on the artillery at the center. Seized, recaptured, and seized again the cannons were silenced with most of the artillerymen dead or wounded. After several hours the Indians mounted a flanking attack to cut off St. Clair's army from the road and possible escape. Panic set in, and the American army abandoned the field in the early afternoon, the men throwing away their weapons as they ran. The road was strewn with equipment for several miles.

As the battle was fought, one witness reported: "the ground was covered with the bodies of the dead and dying, the freshly-scalped heads were reeking with smoke [in] the heavy morning frost . . . [looking] like so many pumpkins in a cornfield in December. And the little ravine that led to the creek was actually running with blood. While the battle raged at one place, at another . . . a party of soldiers grouped together around the fires, doing nothing but presenting mere marks for the enemy. They appeared stupefied and bewildered. . . . At another point . . . soldiers had broken into the marquees of the officers and were eating the breakfast."[13] The Indians were led by a most impressive war chief "six feet in height, about forty-five years of age, of a very sour and morose countenance. . . . His dress was Indian hose and moccasins, a blue petticoat that came half way down his thighs and European waistcoat and surtout. . . . [an] Indian cap . . . hung half way down his back . . . almost entirely filled with plain silver broaches."[14] St. Clair wore a "rough capped blanket coat and a three cornered hat" and sported a long "queue and large locks, very gray, flowing beneath his beaver [hat]."[15]

Several months later James Wilkinson led a small expedition to the site of the battle to recover the cannon and bury the dead. Bodies lay along the road for four miles "many dragged from under the snow and mutilated by wild beasts."[16] One witness wrote: "the great body of the slain were within an area of forty acres. The snow being deep the bodies could be discovered only by the elevation of the snow where they lay. They had been scalped and stripped of all their clothing that was of any value."[17] The bodies were blackened by frost and exposure, but little decayed as the winter had been early and severe. A large pit was dug and the dead buried.

The dead on many battlefields were never buried. The site of Braddock's defeat was such a place. From the 1760s through the 1780s the site was a popular tourist place. Visitors combed the woods and later the cultivated fields for bones, weapons, and other souvenirs for, as John May reported in 1788, the "bones of the slain are plenty on the

ground."[18] Highly romanticized, the battle site was still a popular tourist attraction in the 1830s. The Englishman Charles Hoffman reported,
"There are a few superb oaks still standing which . . . must enhance
the value of the place with all faithful ghost-believers and pious lovers
of the marvellous—the dim form of the red savage, with the ghostly
spectre of his pallid victim shrinking before it, it is said, may be seen
gliding at time among the hoary trunks."[19] Along with the remnants of
the few remaining forts, battlefields were the only specie of historic
site recognized by travelers in the early nineteenth century other than
the Indian mounds.

Frontier Forts and Stations

Forts were built to protect the Ohio Valley's white and dependent
black populations during the various Indian wars. The forts were usually garrisoned by army regulars. The larger installations, such as
Fort Pitt, covered ten to twenty acres with outlying earthworks and
inner palisaded walls of large timbers set vertically in the ground. The
forts usually sported large blockhouses in the corners where exterior
walls joined. Interior spaces were given to open assembly grounds,
barracks, officer's quarters, and powder magazines. Adjacent spaces
were usually stripped of vegetation to provide unobscured lines of fire.
A post garden and night pasture might be located there. Most forts
presented a stark appearance, lacking shade from the summer sun and
shelter from the winter wind. Purely functional as defensive bastions
they also symbolized the European and later the American presence.
Whenever possible forts were built to impress as, for example, Campus
Martius, the first fort constructed at Marietta, Ohio, in 1791. Intended
to be the capital of the Northwest Territory, the fort's two- and three-
story log buildings with their steeply pitched gable roofs and towers
seemed to loom above its two palisaded walls.

The frontier station was much more important to the protection of
the common settler. Stations varied from small forts to single fortified
houses sometimes surrounded by a palisade. Boonesboro, one of the
larger stations in Kentucky during the American Revolution, contained
some thirty houses arranged with their back walls connected in a
common perimeter. Livestock was quartered in the interior court.
When threatened by Indian guerilla bands, hundreds of people were

"forted" in such places for months on end. Manure and other filth accumulated; disease was rampant. Most stations only consisted of single cabins. In southern Indiana during the War of 1812 roofs were removed and cabins fortified by adding a second floor jutting out over the first floor walls. Through slits in the upper flooring defenders could fire down on attackers. One traveler saw dozens of these structures on the road from Louisville to Vincennes.[20]

Frontier stations were usually disbanded after each Indian War. Individual cabins were moved onto settlers' nearby farms. Sometimes one cabin might survive on site as a farmhouse. Some of the larger stations, those strategically located along the system of traces and trails, developed into towns, as did Kentucky's first station, Harrodsburg, established in 1775. Boonesboro became the most famous of the Kentucky stations thanks to the publicity John Filson gave Daniel Boone in the book, *The Discovery, Settlement, and Present State of Kentucke*.[21] In May of 1840 the English traveler James Buckingham attended the sixty-fifth anniversary celebration of the station's founding. The ceremony lasted three days with over 10,000 people attending.[22] It included religious services, barbecues, and political orations all intended to celebrate the heroism of the preceding generations who had braved the savage Indian and conquered the wilderness in the isolated frontier stations.

Most of the large forts encouraged immediate town development. The toponym, "Fort Pitt," designated as much the town built adjacent to the fort as it did the fort itself. After the fort's abandonment its site was quickly urbanized. Charles Hoffman, visiting Pittsburgh in 1833, noted that at Fort Duquesne "there remains now but a small mound, containing perhaps a couple loads of earth; Fort Pitt may be more easily traced; part of three bastions about breast-high, stand within different private enclosures, and a piece of the [wall] which within a few years was in complete preservation, may still be discovered among the piles of lumber in a steam saw-mill yard."[23] Only the brick powder magazine survived. Hoffman noted: "In a country like ours, where so few antiquities meet the eye, it is melancholy to see these interesting remnants thus destroyed. The Pittsburgers, however, I fear are more bent upon increasing their . . . 'store' than on beautifying the favoured spot."[24] Thus the forts were destroyed once they became functionally obsolete.

Conclusion

War was a way of life in the Ohio Valley for over three generations. Between 1752 when the French defeated the Miami Indians at Pickwallany (forcing them to sever trade relations with the British) until 1813 when William Henry Harrison defeated Tecumseh and his British allies at the Battle of the Thames in Ontario, the Ohio Valley Indians fought in four major wars. War was the norm and not simply the unusual interlude between periods of peace and prosperity.

At issue was control of the land and vast resources of the Ohio Valley. Although the conflict was played out in the vicious and bloody fighting of guerilla raids and more formal battles, the outcome was really decided by the superior technology and overwhelming numbers of the American nation. The Indians, dependent upon the fur trade and uprooted from traditional life ways, might have achieved economic and political parity with the Americans salvaging claims to small portions of the Ohio Valley for their effort. But, in retrospect, they were simply numerically too inconsequential to have blocked American expansion beyond the Appalachians.

Direct benefits were few for the American who served in a western campaign against the Indians. Besides the feelings of adventure, honor, and retribution which survivors brought home to family and friends were images of western lands essentially unpeopled and soon to be released to American settlement. Each campaign against the Indians increased the land hunger of the whites as accounts of the rich lands held by the Indians circulated widely. Many soldiers returned to settle in areas visited during wartime. Some veterans were granted land for their military services. For example, Virginians who served in the American Revolution were granted land rights in southern Ohio. The men who served under George Rogers Clark received rights to land in southern Indiana. But, by and large, the common soldier had only a minimal pay and the privations of the campaign as recompense for his effort.

Warfare accelerated American settlement in the Ohio Valley. Not only were questions of territory and land ownership more rapidly settled in favor of the whites, but each military activity fostered road construction giving greater access to Indian territories. Trade linkages were strengthened as eastern merchants competed to supply the enlarged and newly established garrisons. Trade encouraged the growth of towns, and towns encouraged agricultural settlement. Beyond the images of brutality and individual heroism, impersonal forces were at work hastening the decline of aboriginal life ways and accelerating the conversion of the wilderness to farms and urban places.

War provided opportunities for travel. Campaigns into the West marked the initial opportunity for most to leave home for an extended period of time. Most armies primarily consisted of teenagers and young adults. The thirst to see new and exotic places was probably as strong as any sense of patriotic mission and probably much better understood by those so willing to sacrifice their lives. In many ways warfare, particularly military campaigning, was a form of travel.

6 PASTORAL IMAGES

Tis I can delve and plough, love,
And you can spin and sew,
And we'll settle on the banks
of the pleasant Ohio.

Folk Song

Farmers dominated the expanding frontier. Although towns and their urban populations were an integral part of western expansion, most settlers came as farmers to pursue agrarian lives. Their goal was to create a garden in the wilderness: to pursue, as one traveler stated, "the design for which our first parents were placed in Eden . . . [the] keeping and dressing of a great garden."[1] Many travelers participated directly in the pageant as westward movers and seekers of fortune. Others merely observed the process by which the wilderness was surveyed, sold, settled, and developed as a pastoral landscape. The act of converting the wilderness into farms was considered the great American achievement of the late eighteenth and the early nineteenth century.

Frontier Settlement

Rural settlement evolved in stages, or so it was generally believed. Different types of settlers succeeded one another on the frontier.[2] First came the "squatter," often a hunter, who cleared a few acres and remained until he had saved enough money to buy a farm elsewhere or was expelled by the real proprietor. Next came the "small farmer" with money sufficient only for a down payment on land he hoped to buy on installments. He cultivated ten or thirty acres to feed his family, with sufficient surplus to reduce his outstanding debt. Finally, the wealthy or "strong-handed" farmer appeared. He owned from 500 to 1,200 acres, placed a quarter under immediate cultivation, and raised livestock and other crops which he marketed through New Orleans or other towns. Sometimes pioneer families remained in a single place succeeding through the various stages, but more often an area experienced actual shifts in population: the hunters and squatters moving with the depletion of the game and the initial farmers selling out their "improvements" to move farther west in search of bigger farms where land was cheaper.

WESTWARD MIGRATION

Population spread rapidly across the Ohio Valley as settlers sought opportunities in new areas. The frontier did not expand westward as a single wave, but rather it jumped by leaps and bounds. Exclaves of settlement were created, the intervals eventually filled by later migrants. In 1790 there were four areas of settlement in the Ohio Valley with at least six people per square mile: southwestern Pennsylvania around Pittsburgh, the Blue Grass Basin around Lexington in Kentucky, East Tennessee centered on Knoxville, and the Nashville Basin of Middle Tennessee. By 1850 population density throughout the Ohio Valley had reached this level except in several bypassed areas in Appalachia and the wet prairies of northwestern Indiana and northeastern Illinois. Population growth resulted from a high rate of natural population increase as well as migration. Large families were practical, as children aided in clearing the land and in operating the farms.

Migrants were seen everywhere along the routes which led to the interior. Some came in big lumbering Conestoga wagons with four and six horse hitches, but most came in smaller farm wagons pulled by only one or two horses. Most wagons had a "tilt" or canvas cover stretched on hoops. The families walked before, behind, or rode, according to the weather, the road, and their custom. Morris Birkbeck, himself a migrant to Illinois on the National Road in Pennsylvania, reported: "The New Englanders, they say, may be known by the cheerful air of the women advancing in front of the vehicle; the Jersey people by their being fixed steadily within it; whilst the Pennsylvanians creep lingering behind, as though regretting the homes they have left."[3] Many families left the roads for flatboats or steamboats at such places as Brownsville on the Monongahela River and Pittsburgh and Wheeling on the Ohio.

LAND DIVISION AND SALE

Land survey was a first step in the settling process. South of the Ohio River, where the land laws of Virginia, North Carolina, and other states prevailed, individuals assumed the responsibility of surveying their own farms according to the metes and bounds survey system. Using ridge lines, creek bottoms, trees, and other prominent features in the landscape, the prospective settler entered at the county courthouse a crude map of his farm along with his deed of purchase. Confused and overlapping boundaries produced court litigation, and many farmers or their children later moved north of the Ohio River expressly to escape these legal entanglements. In the public domain of the Old Northwest, Congress adopted the "township and range" system of land division. Ideally, the land was surveyed in six-mile squares before the settlers arrived, each of these townships being divided into thirty-six sections of 640 acres each. Although Congress initially sought to sell land by the section, later land legislation allowed sale of smaller 320-acre and then 160-acre parcels. The 160-acre farm neatly subdivided into four forty-acre plats which were frequently sold separately by private land owners.

Federal survey lines were marked on trees or indicated by stakes on the treeless prairies. Locational information was sometimes carved on "boundary trees" at the corners of the sections. Once an area was surveyed and marked the land was auctioned at the district land office. When Morris Birkbeck visited Chillicothe, Ohio, in 1817, the best government land sold in 160-acre parcels for as much as $12 an acre; only the least desirable acreage sold at the $2 minimum.[4] One-fourth of the sale price was due on purchase with the remainder to be paid by installments over five years. The land laws changed frequently, but, in general, farmers were allowed to buy public land in smaller parcels and at lower minimal prices with each successive change after 1800. At each land office a large map indicated the government lands still available.

Land value varied not only with the inherent fertility of the soil, but

with the "improvements" made. Henry Fearon, also visiting at Chillicothe in 1817, found improved farms bringing $8 to $30 on the open
market.[5] Improvements usually comprised a rough log cabin and
twelve to twenty acres under cultivation. Factors influencing a farm's
worth included the distance from the town and the convenience of
shipping produce. Supposing no improvements to have been made,
Fearon found a general decay in the value of land outward from Chillicothe, then the state capital. "Those [farms] within five miles are
from $20.00 to $40.00 per acre; five to ten miles, $10.00 to $20.00; ten
to fifteen miles, from $5.00 to $15.00," he wrote.[6]

CLEARING THE LAND

After purchase, settlers turned to clearing the land. A husband, often
accompanied by an older son, a brother, or brother-in-law, journeyed
west to clear a few acres and plant a crop before returning east for his
wife and children. Harry Toulmin, who wrote several short books for
the prospective emigrant to Kentucky, believed that "an industrious
man" working alone could open three acres of land in the autumn and
winter.[7] With half an acre reserved for vegetables, the remainder
would return seventy-five bushels of corn, half of which would be
needed to support a family of four. Surplus could be sold to buy salt,
gunpowder, and other necessary items not manufactured on the farm.
In the second autumn and winter two additional acres could be
cleared. Even with one acre given to flax or hemp to provide linen, the
second year's corn crop of 125 bushels would provide sufficient surplus
to buy a horse and a plow.

Large trees were killed by girdling: stripping the bark in bands
about two feet above the roots. Small trees and bushes were cut, piled,
and burnt. The ground was broken with a hoe or a light plow and the
corn planted in the ashes around the dead trees. "The thin stems of
Indian corn . . . contrasted with . . . the skeleton trees towering
above," one observer wrote; "Life and desolation were never brought
closer together."[8] The dropping of twigs and bark and then of larger
limbs continued until the trees were cut down leaving only stumps in
the fields. Stumps sometimes survived for decades. The rate at which
land could be cleared varied with the type of vegetation, the topography, and the dedication of the farmer. William Faux estimated that the
average adult male could clear five or six acres every year.[9] Cleared
land was worth four or five times its original price.[10]

Most European travelers disapproved of what often seemed the wanton destruction of the forests. "Through the Union," exclaimed William Oliver, "the inhabitants seem to be executed by a spirit of extermination against trees."[11] James Buckingham regretted the lack of "some law or regulation obliging those who cleared their lands by the public road, to leave at least one row of trees standing on each side the highway to afford shade, shelter, and beauty."[12] But American settlers little appreciated trees except as obstacles to be removed in favor of cultivation or as resources to be converted into fences, barns, and houses, or to be used as fuel.

New difficulties were encountered when settlers moved out onto the prairies. There the trees were valued more. Most early prairie settlers chose forest peripheries which mixed the rich prairie soils with accessibility to woodlots. But the breaking of the thick prairie sod was the major obstacle to prairie settlement, followed by the lack of water on the dry prairies and the excess of water on the wet prairies. A whole new technology of heavy steel plows, deep wells, and drainage ditches ultimately made prairie cultivation practical on a large scale. Before the Civil War most wet prairie areas specialized in livestock grazing. The English prairie settlement around Albion, Illinois, was an exception. Led by Morris Birkbeck and another wealthy Briton, George Flower, a small English population had established itself by 1820. Albion became the objective of many British travelers, and the merits of the settlement were hotly debated in the travel literature through the first decades of the nineteenth century. A heavy plow and four horses were necessary in breaking the thick prairie sod according to one of the settlers, John Woods.[13] The first plowing added $5 to the worth of the land and the second plowing another $4.[14]

FRONTIER STEREOTYPES

Observers were almost unanimous in declaring the frontier the salvation of the lower classes whose poor prospects in the East and in Europe necessitated a fresh start. William Oliver advised from Illinois: "Let no one whose prospects are good at home rashly think of emigrating. The poor, those who see unavoidable difficulty approaching them, and such as have families without any adequate provision for them, are the proper immigrants to a new country, where thews and sinews are convertible into wealth."[15] Stories of success and failure were frequently thrust upon the traveler. A Princeton, Indiana, farmer from

Chatteris, England, bragged to William Faux that he could "live and live well."[16] He owned 300 acres "free from all poor-rates, parsons, and tax gathers," and he would be able to give each of his children 100 acres to work on instead of "the highway or Chatteris work-house."[17]

For the middle-class farmer less concerned to convert brawn into capital gain, it was best to purchase farms already improved with the intent ultimately of pursuing commercial agriculture. This required considerable capital investment. The Ingle family, also settled near Princeton, Indiana, spent $1,240 in 1817 establishing a farm.[18] Their expenses are detailed (Table 6-1). Labor on the frontier was not always dependable, as Morris Birkbeck complained to Elias Fordham, an English visitor: "The smith has no iron; you buy it, then he has not coal. The wheelwright is gone a hunting, or is drunk, or attending a lawsuit. The saddler and collar maker will sell the articles you have ordered to the first comer. You are sure of nothing."[19] Birkbeck decided not to cultivate his land, but purchased his food supplies at nearby New Harmony, Indiana. Wealthy farmers who had come prematurely to the frontier often reverted to land speculation, dividing and selling their farms. Many divided and leased their land to tenants. In Kentucky, François Michaux found most tenants obligated to clear and enclose eight to nine acres, build a log cabin, and pay the landlord

Table 6-1. Investment of the Ingle Family in Settling near Princeton, Indiana, in 1817

Expenditure	Cost
Entry of half section (320 acres)	$ 160
House, stable, smokehouse, pigsty, hen house, corncrib and barn . . .	180
2 horses, 2 plows, wagon, and harness	300
Axes, hoes, harrows, spades, and shovels	34
2 cows, and 4 sows in pigsty	56
Clearing and fencing of 20 acres of land	130
Ploughing, planting, hoeing, and turning	130
Twelve months' maintenance of family	250
Total	$1,240

Source: William Faux, *Memorable Days in America: Being a Journal of a Tour to the United States* (London, 1823), p. 255.

eight to ten bushels of corn for each acre planted.[20] Corn yields averaged forty bushels to the acre.[21]

For each successful and satisfied settler there were clearly as many who were disappointed. The frontier was "the world beyond the grave of disappointed hopes," one observer wrote in 1840.[22] Toulmin warned prospective migrants to Kentucky:

> There always have been and there always will be persons whose sanguine expectations end in disappointment and disgust. They complain of a want of beauty in the face of the country; of the heat of the summers and the cold of the winters; of the difficulty of procuring servants and the uncertainty of keeping them . . . ; of the prevalence of flies and frogs; of the irreligion, or bigotry, of the people; and above all of the dearness of European commodities.[23]

A transplanted Yankee living near Springfield, Ohio, complained to one traveler of bad water, bad roads, ignorant people, sick milk, sick wheat, "a plenty of ague," poor markets, and high prices.[24]

The frontier was a raw place lacking the refinements of established society. Frontier settlers were stereotyped accordingly. To many Easterners, noted Harry Toulmin, the western population was "an idle, dissolute, quarrelsome, insolent set of adventurers . . . too vicious or too poor to live where they were born."[25] At best the frontier was a new place requiring decades to reach the levels of refinement known in the East. The frontier was a place of crass repetition. One visitor wrote: "There is little in a scantily peopled territory to excite speculation. He that has seen one settler in the backwoods has seen a thousand."[26] Many Europeans complained of the lack of fine architecture and the low levels of maintenance given what architecture there existed. James Flint wrote: "Almost every object bespeaks a want of capital. Fine houses are brick . . . of two stories covered with shingles and frequently unfinished within; and where the work is completed, it is usually in a bad style; the windows often broken; and the adjoining grounds perhaps studded with the stumps of trees, overgrown with rank weeds; or rutted by hogs."[27] It was a mistake "laying out" money in improving and beautifying property, for such improvements yielded little return.

Travel on the frontier required a new point of view. Everything was new. "The traveler . . . beholds the beauties of nature in rich luxuriance, but he sees no work of art which has existed beyond the memory of man" for "the inhabitants are all emigrants from other countries;

they have no ruins . . . nothing romantic or incredible with which to regale the traveler's ear," James Hall wrote.[28] "To acquire an adequate knowledge of such a country," Hall continued, "requires extensive personal observation. It is necessary to examine things instead of books, to travel over this wide region, to become acquainted with the people, to learn their history from tradition, and to become informed as to their manners and modes of thinking, by associating with them in the familiar intercourse of business and domestic life."[29]

No brand of nineteenth-century romanticism was more potent than the frontier's cult of the common man. Hardship became a testing ground, and simplicity became a virtue. The settler who tamed the wilderness became a folk hero. But by the mid-nineteenth century travelers to the Ohio Valley no longer encountered the raw frontier. Towns and cities and a mature agrarian landscape had evolved, and the frontier had become the region's past, its history. Many travelers expended as much energy imagining this past as describing the contemporary scene. Henry Tuckerman mused "on the union of beauty and terror in the life of a pioneer," the "wide, umbrageous solitudes he loved," and the "contentment he experienced in a log hut."[30] He wrote, "The senses became acute, the mind vigilant, and the tone of feeling chivalric under such discipline. . . . Life has a peculiar dignity, even in the midst of privation."[31] Each locality had its heroes, and although local expressions of esteem were rarely as eloquent as Tuckerman's prose, they were usually more to the point. The backwoodsman Peter Weaver was remembered in the 1850s around Lafayette, Indiana, as having "killed more deer, wolves, and rattlesnakes; caught more fish, found more bee trees, and entertained . . . more land hunters, trappers, and traders, than any private citizen between Vincennes and the mouth of the Salimony [Creek]."[32]

The isolation on the frontier, it was believed, made men and women more resourceful or more reliant on their own capabilities. Out of this self sufficiency came innovation and the perfection of old cultural modes. Through the nineteenth century Daniel Boone remained the Ohio Valley's principal folk hero. Tuckerman could write,

> without political knowledge, he sustained an infant settlement; destitute of a military education, he proved one of the most formidable antagonists the Indians ever encountered; with no pretensions to a knowledge of civil engineering, he laid out the first road through the wilderness of Kentucky; unfamiliar with books, he reflected deeply and

attained to philosophical convictions that yielded him equanimity of
mind; devoid of poetical expression, he had an extraordinary feeling for
natural beauty, and described his sensations and emotions, amid the
wild seclusion of the forest.[33]

The frontier past had been imbued with many of the heroic character-
istics of the East. The frontier had been a "nursery of character."[34]
Later, the prominent historian Frederick Jackson Turner amplified this
sentiment. His "frontier thesis" attributed America's very cultural and
political identity to the anvil of frontier isolation.[35]

Agriculture

Although there were certain common denominators, different farming
systems and crop emphases developed in different sections of the Ohio
Valley. Emphasis on livestock, particularly hogs, characterized the entire frontier. Left to browse in the woods, the swine fed on acorns and
roots, but with the clearing of the forests hogs were fattened increasingly on corn. Corn cultivation was also ubiquitous, and cornmeal was
the mainstay of the frontier diet. On this base other crops were introduced. The Kentucky Blue Grass specialized in hemp, mules, and
horses as well as tobacco. By the Civil War, the area north of the Ohio
River had become the nation's wheat belt. To the south in Tennessee
and northern Alabama and Mississippi cotton culture held sway.

Corn attracted much attention. "Cornstalks are often eight or ten
and sometimes twelve to fifteen feet [high]," one traveler acclaimed.[36]
Another was surprised to find ears weighing as much as fourteen or
fifteen ounces and [measuring] nearly three inches in diameter.[37]
Fields were usually prepared with light plows. "Scratches" were made
across the fields at four-foot intervals and then again at right angles.
Where the furrows intersected seeds were planted and covered by hoe-
ing.[38] Weeds were chopped periodically, although the less ambitious
might ignore the fields until harvest. The cornstalks were cut with
large knives and piled in shocks. Frequently corn was left uncut, the
ear alone being pulled and stored in corncribs. Cattle were usually
turned into the fields for a few hours each day during the winter.[39]
Often the entire plant was left standing throughout the winter and the
ears gathered only as needed.[40]

Relatively few farmers bothered to fertilize their land or even to ro-
tate their crops to preserve soil fertility. The common mode of man-

aging a farm was to cultivate a field until it was exhausted and then clear new land.[41] The use of manure was considered a waste of time, for labor was dear and land cheap.[42] One traveler wrote, "Farmers will not unfrequently pull down and remove sheds in the fields, sooner than incur the trouble and expense of clearing away the . . . manure that has accumulated in them."[43] Crop rotation, first introduced in the Ohio Valley in southwestern Pennsylvania and eastern Ohio, usually involved a sequence of corn, oats, wheat, rye, and clover in that order.[44] Farmers might allow fields to lie fallow for a few years when yields began to decline.[45]

Livestock provided the frontier farmer with ready cash to retire outstanding debt on his land. Most small farmers kept ten to twenty brood sows, each producing six to eight pigs twice a year. "The young pigs run with the sows in the woods and mature without attention or special feeding," J. G. Harker, a German settler at Wartburg in East Tennessee, wrote.[46] Acorns, chestnuts, walnuts, and persimmons were their favorite foods. Hogs were slaughtered each fall and the pork smoked or packed in salt for shipment, or the animals were driven on the hoof to market. Cattle also ran in the woods. Europeans were amazed that cattle were not housed in the winter. The cattle were "kept in the open amidst ice and snow with which their backs are covered," the German, Prince Maximilian, reported during his stay at New Harmony, Indiana.[47] Harker observed in Tennessee that farmers bought year-old stock in the spring at $1.50 to $2.00 a head and let the cattle run in the woods for two and one-half years giving them only salt and corn during the coldest winter months.[48] In August of the third year they were shipped south or to Baltimore by way of the Great Valley of Virginia where they sold for $8 to $12 a head.[49] English travelers were surprised by the lack of sheep in the landscape and the lack of mutton in the taverns. Few Europeans ever adjusted to the steady diet of salt pork.

Cotton and tobacco culture gave a special look to the landscape. Travelers first saw cotton growing near the Kanawha River as they descended the Ohio River from Pittsburgh.[50] William Faux encountered it as far north as Princeton in the Wabash Valley of Indiana.[51] In 1802 the young French naturalist François Michaux observed that Tennessee farmers cultivated little else but cotton, growing only enough corn, hemp, and tobacco for their own use.[52] Michaux calculated that a man, his wife, and two or three children could earn $250 a year from a four-acre field capable of earning only $50 in corn.[53] Of particular in-

terest to travelers were the cotton gins which made possible the cultivation of short staple cotton. Fortescue Cuming saw at Henderson,
Kentucky, "a patent machine which gins, cards, and spins cotton, all
at once, by one person . . . turning a wheel. It is ingenious and simple
and occupies no more room than a small table.[54] Most of the tobacco
was produced in Kentucky and Tennessee. Both tobacco and cotton
cultivation required intensive labor and, thereby, encouraged the per-
petuation of slavery south of the Ohio River.

Life on the farm was ordered by the seasons. New land was cleared
in the late fall and winter, months which also found the farmer erecting farm buildings, improving fences, and repairing equipment as well
as beating hemp and flax, and threshing wheat.[55] In the North, February was also the month for making maple sugar. Oats and flax were
usually sown in March or April and corn and hemp in May or June.
July and August were given to cultivating the corn and pulling and
securing the flax in stacks. In September and October the corn harvest
began, and wheat, rye, and barley were sown. Tobacco was set out
from seed beds in May and harvested in September; cotton was planted
in the spring and harvested through the fall. Fall was everywhere a
time for butchering.

Shortage of labor characterized western agriculture. Consequently,
farms appeared poorly kept to the eyes of Easterners and Europeans.
As William Faux astutely observed: "The great object is to have as
many acres as possible cleared, plowed, set, sown, planted, and managed by as few hands as possible; there being little capital and therefore little or none to spare for hired labor. Instead of five acres well-
managed, they must have twenty acres badly managed. It is not how
much corn can be raised on an acre, but how much from one hand or
man, the land being nothing in comparison with labor."[56] South of the
Ohio River, slavery offered landowners a means of overcoming the
general labor shortage.

SLAVERY

Nothing distinguished agriculture in the South more than slavery. In
1819 Timothy Flint wrote from Kentucky: "I am now in the region
where the farmers designate their agriculture by the term 'raising a
crop.' They do this when a planter, with a gang of Negroes, turns his
principal attention to the staples of the country: hemp, flour, tobacco."[57] The Bullet plantation near Louisville was selected by Harry

Toulmin as typical of Kentucky's larger farms.[58] The property consisted of 500 acres of which 150 were under "fence and cultivation." Fifty-five acres were given to corn, two acres to hemp, twelve acres to an apple and peach orchard, garden, and enclosed pasture, and twenty acres to tobacco. Besides the Bullet family of six, an overseer, his wife, and child, as well as fourteen slaves, lived on the farm. The latter included two spinners, a carpenter, a gardener, and hostler in addition to house servants and field hands. Operating expenses and revenues for 1793 are given (Table 6-2). It cost slightly less than $200 a year to maintain the slaves. The overseer or farm manager received an annual income of $170 (as a ten percent share in the year's crops) in addition to living expenses figured at $30.[59] The cost of the overseer equalled the expense of maintaining fourteen slaves. The landowner received an annual income of $639, or approximately three times that amount.[60] Wealth was thus pyramided in the plantation economy to the principal benefit of the landlords.

Most travelers came to the southern portion of the Ohio Valley with well-formed opinions concerning slavery. Few did little more than validate their expectations. As one traveler admitted, "It is impossible for a casual traveler to form an exact estimate of the real condition of the slaves."[61] Most saw slavery as a degrading, inhuman system of labor. Most travelers found the slaves despondent. One traveler noted that slaves in the fields "exhibited no life, no activity, in their occupation; but seemed to drag themselves along, as if existence were a weariness" and they seemed "careless as to the amount of work done."[62] "[They] run about with a wonderful display of muscular activity," another observed, "but there is a sad lack of mind in it. They are active in body to avoid vituperation, but their minds are dormant, because they have no interest in their work."[63] An attempt to question a slave usually brought a carefully guarded reply. Travelers relied primarily on whites for their information or reached conclusions through inference or deduction.

Slavery was seen to degrade the whites as well as the blacks. As James Flint put it,

> The baneful effects of slave-keeping are not confined to negroes. . . . The necessity of personal labor being removed from the master, he either indulges in idleness, or spends his time in amusements. . . . His progeny, seeing that every sort of useful labor is performed by the slaves, whom they are taught to regard as an inferior class of beings,

Table 6-2. Income Statement, Bullet Farm, Jefferson County, Kentucky, 1793

Annual Expenses:

Every Negro (14) has 7 yards of linen	$ 41
" " " 5 yards of Kendal cotton	47
" " " 1 pair of shoes	23
Every horse has 60 bushels of corn	90
Every slave has 20 bushels of corn	70
The overseer, having a wife and child, has 60 bushels of corn	15
The cattle and hogs consume 200 bushels	76
Every hand has 100 pounds of pork	33
The overseer has 600 pounds of pork	14
The slaves, overseer, and stock consume 12 bushels of salt	12
The smith work in repairing wagons, etc.	35
20 hogsheads to hold tobacco	20
The wagonage of 600 bushels of corn	37
Grain for seed	18

The wages of the overseer are one-tenth of the whole produce, which was:

300 bushels of corn	$75	
60 bushels of wheat	40	
2 hogsheads of tobacco	47	
200 pounds of hemp	8	170
Taxes		16

Total Expenses	$ 747

Annual Revenues:

Sale of 300 bushels of corn	$ 675
Sale of 60 bushels of wheat	360
Sale of 2 hogsheads of tobacco	423
Sale of 200 pounds of hemp	72
Total Revenues	$1,386
Income	$ 639

Source: Harry Toulmin, *The Western Country in 1793, Reports on Kentucky and Virginia* (San Marino, Calif., 1948), p. 34.

naturally conceive that the cultivation of the earth is a pursuit too degrading for white men. . . . We need not be surprised with the multitude of idlers, hunters, horse-racers, gamesters, and dissipated persons.[64]

Work seemed less well organized and poorly executed in the slave states. Slave labor was thought to be ineffectual given the slaves' assumed disposition to avoid work.

Most travelers agreed that the slave population in western Virginia, Kentucky, and Tennessee were well cared for in comparison with the Deep South, particularly Mississippi and Louisiana where very large plantations used gang labor. In the Ohio Valley few slave owners owned more than two or three slaves. Slaves often became members of white households, although playing subservient roles. This didn't lessen the slave's deprivation. One traveler wrote, "I am bound to say that their condition is one of comfort and that the slaves are generally . . . 'fat and sleek'; indeed, viewed as cattle, I believe the slave is well treated, in general, in Kentucky. It is when I view him as a man that we are shocked at the barbaric ignorance, degradation, and immorality in which he is kept."[65] A few defended slavery. Lillian Foster found the black slaves, "a happy contented race: comfortably clad and well fed. . . . Masters here do not require more than one third of the labor from a slave that a northern man does from a hired servant."[66] Others saw the slave's condition as no worse than that of industrial laborers elsewhere. "The difference in point of comfort between a negro cabin in Kentucky and the cottage of a Wiltshire or Dorsetshire laborer is not so great as a philanthropic Englishman might wish," one British visitor penned.[67]

On the very large plantations of the Ohio Valley, one found the slaves stratified socially. House servants benefited from their close association with whites, often sharing in the amenities of fine living, albeit in the kitchen house or back rooms. The field hands enjoyed few amenities and were often worked in labor gangs by insensitive overseers. In 1810, a good field hand between fourteen and thirty years of age cost $350 to $400.[68] Slaves were frequently hired out, their owners receiving their wages. Often slaves retained some of their earnings using it to purchase freedom. William Owen met at Louisville a black man who had saved over $1,900 to buy his freedom and that of his wife and child.[69]

Rural Landscape

Farm buildings, their function, and their spacing gave the rural landscape a distinctive image. Travelers used architecture as a means of identifying the West as a distinctive place. Houses, the most frequently mentioned settlement features, seemed to tell the travelers much about the origins of people and their success. Other farm buildings told about the prevailing crops and the manner in which the work was done. Log cabins were the dominant species of house on the frontier, although the more affluent farmers usually replaced their cabins with brick or heavy frame and clapboard houses as soon as possible. Barns were rare, even though a great diversity of small, specialized log farm buildings could be seen in most places.

LOG CABINS

For many travelers the log cabin symbolized the frontier (Fig. 6-1). Few failed to investigate their construction and partake of life within. William Oliver's description of "raising" a log house is perhaps the best available.[70] The farmer made extensive preparations: logs for the walls were cut to proper length and hewn on opposite sides to approximately nine-inch thickness. Joists and spars as well as shingles and clapboards were also prepared using yellow poplar and black walnut whenever available. With the materials assembled at the site, neighbors arrived to spend a day erecting a shell of horizontally-laid logs dovetailed together. Those most skilled with the axe manned the corners, fitting and squaring off the logs as they were raised along spars temporarily propped against the walls. Ideally, two teams worked to build opposite sides of the house simultaneously. Only where a cabin was to be fortified were logs carefully fit together to prevent attacking Indians from firing between the crevices. Logs were usually separated by two to three inches, the intervals "chinked, daubed," or "mudded": filled with wood chips and plastered with clay or mortar. The two hewn sides formed a cabin's outer and inner walls, although clapboards about four feet long and a foot wide were often nailed on exterior walls or held in place by traverse spars pegged at intervals.

After the logs had been set in place, openings were sawed out and framed for the doors and fireplace. Most cabins had two doors on opposite walls for light and air circulation. The German, J. G. Harker, found the American settlers' use of doors peculiar. "The Americans . . . have no idea . . . what a door is for," he wrote. "I have seen them keep both doors open during very cold weather, sit close to the burning fire place, and have a sheet of calico stretched from ceiling to the floor to protect themselves from the biting cold wind. . . . It is also a fact that when an American goes in or out of the house of a German, he never closes the door."[71] The fireplace was usually located in one of the gable ends. Chimneys of wood, plastered with mud, were the most

Figure 6-1.
A Typical Frontier Cabin. (*Harper's New Monthly Magazine*, Nov. 1857)

common. Fortified cabins had interior chimneys, for attacking Indians could easily detach an end chimney and gain entry. Few cabins were built with windows owing to the lack of glass on the frontier. Windows were usually added later. Cabin floors were of pounded dirt or made of short "puncheons" split from logs and pegged down on longer sleepers laid beneath. If a sawmill was handy, floors might be made of planks. Oliver estimated the cost of a large, well-constructed log house with a brick fireplace, interior plastering, and finished floors, at $133.[72] His estimate assumed hired labor and the use of the finest materials. Most log cabins, however, were valued under $25. Few anticipated that their log houses would be permanent.

Log cabins were usually of a single story, sixteen to twenty feet long, and twelve to sixteen feet wide.[73] Most had a single room with an unfinished loft under the roof where the children slept and where food and other items were stored. Furniture commonly included a table, some chairs, and several beds with mattresses filled with corn shucks. Clothing hung on the walls along with at least one long rifle. An overnight stay in a log cabin was an adventure for travelers not used to the primitive frontier. William Faux wrote of the Ingle cabin in Indiana: "[A] heavy battering rain . . . poured rain down upon our beds. Great lumps of clay, or daubing, stuffed between the logs, also kept falling on our heads. . . . We needed an umbrella."[74] The loosely constructed log cabin was very difficult to keep clean, and for most settlers household dirt was accepted as a part of life. This acceptance frequently continued long after log cabin conditions had disappeared. Morris Birkbeck wrote, "The American was bred in a cabin: this is not a reproach; for the origin is most honourable: but as she has exchanged her hovel of hewn logs for a mansion of brick, some of her cabin habits have been unconsciously retained."[75]

GENTRY HOUSES

Successful farmers usually replaced their log cabins with frame or brick houses or substantially improved and added to their cabins to simulate frame structures. The intention was to symbolize worldly success. Houses were often located on hill tops in order to afford "a view." The wealthier landowners often landscaped their grounds with decorative trees and shrubs and provided their houses with ceremonial drives and walks from which the house could be admired. The farm of William Henry Harrison at North Bend, Ohio, near Cincinnati was an example noted by many travelers. The house originally belonged to Harrison's father-in-law, Judge John Symmes, whose large land purchase and colonizing scheme had led to the initial settlement of southwestern Ohio. Mrs. Harrison had been responsible for partially landscaping the grounds before her marriage. Thomas Ashe, the British traveler, found her an accomplished botanist. "She is forming a shrubbery," he wrote, "which will be entirely composed of magnolia [*Magnolia tripetala*], catalpa [*Catalpa speciosa*], pawpaw [*Asimina triloba*], rose [*Malus angustifolia*], and . . . all others distinguished for blossom and fragrance."[76] The house was a two-story log cabin covered with long clapboards to simulate a frame house. It was extended with frame appendages and sported a long porch facing the Ohio River. The original log house figured prominently in the presidential election of 1840 when Harrison's supporters pictured him as a simple country farmer sitting on his log cabin porch with a cider barrel. At his death, Harrison was buried near the house. The house and the tomb, set in a parklike setting high on the bluff, were major landmarks for steamboat passengers on the Ohio River.

The Kentucky Blue Grass around Lexington was the district most noted for gentry houses and estate-like farms. Most houses were two-story oblong boxes with either two or four rooms on each floor. Connected to the rear of most were single-story kitchen houses in which food was prepared and where house servants were frequently housed. Travelers took little interest in identifying house types. Most were satisfied to distinguish frame from brick and brick from stone houses, the latter symbolizing the most wealth. Travelers focused more on the life of the house and the activity of the yard in which the slave quarters, usually small log cabins, were located. Washington Irving recorded impressions in his notebook as he approached a plantation near Louisville.[77] The road led through a grove of butternut trees (*Juglans cinerea*) and across a small creek. Passing an old Negro and a dog at a stone gate, the wooden house flanked by slave houses came into view. Blacks of all ages dominated the scene, and before the house the ground was littered with rubbish. A bugle sounded to call the master. "Fat negro wenches" were drying apples and peaches on a board under the trees, and in nearby fields Negro boys were exercising race horses.[78] On many estates, planters kept tame herds of deer, elk, and even buffalo to the amusement of visitors.

FARMSTEADS AND FIELDS

In addition to houses, most farmsteads contained outbuildings housing stock, equipment, grain or serving other specialized functions. Only in western Pennsylvania and eastern Ohio were general purpose barns early introduced. Where Pennsylvanians settled, barns were often two-story, heavy frame structures built over basements of brick or stone. Second stories were reached by embankments. Sometimes called "Swiss barns," these structures were thought to have been initially introduced in southeastern Pennsylvania by German-speaking settlers from Switzerland. Where New Englanders settled, small frame barns of a single story were seen. Elsewhere in the Ohio Valley individual farm buildings built of log predominated. Most farms had a corncrib, a stable, a pigsty, an equipment shed, and a smoke house. Smoke houses "built much as dwelling houses, only slighter and not often mudded," were common around Albion, Illinois, in 1820 John Woods wrote.[79] Corncribs were similarly built, but raised a few feet off the ground. "Corn and pig pens with cart and wagon lodges are yet scarce. . . . I have seen no barn . . . although . . . a person at Birks Prairie has

built a threshing floor to which he purposes adding a barn," he continued.[80] Most barns in the Ohio Valley were combinations of two or
four log cribs covered with a single roof. Unfortunately, travelers were
little concerned with farmstead architecture, and there is little to learn
about these barns from their observations.

Fences, on the other hand, attracted much attention, especially from
the British travelers used to orderly hedge rows and stone walls. Particularly offensive to refined tastes were the "worm" or "zigzag" fences
made of split rails. One Briton wrote, "instead of the fragrant quickset
hedge there is a 'worm fence'—the rudest . . . barrier known in the
country—which consists simply of bars, about eight or nine feet in
length, laid zig-zag on each other alternatively."[81] The "post and rail"
fence was constructed of posts about six feet in length sunk in the
ground eight to ten feet apart with four horizontal rails laid into mor-
tises cut in the posts. But worm fences, the easiest to construct, were
the most common. "Any man of ordinary physical powers can put up
200 yards of a rail fence in a day, or fence about thirty acres in a
week," William Oliver wrote.[82] These fences usually lasted about ten
years.

Even in the most densely settled areas, forest remnants remained. As
one observer put it, "fine forests . . . are everywhere left standing isolated in the midst of cultivated tracts making . . . links in [a] chain of
woodland . . . across the country."[83] In the areas of tobacco cultivation considerable land was left uncleared or was abandoned to the
forest, being held in reserve or being exhausted and in fallow. Fields
were small, rarely exceeding ten acres, and irregularly shaped to con-
form to topography, although most farmers evidently sought a square
shape to accommodate cross plowing with light plows. The township
and range system had not yet brought the checkerboard pattern to
lands settled from the public domain. Roads followed Indian trails and
game traces and led from one farm to another in the most convenient
manner.* If travelers saw differences in the layout of fields from one
section of the Ohio Valley to another, they did not report it in their
journals.

A few naturalists noted the prevailing ground cover along the roads,
in the pastures and fields, and along the fence lines. At New Harmony,

* Roads did not adhere to the section lines in the flatter areas until the late nineteenth century when state legislatures abolished the open range. Farmers were
required to fence their farms, and roads on the section lines made for less fencing.

Indiana, Charles Lyell was surprised by the number of European species evident. He wrote: "Many European plants . . . are making their way here, such as the . . . thorn-apple (*Datura stramonium*); and it is a curious fact, which I afterward learnt from Dr. [Robert] Dale Owen, that when such foreigners are first naturalized they over-run the country with amazing rapidity and are quite a nuisance. But they soon grow scarce and after eight or ten years can hardly be met with."[84] One European species thrived so well around Lexington, Kentucky, that it gave its name to the district. Bluegrass (*Poa pretensis*) gave a carpetlike appearance beneath the oaks, hickories, and chestnuts left standing in the woodland pastures. The road between Lexington and Louisville "flourished" with camomile (*Anthemis noblis*), mullein (*Verbascum thapsus*), and clover (*Trifolium*) in the 1840s.[85] In the 1790s, on the other hand, earlier travelers had reported a predominance of native cane (*Arundinaria macrosperma*) and wild rye (*Secale cerveale*).[86] The German, J. G. Harker, noted in East Tennessee that wild violets (*Viola cucullata*), ragwort (*Senecio aureus*), thistle (*Cirsium vulgare*), plantain (*Plantago major*), mullein, and ironweed (*Vernonia altissima*) predominated along fence lines; all were "familiar forms . . . [or] ones closely related to those of [the] fatherland."[87]

Rural Neighborhoods

Signs of rural community were slow to appear on the frontier. Settlers were preoccupied with establishing farms and providing subsistence for their families. Nonetheless, concern with schooling and religion ultimately led to the establishment of schools and churches in most places. Gristmills and rural stores also appeared, giving focus to rural localities. Where New Englanders settled in Ohio the process of establishing a sense of community proceeded more rapidly, helped along by the institution of township government derived from the New England town heritage. Yet even in Ohio the settler's sense of belonging to a township was often negligible. "I have asked many people what township they lived in and they could not tell," one traveler wrote.[88] Most people identified with the county as a geographical unit, probably because it was readily symbolized by a town with a courthouse.

The camp meeting and the cemetery stimulated the sense of rural neighborhood. John Woods observed that settlers "most commonly bury their dead near the place where they die and erect a small pale fence round the grave, to prevent its being disturbed."[89] James Hall noted that it was "not unusual to see these spots surrounded with weeping willows, or hedges of privet [*Ligustrum*] or lilac [*Syringa*], which give them a decent air of seclusion."[90] Hall added: "when a place is thus consecrated, it is restored to by all the families connected by relationship with the proprietor . . . and frequently by all the neighbors indiscriminately. The next step in the process of improvement is the establishment of public grave-yards, which is usually effected by religious communities."[91]

The Great Revival movement which swept the Ohio Valley frontier between 1797 and 1805 greatly encouraged organized religion. The camp meeting, introduced as a device to win converts to Christianity and to stimulate the organization of permanent congregations, continued well into the nineteenth century. The Methodist bishop Francis Asbury described one meeting held in 1810 in Sumner County, Tennessee: "The stand was in the open air, embosomed in a wood of lofty beech trees. Ten ministers of God, Methodists and Presbyterians, united their labors and mingled with the childlike simplicity of primitive times. Fires blazing here and there dispelled the darkness and the shouts of the redeemed captives, and cries of precious souls struggling into life, broke the silence of midnight."[92] Orators, playing on crowd emotions, often worked participants into frenzies, much to the amusement of visitors. The camp meetings offered excitement and emotional release from the isolation of the farm and the routine life of farming.

Although structures symbolizing rural neighborhood were slow to evolve on the landscape, this did not mean that neighboring was unimportant. James Flint wrote, "The new settler in the woods is soon so well known among a wide circle of neighbors that almost any person within ten miles . . . can direct the stranger to his residence."[93] Another traveler noted: "As social comforts are less under the protection of the laws here . . . friendship and good neighborhood are more valued. There is more genuine kindness and politeness among these backwoodsmen, than among any set of people I have yet seen in America."[94] William Hall and a neighbor estimated the population of the neighborhood near Albion, Illinois. Seven hundred sixty people lived on Deer, English, Birk's, Burnt, Village, and Long Prairies, but "we had only our own knowledge to guide us and most likely omitted several families," he wrote.[95]

Communal Settlements and Colonies

The sense of community was strongest where settlers banded together in religious communities, as did the Shakers, or where they found themselves ostracized in rural colonies, as were the free blacks in Ohio and Indiana. Although these types of settlement were rare, their uniqueness was an attraction to travelers.

Several Shaker communities evolved in the Ohio Valley during the religious fervor of the Great Revival. The largest were at Union Village near Lebanon, Ohio, and at Pleasant Hill near Harrodsburg, Kentucky. Property was held in common and celibacy was practiced; but it was the unusual form of worship, involving dancing and shaking, which most set apart the members of "the Union Society of Believers in Christ's Second Appearing." Communities were divided into "families," each living in its own large, three-story dormitory and managing its own farm. Most visitors agreed that the Shaker settlements were exceptionally clean. The Shakers were also known for their manufacture of wagons and the production of furniture and household implements. New Harmony, Indiana, was another communal village frequently visited by tourists. First settled by Germans under the leadership of George Rapp, the town was subsequently sold to Robert Owen, a Scottish industrialist, who attempted unsuccessfully to found a communistic society.

The English minister Edward Abdy was especially interested in the American black population, not only the slaves in the South, but the freedmen in the North as well. In 1834 near Madison on the Ohio River in Indiana he found a small colony of liberated slaves. Eleven families owned some 500 acres of land, growing wheat, oats, rye, hemp, and tobacco.[96] "While they were clearing their farms of timber, they were unmolested," he wrote; "but now that they have got the land into . . . cultivation, and are rising in the world, the avarice of the white man casts a greedy eye on their [land]."[97] They were "pestered and plagued" by the whites with offers and inducements to give up their farms and go to Liberia. As blacks, they had little protection under the law. They derived no benefit from the school tax, had no political privileges, and could not give evidence against a white person in court although Indiana then called itself a "free state." In Ohio, near Georgetown, Abdy found another colony of nearly 600 blacks. "At all events," he was told by a white tavern keeper, "we can get rid of those settlers; they are an eye-sore and a nuisance and they have no business among us."[98] The opportunities of the frontier were not shared equally by all.

Sectional Differences

Travelers sought to identify differences from place to place. Not only were they interested in the various elements that generally constituted the rural scene, but they sought subtleties of sectional variation. What were the landscape cues that told a traveler he was in a different country? It largely depended upon the traveler. In northeastern Ohio New Englanders had settled in Connecticut's Western Reserve, whereas southerners dominated Virginia's Military Reserve in the south-central portion of the state. The rather biased Yankee, John Wright, wrote:

> The difference between industry and indolence was never more strikingly displayed then in the two sections. . . . The beautiful rolling land, the ever varying scenery, the extensive improvements, the elegant, painted houses, the lofty spires of the village churches, and even the sportive groups of decently clothed well-behaved children . . . form so strong a contrast with the dull uniformity of the land, mean habitations, slovenly apparel and coarse manners of the people of the lower country, that the traveler is almost led to believe himself transported to a land inhabited by a different order of beings.[99]

But few travelers distinguished sectional differences within states. Most looked for broader variations.

What distinguished East from the West? Some could answer in a single sweeping phrase. The West, one traveler wrote, was "log cabins, ugly women, and tall timber."[100] Another described the West as "badly built houses, windows without glass, dirty children, lean mongrel cows, barns in ruins, patches representing gardens . . . choked up with weeds and every appearance of discomfort."[101] To others the West was less a man-made phenomena and more a fact of nature. "The only change I observe in the face of the county," Charles Hoffman wrote, "is that instead of being broken up into small hills, where forest and cultivation are most happily mingled . . . the vales here spread out into plains; and, the high grounds receding, swell off till they show like mountains in the distance."[102] The West was a way of thinking. "One acquires as he proceeds westward, largeness and expansion of his ideas. . . . thought swells away into the vast dimensions of the majestic rivers and boundless tracts of country over which the eye expatiates," another wrote.[103] The West was a state of mind. The Swedish traveler Fredrika Bremer inquired, "What is there better here in the western states than in those of the East?"[104] She was answered, "More freedom and less prejudice [and] more regard to the man than to his dress and his external circumstances: a freer scope for thought and enterprise."[105] The past was an eastern thing. The West belonged to the future.

What distinguished North from South? This was a question of increasing controversy as the nineteenth century wore on. Travelers sought to find differences in landscape between slave and free-soil states. Often the search began on the deck of an Ohio River steamboat as passengers compared the Ohio, Indiana, and Illinois banks with those of Virginia (now West Virginia) and Kentucky. Most thought they saw a marked difference in favor of the free-soil states. One traveler wrote in 1825: "The contrast between Ohio and Kentucky is striking and the baneful influence of slavery is very soon discovered. Instead of elegant farms, orchards, meadows, corn and wheat fields carefully enclosed, you see patches planted with tobacco, the leaves neglected, and instead of well-looking houses [you see] cabins . . . bearing a resemblance to pigsties."[106] Charles Dickens observed in 1842, "Where slavery sits brooding . . . there is an air of ruin and decay."[107]

Those who left the river had their expectations validated. One traveler wrote in the 1850s:

> The moment you cross the Ohio you are painfully struck with the contrast, and as you advance into the interior things get worse and worse. You miss entirely that progress which is the charm of the East and the wonder of the West. Here things seem all at a standstill; there is no go-aheadness. . . . Nowhere do you hear that extraordinary combination of hammering, planing, and sawing which . . . announces a new and bustling settlement.[108]

James Buckingham saw in Kentucky a "general absence of neatness and cleanliness," for "the great bulk of the laborers were negro slaves whose air, dress and general appearance, sufficiently manifested their indifference to everything but their own ease, and their desire to escape from labor."[109] Although Buckingham had seen no differences between Ohio and Kentucky on the Ohio River, "here in the interior the difference was too great to escape the perception of the most careless observer."[110]

Creating a Garden

Conversion of the Ohio Valley to agriculture was an accomplishment that seemed to mark the Americans as a chosen people. Had they not followed the Creator's will by conquering the heathen savage to evolve a garden in the wilderness? Caleb Atwater, a Yankee transplanted to Ohio, relayed a universal feeling when he wrote: "Here every farmer in the world may become a freeholder in rural bliss. No poor man in the eastern states . . . has any excuse for remaining poor. . . . He who made him . . . created this country for his use. . . . it has been given to him by God, who has commanded him to cultivate and enjoy it."[111] The Easterner, Thaddeus Harris, wrote:

> When we see the forest cleared of those enormous trees . . . we cannot help dwelling upon the industry and art of man, which by dint of toil and perserverance can change the desert into a fruitful field. . . . when the silence of nature is succeeded by the buzz of employment, the congratulations of society, and the voice of joy. . . . when we behold competence and plenty springing from the bosom of dreary forests,—what a lesson is afforded of the benevolent intentions of Providence![112]

The process of settling the West intrigued most travelers. Out of the raw frontier a virtual garden was made to bloom. Timothy Flint, one of the early West's best-known literary champions, wrote of the sequence. Traveling out from Cincinnati in 1819, he saw smoke rising from the woods; he heard "the stroke of the axe, the tinkling of bells, and the baying of dogs, and saw the newly arrived emigrant."[113] "Pass this place in two years," he predicted, "and you will see extensive fields of corn and wheat; a young and thrifty orchard . . . the guaranty of present abundant subsistence and of future luxury. Pass it in ten years, and the log buildings will have disappeared. The shrubs and forest trees will be gone. The Arcadian aspect of humble and retired abundance and comfort will have given place to a brick house, with accompaniments like those [of] older countries."[114]

Yet, the garden was made to bloom in different ways in different places. South of the Ohio River slavery enabled a planter aristocracy to evolve. Large estate houses stood beside the slave cabins: a contrast in wealth and poverty, freedom and servitude. North of the Ohio River the anti-slavery and liberal land policies of the Federal Government encouraged the small family farm. Farmers from Kentucky and Tennessee, discouraged in their competition with slave labor and frustrated by the confusion of land titles, moved North in large numbers. In Ohio, Indiana, and Illinois they joined settlers from New England and the Middle Atlantic states and foreign immigrants from Britain and Germany. To the South, capital was invested increasingly in slaves and land in pursuit of tobacco and cotton profits. To the North, agriculture was as diversified as the population was cosmopolitan. The cleavage between North and South was clearly apparent in the rural scene. In the decades preceding the Civil War the Ohio Valley ceased to be a western frontier. Two distinct regions had emerged with the Ohio River a clear division line: the "Upper South" contrasted with the "Lower Middle West."

7 URBAN IMAGES

I inquired what lions the town offered of interest to a traveller. I found there was little . . . unless I wished to go through the pig-killing, scalding, and cutting process again; but stomach and imagination rebelled at the bare thought . . . so I was fain to content myself with the novelty of the tobacco pressing.

Henry Murray

Nothing symbolized American progress like the towns and cities of the Ohio Valley. Not only did Americans convert the wilderness into a garden, but within the garden the seeds of urban civilization had been sown to bear the early fruits of a new commercial and industrial age. Cities like Pittsburgh, Cincinnati, and Louisville sprung to full maturity in a single generation. Urbanism was always an integral part of the Ohio Valley frontier. The French, English, and American fur trades had centered at urban places. Initial American settlement required military protection, and most forts evolved into towns. The earliest pioneer farmers sold their surplus crops to town merchants who supplied both necessities and luxuries in return. Towns nurtured the region's first large-scale manufacturing, and government, both at the county and state levels, centered in urban places.

The relative few who lived in towns experienced a distinctive environment by rural standards. A town was clearly man's creation where nature was more completely subverted. Towns were compact, and population densities were high. Towns were solidly linked to outside places with a constant circulation of people and goods. People were more varied making for more excitement. In many ways urban places were more dangerous, for disease and criminality often accompanied overcrowding, especially where the new factory system of labor routinized daily life at or near poverty levels. Wealth was concentrated in the cities. The gentry displayed their affluence in large town houses which contrasted sharply with the residences of the poor. Yet, town life held hope to all. Urban places had a "get rich" aura which promised success to those who worked hard.

Not surprisingly, travelers spent more time in the towns and cities of the Ohio Valley than in her rural areas. Urban centers provided the facilities which catered to travelers. The towns were nodes in the evolving circulation system along which the travelers moved. Travelers described the typical aspects of the Ohio Valley's urban landscape, but they also sought distinction in the look of the towns from place to place. How did small towns differ from large ones? Did they perform different functions? Was the architecture different? How were they organized spatially? What made each place distinctive unto itself?

In 1800, only ten places had more than 500 people; the two largest towns, Lexington and Pittsburgh, had only 1,795 and 1,565 people respectively.[1] By 1850 over 300 towns had attained populations of 500 or more people; the three largest cities, Cincinnati, Pittsburgh, and Louisville, had 130,700, 75,200, and 54,200 people respectively.[2] Cincinnati was the sixth largest city in the United States, behind New York, Philadelphia, Baltimore, Boston, and New Orleans.

Towns grew along the transportation routes, especially where people and commodities were exchanged between land and river routes. At Brownsville, Pittsburgh, and Wheeling, various roads from Philadelphia and Baltimore met the headwaters of the Ohio. Louisville was also a "break of bulk" point, for, except at high water, steamboat cargoes were unloaded and carted around the rapids there. Two separate river fleets evolved. Only large vessels were economical below Louisville, but only small steamboats could operate on the narrower and shallower river above. Even after the canal at Louisville was completed, the two fleets continued to exchange passengers and freight across the Louisville levee. Given its central location, Cincinnati was a logical place to ship farm commodities to New Orleans and for migrants, coming from the East, to leave the river for new farms in the North and West. Lexington grew at the center of Kentucky's Blue

Grass area, the Ohio Valley's most prosperous agricultural district. Most towns larger than 500 people were river towns served by flatboats and later by steamboats, but Lexington was unique, for the city was not located on navigable water.

Towns evolved at intervals along the major roads. Zanesville, Lancaster, and Chillicothe grew where Zane's Trace from Wheeling crossed the major rivers of southeastern Ohio (Fig. C). Most migrants on the Ohio River bound for the Kentucky Blue Grass disembarked at Limestone (later called Maysville), climbed the steep bluff a few miles to Washington, and then struck out for Paris and Lexington (Fig. C). Those who went farther west to Louisville passed through Frankfort at the fording place on the Kentucky River. The National Road generated several large towns: Columbus at the crossing on the Scioto River, Springfield in Ohio and Richmond in Indiana on major tributaries of the Miami River, and Indianapolis and Terre Haute at the White and Wabash rivers in Indiana (Fig. F).

The canals and railroads initially reinforced the river towns. The canals of western Pennsylvania, Ohio, and Indiana had been built as trunk lines connecting Lake Erie and the Ohio River, although they actually functioned more to funnel freight short distances to river ports (Fig. G). The first railroads, on the other hand, had been built as feeder lines; but by the 1850s they had come to form north of the Ohio River an integrated network of trunk lines (Fig. H). The canals and the railroads stimulated urban growth away from the major rivers at places like Dayton and Indianapolis. Railroad building languished south of the Ohio River. During the Civil War the line from Louisville to Atlanta through Nashville and Chattanooga provided the only linkage between the Deep South and the Middle West.

Town Morphology

Even the largest cities could be glimpsed in a single view when seen from the vantage point of a nearby hill (Fig. 1-3). As most towns were river oriented, sprawling across an adjacent floodplain or terrace, they could also be easily viewed from the water (Fig. 7-1). During the early years, before trees were planted along a town's streets and around its houses, a town's plan boldly stood out on the landscape. In nearly every town the streets met at right angles in a grid pattern. Streets varied in width, with the principal business avenues often 100 feet or wider in

Figure 7-1.
View of Steubenville, Ohio, c. 1850. Whole towns could be seen in a single view. (Robert Sears, *A New and Popular Pictorial Description of the United States*, New York, 1856)

order to accommodate turning wagons. The regularity and spaciousness of the streets gave Ohio Valley towns a planned look.

Streets were slowly improved through the nineteenth century. Sidewalks and stepping stones had been laid down in most towns by 1810. By 1830 major streets in most places had been entirely paved with stone or brick and ornamental trees systematically planted. In Huntsville, Alabama, the Pride of China (*Melia azedarach*) made a spectacular display in bloom.[3] In Lexington, the Kentucky coffee tree (*Gymnocladus dioicus*) was a favorite planting.[4] Other popular species included black locust (*Robinia pseudoacacia*), red maple (*Acer rubrum*), American elm (*Ulmus americana*), catalpa (*Catalpa speciosa*), and sycamore; but Lombardy poplar (*Populus nigra*) was probably the most widely used tree in a town's earliest years owing to its fast rate of growth. At a distance, most towns looked like a formal garden surrounded with bluffs still covered by the original forest. The exotic species which lined the streets brought a sense of order and the image of human control over nature. At close view, the paved streets with their foliage provided a clean, pastoral look. After 1830, however, less care was taken to plant trees. Many streets lost their trees to street widening, sewer construction, and other improvements. Tree planting became more the prerogative of private landowners, and the public streets became more utilitarian and less esthetic.

The main commercial street of the typical river town either paralleled the river or ran perpendicular to it, terminating at the levee, a paved area for the accommodation of steamboats and flatboats. In Chillicothe, Ohio, for example, Water Street paralleled the Scioto River for about half a mile containing some ninety houses in 1810, although the river had already begun to erode the bank, collapsing buildings into the water.[5] Main Street, located one block away, received most of the new business buildings thereafter. Market Street, of equal width, ran perpendicular to the river and contained the market house. Market Street was Chillicothe's "main cross street" and was intended as its second most important thoroughfare. In inland towns, highways created the principal streets. Along the National Road, towns rarely consisted of more than a single street, with houses strung out along the highway's right of way.

Log cabins predominated in a town's first decade, to be succeeded by frame buildings covered with clapboard or buildings of red brick or stone. All varieties of building material were evident to the travelers at any one time in any one place. Along the National Road in Ohio, Fortescue Cuming noted a predominance of white clapboard buildings with green jalousie window shutters and shingled roofs painted red.[6] Clapboards and shingles were usually of white pine, white oak, cedar, or yellow poplar, woods easily split with an axe. Rafts of white pine were floated down the Allegheny and Ohio Rivers from western New York and western Pennsylvania, and red cedar was brought down the Kentucky and other rivers in the South to supply the exaggerated building needs of Cincinnati, Louisville, and the other large cities. Clapboards were cut about twenty inches long, six inches wide, and three-quarters of an inch thick. Boards on a facade usually lapped each other lengthwise by about ten inches. Generally, there were two layers, with the outside set sloping opposite to the inside set.[7] Clapboarding required constant repair, and more than one traveler commented on the dilapidated appearance of most frame houses.

After 1820 commercial buildings and houses of the urban gentry tended to be of red brick or of stone construction. This was particularly true in the larger towns where rebuilding along the waterfronts

Figure 7-2.
High Street in Columbus, Ohio, in the 1850s. Shown is the statehouse and
the new commercial "blocks." (*The Ohio Railroad Guide, Illustrated*, Columbus, 1854)

and main streets saw blocks of substantial brick store fronts rise (Fig.
7-2). The brick was usually fired on the site, but, as one traveler observed, they were often badly made and "fall to pieces within half a
century."[8] Brick gave the illusion of permanence, but the soft and per-
meable quality of the early varieties necessitated constant maintenance. Stone was usually quarried in nearby river bluffs. At Chillicothe
a whitish brown limestone was used.[9] At Frankfort a "good marble of
a dusky cream colour, veined with both blue and red" was popular.[10]
Stone quickly darkened once exposed to wood and coal smoke.

Even those travelers interested in architecture failed to describe in
detail the buildings they saw. Only when construction materials, size
and form, or decorative styles were unusual were details provided. One
visitor noted at Washington, Pennsylvania, that chimney tops were
generally of white sandstone resting on bricks which gave "a neat appearance."[11] At Columbus, Ohio, another observer puzzled, "Why
should tin drop-spouts be used instead of wood or lead?"[12] Before 1810

there was little difference between the rural and urban houses of any locality. More two-story houses could be found in the towns, but nearly all were small oblong boxes with one of the long sides facing a street. As building lots were further subdivided, individual houses sometimes abutted one another, providing a continuous facade along a street. Where building height and roof lines suggested total integration, a building "block" was said to exist.[13] These were most common along waterfronts and along principal business streets. As pressure for land increased in commercial areas after 1810, more buildings were built with their narrow sides facing the street, thus squeezing more businesses into a given block. In residential areas houses tended to be free-standing, often with decorative gardens in front and vegetable gardens, stables, and other outbuildings in back. Travelers noted differences in architectural style, but paid little attention to defining distinctive decorative modes. "Modern fashions prevail," one traveler wrote, although "here and there some 'old fogy' defies the order of the day, and builds as his grandfather used to build."[14] Federal and Greek Revival styles predominated through the 1830s with Italianate and Gothic Revival ideas introduced into the larger towns in the 1840s.

Most urban structures were built on speculation and most were rented to their occupants. As towns matured old buildings were replaced, but not necessarily destroyed. Buildings were recycled: moved to new locations on new streets toward the edge of town. Mrs. Trollope wrote from Cincinnati, "One of the sights to stare at in America is that of houses moving from place to place."[15] Daniel Drake, writing as a physician, thought most urban houses inadequate.[16] Walls were too thin on frame houses for effective winter heating, and the lack of porches meant undue exposure to the summer sun. Most of the houses built on speculation lacked cellars and were poorly ventilated and were "filthy" through "perpetual decay and decomposition."[17] Walls built of brick and stone were often "covered with condensed vapor," and rotting foundations produced noxious "gases or malaria," he continued.[18] One traveler observed that houses were so poorly built that twenty years was "amply sufficient to clothe them in a garb of antiquity."[19]

Towns measured their success by the number of buildings constructed, particularly the structures of special size and function that, more often than not, had outstanding architectural decorations. As most towns were small, travelers could easily count the buildings. Standing above Chillicothe in 1807, Fortescue Cuming counted 202 log and frame houses and four of brick.[20] But special landmarks attracted his attention: the market house, a narrow single-story structure with green shutters and a belfry, the courthouse with its small belfry, and the Presbyterian church of brick and the smaller frame Methodist church. The state capital building was slightly elevated above the town on a hill. Cuming observed that the town contained six taverns, each with a sign hung from a post before the door; fourteen buildings contained stores and one store contained the post office.[21] A few of the wealthier residents had built large suburban houses on the bluff overlooking the town.

Deserted properties were common given the rapid turnover of population in most places. This was particularly true of towns with declining fortunes like Chillicothe which lost the Ohio state capital to Columbus in 1812. Towns did not always live up to their early promise. Streets did not always completely fill in with buildings. The vacant lot, abandoned or held in speculation, was a common urban feature. Jimson or Jamestown weed (*Datura stramonium*) and mullein were the most common weeds seen in these vacant spaces by the botanist François Michaux.[22] Both species were avoided by the hogs who freely roamed the streets and the unfenced properties of every place.

In many towns a courthouse was often the central feature. Courthouses were usually located in a public square along with a small gaol or jail and, in Virginia and Kentucky, stocks and a whipping post. Business districts usually evolved around these squares unless some other attraction, like the commerce of a waterfront, encouraged commercial growth elsewhere. In the early nineteenth century most courthouses were small two-story brick or stone boxes with gently sloping pyramidal roofs surmounted by small belfries or cupolas. Most were plain, but the fancier of the species sported the entablatures and columns and the porticoes or less prominent pilasters of the Classical Revival style. Near most courthouses were small single-story, frame buildings containing lawyers' offices. In the summer, one observer wrote, the lawyers sat at their doors in wicker chairs like spiders "waiting to snare the silly fly."[23]

Travelers, particularly foreign visitors, were curious about the western courts. Timothy Flint observed that it was popular to be "democratic" in the courtroom where the lawyers observed "meanness and slovenliness" of dress and where the language was an "amusing compound of Yankee dialect, southern peculiarity, and Irish blarney."[24] Flint wrote: " 'Him' and 'me' said this or that. 'I done it' and various phrases of this sort, and images drawn from measuring the location of land purchases; and figures drawn from boating and river navigation, were often served up, as the garnish of their speeches."[25] Americans of the period did much "calculating" and "reckoning" in their conversations.

Henry Baxter, having brought a large lumber raft down the Ohio River, spent several months in Warsaw, Kentucky, selling lumber. There he observed the local political campaign and election of 1844. The courthouse square was jammed with people on election day, for farmers had come to town to vote and influence their neighbors' votes. When the polls opened the crowd surged forward to the front door of the court building. There sat the election judge. "How do you vote? The full Whig ticket, is answered. Back out, sir . . . give place to others . . . your vote is down."[26] Soon a throng of men and boys, one carrying a hemp stalk with the local Clay Club banner, beseiged the courthouse "with such tremendous shouting that the officers were obliged to suspend voting until silence could be restored," Baxter wrote.[27] Western elections were notorious for their disorder. At Somerset, Pennsylvania, in 1818, another traveler wrote that he had never seen such a scene among civilized people. There was betting, drinking, and quarrelling, and "they kept up their carousal through the night, screeching like savages, beating drums, throwing of rocks against buildings, making such a dim, that I was unable to . . . sleep."[28] But other travelers, expecting disorder on election day, were pleasantly surprised. James Buckingham saw "no flags or banners, no processions, no distinquishing colours or badges, no bands of music, no open houses for the voters, and no treating or entertaining of any kind" at Blountville, Tennessee, in 1840.[29]

As a courthouse promised prosperity to a town, so also did a statehouse. State government meant a small payroll for government employees, the spending of state legislators and others who visited the place on government business, and visibility as a town of distinction. The earliest statehouses were small; indeed, they were little larger than courthouses. The first capital building at Frankfort, Kentucky, was a small, two-story oblong box of rough marble with a cupola at the center of the roof. One traveler was told with pride that the building contained 1,368 panes of glass.[30] This first building was destroyed by fire in 1813 to be replaced by a larger Greek Revival structure with a dome and portico supported by six Ionic columns. In the Senate Chamber and Representatives' Hall hung the portraits of LaFayette, Daniel Boone, and William Henry Harrison.[31] The public grounds comprised some four acres landscaped with trees, shrubs, and a small fountain. During the 1840s a railroad was constructed across the front of the capital grounds. Frankfort's principal business streets were immediately adjacent.

James Alexander visited the State Senate at Nashville in 1839. Europeans, like Alexander, were generally surprised by the decorum (or lack of decorum) in such assemblies. The delegates sat at separate tables, "and every man of them," he wrote, "was balancing himself on the hind legs of his chair, with . . . dusty boots on the table among the writing materials. They spoke to each other, coughed, chewed tobacco, and spat on the floor; some walked about with their hats on, or opened a window and leaned over it with their backs to the company."[32] A proposed law restricting the movement of slaves into the state was under debate. A massacre of seventy whites had just occurred in Virginia, and many were alarmed that the violence would spread to Tennessee.

Churches, cemeteries, colleges, and schools caught the traveler's eye as symbols of social progress. Most churches were small frame buildings capable of seating but a few hundred people. With simple gabled roofs (one gable facing the street) churches sometimes had two entrances, one for men and one for women. Small belfries were common; steeples were rare. The more prosperous congregations built in brick. Traveling ministers were particularly interested in church layout. The Episcopalian church at Madison, Indiana, was laid out "with due regard to ecclesiological principles," Henry Caswell wrote.[33] He continued: "The seats are all without doors, the roof is open, the altar occupies its proper place in the chancel, and prayers are read from a lectern at the left. The pulpit is placed in the right and is in a perfect contrast to the huge rostrum occupied by the preacher in too many . . . American churches."[34] Before 1820 the Quakers built the most impressive church buildings. The annual and quarterly meetinghouses at such places as Mount Pleasant, Ohio, and Richmond, Indiana, seated upwards to 1,000 people in large rooms divided by movable partitions.[35] After 1840 the Roman Catholics built the largest churches in Cincinnati, Pittsburgh, and the other large cities.

Protestants were generally buried in public cemeteries located at a town's edge. Roman Catholics usually established separate, but nearby, cemeteries. The cemetery at Frankfort, Kentucky, was one of the first to be elaborately landscaped. Located at the edge of a cliff high above the Kentucky River, the visitor looked directly down on the town. Carriage drives, grass, and decorative trees and shrubs provided a parklike environment. A large war memorial was built in 1851: a column set on a large granite base on which the names of the battles where Kentuckians had fought were inscribed along with the names of the officers killed. Atop the column stood the Statue of Victory, and at each corner of the base stood a "colossal figure of an eagle, symbolic bird of America—emblem of liberty, independence and courage, bidding proud defiance," Isabella Trotter wrote.[36] The tomb of Daniel Boone was situated nearby beneath two large sycamores. The spot was planted as a cane break. Mrs. Trotter observed that the remainder of the cemetery had been appropriately planted with the "solemn" yew and the cypress, "emblem of mourning," but lacked the weeping willow "to shed its melancholy yet pleasing influence around."[37] Vestiges of the original forest often survived in these "cities of the dead." "Like all American cemeteries," Charles Weld wrote of Cincinnati's Spring Grove burial ground, "this is a scene of great natural beauty, contrasting strongly, but delightfully, in its hushed repose with the clamor and restlessness of the city."[38]

Colleges were usually housed in a single building with the president's house adjacent. At Lexington, Kentucky, Transylvania College occupied a large, three-story building at the west edge of town. The surrounding lawn, an acre in extent, was fenced, and walks radiated outward from the main building. Following a fire in the early 1840s, the college was rebuilt in Greek Revival style with a "Doric portico, of chaste proportions, but disfigured by the bad taste . . . of making the flights of steps too high and too steep . . . to the great discomfort of those who approach these buildings," James Buckingham wrote.[39] Students roomed in private homes. In most towns grammar schools were first conducted in private houses and then in houses converted to classrooms. After 1820, however, a distinctive style of school architecture emerged. Schools looked like courthouses, small boxes of two or three stories, many with belfries.

Economic Functions

Commerce provided towns their principal support. Most merchants started by selling a general line of merchandise in small frame or brick warehouses. As one traveler observed at Lexington in 1824, "One indication of a new country is . . . [the] variety shop; each one keeping piece goods, groceries, cutlery, porcelain, and stationery, in different corners; there not yet being that partition in trade which we meet in older states."[40] Much business involved barter, as specie was in short supply in the West. Manufactured goods brought from the East or imported through New Orleans were exchanged for agricultural commodities brought from an area's farms. At Lexington in the 1790s, tobacco, salt pork and beef, butter, cheese, tallow, hemp, flax, lard, flour, and hops were mentioned by Harry Toulmin as common in trade.[41] Tobacco, which sold for $2 per hundredweight in Lexington, brought upwards to $5 per hundredweight at Philadelphia.[42] Most merchants formed partnerships. Every six months one partner traveled east to buy new merchandise while his counterpart tended store. Toulmin reported that Philadelphia prices were generally marked up sixty percent at Lexington on eastern goods.[43]

Manufacturing activities evolved rapidly. By 1840 even the smallest towns had mills for grinding corn, milling wheat, and sawing lumber for local consumption. Industries that produced manufactured goods for export proved the greatest stimulus to urban growth. Distilleries, ropewalks, and tobacco processing houses in Kentucky; glassworks, iron foundries, and boatyards in western Pennsylvania; and packing plants and implement factories in Ohio made large towns of small places. Large-scale manufacturing required access to raw materials and markets. A prosperous town was one well located in the region's evolving transportation system.

Manufacturing brought a new way of organizing industrial labor. The factory replaced the workshop and the home. Work was formally and impersonally organized, with individuals performing highly specialized and routine tasks. Some saw it as a new form of slave labor. One Yankee merchant visiting Pittsburgh wrote: "The workmen are kept in complete slavery; when the bell rings they are compelled to attend punctually. They keep to work and drink whiskey. The taverns and grog-shops are crowded morning and night."[44] In 1818 John Melish reported male laborers at Pittsburgh earning about $0.75 a day or $234.00 a year.[45] For the typical family, he figured house rent at about $55 per annum and coal for one fire at $18.[46] For a day's work the ordinary workingman could procure forty pounds of flour, twenty pounds of beef, twenty-seven pounds of pork, or three bushels of potatoes.[47] The family of the typical factory worker survived just above the subsistence level.

By the 1840s foreign immigrants had come to fill most of the industrial jobs in places like Pittsburgh and Cincinnati. One Englishman observed with some exaggeration: "Hardly a single American ever works in a coal pit, or, indeed, performs any analogous task. This is done for him by the labouring hands of all portions of the world. At present the Yankee seems to imagine that his calling is to furnish the . . . plan, the scheme, the head, but it belongs to Europeans and Africans to find the hands to do the drudgery.[48] Women were also employed in the new factories. In 1835, women's wages varied between $0.87 to $1.25 per day at one cotton mill at Cincinnati; children were paid as little as $0.50 a day.[49] Charles Lyell arrived at Pittsburgh to find the women of one factory on strike for a ten-hour instead of a twelve-hour working day.[50]

By 1840 most factory buildings were of brick and were located at or near a town's waterfront. Surrounded by yards in which raw materials and equipment were stored, they made no pretense at beauty. Utilitarian values prevailed. Most travelers thought the factories symbolized social progress; only a few saw negative implications. This reflected the small scale of the early mills. Factories blended with other commercial buildings and even with surrounding houses. Rarely was a place totally dominated by factories and their machines. Charleston along the Kanawha River in present-day West Virginia was an exception.

An extensive salt industry was located at Charleston. As early as 1824 sixty-two furnaces were in operation along eighteen miles of river.[51] Salt water was obtained from wells and then boiled in vats, the salt accumulating as the water evaporated. The surrounding forest had been stripped away; the hillsides were bare and eroded. Coal was the chief fuel, and a haze of smoke hung over the salt furnaces constantly. The American journalist Anne Royall observed: "The salt works are dismal looking places; the sameness of the long low sheds; smoking boilers; men, the roughest that can be seen, half naked; hundreds of boatmen; horses and oxen, ill-used and beat by their drivers; the mournful screaking of the machinery, day and night; the bare, rugged, inhospitable looking mountain, from which all the timber has been cut, give to it a gloomy appearance."[52]

Environmental Deterioration

Resources in the West seemed limitless. Caleb Atwater wrote enthusiastically of the Ohio Valley's wood and coal as sufficient to fuel the nation "as long as the sun shines upon the globe."[53] New land, fresh water, and clean air seemed equally inexhaustible. Industrialists stripped the forests, mined the coal, and discharged their mill and factory wastes indiscriminately. Few worried about esthetic values when they built their factories and otherwise influenced urban growth. Air pollution, water pollution, and ugliness in the urban scene were signs of the times.

Air pollution was a serious problem, especially where coal was burned on a large scale. Coal was in general use in the towns of western Pennsylvania, western Virginia, and eastern Ohio. Its use spread down the Ohio River with coal shipped from mines around Pittsburgh. By 1820 coal was also being shipped in quantity down the Kanawha and Kentucky rivers. Wood continued as the prime fuel in towns outside the coal fields and away from the Ohio River.

Pittsburgh was most notorious for its air pollution. Nearly every visitor commented on its smoky circumstance. In 1819 Richard Mason found Pittsburgh "a dirty hole," for "the fogs from the rivers, together with the universal use of stone coal for fires, added to the smoke and dust from the large numbers of mills and manufactories, form a cloud which almost amounts to night and overspreads Pittsburgh with the appearance of gloom and melancholy."[54] He continued: "Coal dust was well ground in until I must say with much truth that I did not see a white man or woman in the place. The more you wash the blacker you get."[55] This description seems not to have been too exaggerated. William Richardson reported that inhabitants dressed in dark clothes because of the soot and smoke.[56] John Wright noted on approaching the town "an immense column of dusky smoke . . . spreading in vast wreaths."[57] The smoke gave a "smutty appearance to everything," he observed.[58] Every object in every house was "stained, soiled, and tarnished," for even the walls of the "most elegant drawing rooms" were discolored, John Clark observed.[59] "I raised the window in my chamber," he continued, "and the room was almost instantly filled with smoke."[60] Several visitors at Pittsburgh had trouble breathing.[61]

The smoke altered the view. The "eternal veil of smoke, which by rending . . . objects less distinct," James Hall observed, "seems to throw them to a greater distance."[62] For one given to the romantic, Pittsburgh looked like "Moscow smoking in ruins" or "the plain of Sodom."[63] But, utilitarian orientations prevailed. Many noted the smoke at Pittsburgh and other places as a sign of progress. The Briton, Thomas Hulme, observing a glassworks on the Ohio River above Wheeling, noted, "This smoke it is that must enrich America."[64] Most travelers thought the residents of Pittsburgh and the other towns oblivious to the filth in the air. One traveler found locals praising the smoky atmosphere of Pittsburgh for "its beauty and glory" as associated "with all the delights and interest of home."[65]

Water pollution was less apparent to travelers, although wastes were universally discharged into surface streams. At a distillery at Carrolton, Kentucky, one traveler saw refuse mash dumped into the Kentucky River. Although a considerable portion was being fed to hogs, their manure was subsequently dumped into the river also.[66] At Cincinnati the refuse of the packing plants was drained into local streams, and one creek ran red in season with the blood of slaughtered animals.[67]

Visual pollution was even less apparent. Newness meant progress irrespective of how ugly it might be. If the new urban scene was raw, it, like the rural frontier, promised eventual refinement. Ugliness could be tolerated, but once tolerated it threatened to become commonplace. Ele Bowen, traveling on the Baltimore and Ohio Railroad toward Wheeling, stopped at the town of Fairmont in present-day West Virginia. Walking in the evening near the falls on the Tygart River, he observed: "Nature has done her part to beautify Fairmont; art has exerted her utmost to disfigure it. Save the suspension bridge, I did not see a single other erection that was not abominable. It has the look of a town grown old in its infancy. Such an array of broken windows and tumble down porches . . . and blackened shanties never before huddled together in a single locality."[68] But somehow, it was thought, the future would heal the wounds. Bowen continued, "Perhaps at some future day, more in accordance with her name and with the beautiful river . . . Fairmont may have hanging gardens, her flowery terraces, and her ornamental Gothic cottages. I have seldom been in a place where my fancy was a more active castlebuilder and landscape gardener."[69]

ENVIRONMENTAL HAZARDS

Streets were laid out and houses erected with little regard for natural hazards, such as floods, or man-induced dangers, such as fire. Annually the lower streets in most river towns were flooded; at least once a decade flood waters completely inundated a town's business district. Few travelers witnessed the serious floods, for with transportation on the rivers shut down towns were relatively inaccessible. But the evidence of flooding remained for months. Travelers saw high water marks on the second and third stories of many buildings.[70] Locals took pride in their floods and nailed boards to trees and painted signs on buildings to indicate high water levels.[71] Most river towns were surrounded by poorly drained marshes in which mosquitos and other disease-carrying insects bred. Louisville was particularly notorious, being surrounded by swamps on the north, south, and west.

Fire was a constant danger. Most towns had volunteer fire companies which not only fought fires, but served as important social and political organizations as well. By 1850, the largest cities had established municipal fire departments. In Cincinnati, fire stations were located on the bluffs where lookouts could scan the town below. Once a fire was spotted, steam pumpers were pulled downhill to fight the blaze. Firemen were directed to fires by signalling devices on the fire station towers. How exciting for a traveler to awaken in his hotel room to the ringing of bells and the shouts of people in the street, the night sky aglow from the blaze of a nearby building. The great steam fire engine at Cincinnati was a real curiosity. It resembled a railroad engine, although it had only three wheels. One witness reported: "The volumes . . . of water, for there are six jets of various sizes thrown by this engine, were enormous."[72] Frequently, fires burned out of control, sweeping from block to block. In 1838, one traveler saw one-half of the houses of Paducah, Kentucky, destroyed.[73] Fires destroyed much of Pittsburgh in the 1840s. Arson was always suspected; speculation centered on disgruntled slaves and property owners after fire insurance benefits.

Government

The travelers paid little attention to municipal and state government except, as in the case of fire fighting in Cincinnati, some unusual technology had been applied to solving a local problem or some new form of social institution, such as a prison or asylum, could be visited. Most travelers thought city governments were relatively ineffectual. Municipal services tended to be supplied by the private sector or by quasi-governmental associations created to solve particular problems. Water supply and street lighting were usually handled by private corporations. In several cities medical colleges were established in association with local hospitals. After 1850 the major business streets in Pittsburgh, Cincinnati, and Louisville were lit by gas lamps, although travelers remarked that they were frequently out of service.

The cities of the West, with their highly transient populations, appeared plagued by crime. Travelers, particularly the Europeans, were shocked at the American custom of carrying dirks and pistols, and more than one traveler witnessed a murder.[74] Most hotels had signs warning against theft. Police departments were organized with uniformed men regularly patrolling the streets on foot. Special attention was given to waterfront areas where taverns, gambling halls, and brothels thrived in rundown buildings near the new warehouses and factories. Blacks and immigrants were blamed by those of the gentry for much of the crime.[75] The state militia took a hand in law enforcement. Armories were maintained in the large cities and martial law declared during civil disorders.

State government was most apparent in the urban landscape through the construction of prisons and asylums. Ministers and other travelers interested in social reform made special efforts to visit these institutions. The state prison at Columbus was three stories high, constructed of hewn limestone, and of the "Saxon style" of architecture.[76] Each wing contained 350 cells, each cell a stone cubicle seven feet long, three and one-half feet wide, and seven feet high containing room only for a narrow cot.[77] The "lunatic asylum" was built, as were the other public buildings, with prison labor. Each sleeping room was "lofty and well lighted: each . . . window [has a] cast iron frame, so that no sign of coercion or confinement is visible," the minister, Edward Abdy, reported.[78]

The Urban Gentry

Most of the travelers who kept journals were of the more educated, affluent classes. Thus they tended to circulate among the elite of the new
western towns. From among the merchants and industrialists there had
emerged an urban gentry. They promoted religion, art, and science
and, as a force for civic improvement, they lobbied for the new hospitals and asylums, sometimes personally underwriting construction.
They sought to promote a "polite society" through frequent entertaining. They were seen as people of cultivated manners and refined
speech who sought to live in style and dignity: to get above the common herd. Professional people, including doctors, the educated clergy,
college professors, writers, and editors and publishers were counted
among their number. Lawyers, however, seemed to have had the inside track. Fortescue Cuming wrote in 1807, "There is a very numerous
class, which assumes a certain air of superiority throughout this whole
country: I mean the lawyers. They . . . arrogate to themselves the
title or epithet of esquire, which the uninformed mass of the people allow them; and as by intrigue, they generally fill all the respectable offices in the government as well as the legislature."[79] Cuming further observed that lawyers tended to occupy the biggest and finest houses in
all the towns.[80]

The gentry hero was the self-made man of business who in semi-
retirement pursued a career in science or literature. One such man was
Ormsby Mitchell, described by several travelers as the "pride of Cincinnati."[81] A graduate of West Point, Mitchell arrived at Cincinnati at
age nineteen as an assistant professor of mathematics at a local academy. In his twenties he practiced law, opened his own academy, organized a railroad company personally surveying several railroad lines,
and established an observatory on Mt. Adams. James Buckingham observed that Mitchell, "though engaged intensely in prosecuting his professional labours," remained "always the practical American, busy to
forward plans for the development of the resources of the country."[82]

Members of the gentry built large houses situated on the bluffs overlooking their towns. These efforts produced the first residential suburbs. Greek Revival architecture predominated before 1840 and Gothic
Revival and Italianate thereafter. Most visitors favorably compared
the western gentry with their eastern counterparts. Timothy Flint

wrote: "The elegance of the houses, the parade of servants, the display of furniture, and . . . the luxury of their overloaded tables, would compare with the better houses in the Atlantic cities, although perhaps, there was a 'gaudiness and glitter,' the result of too great a desire to produce a striking effect upon the eye, which betray a want of taste."[83] Women travelers were particularly interested in house decoration. Isabella Trotter described the typical drawing room of the upper class: "It seems the fashion all over America . . . to leave the space open in the middle of the room and the chairs and sofas arranged round the walls; but there is always a good carpet of lively colours or a matting in summer."[84]

Many of the houses in Cincinnati, Pittsburgh, and other cities were of the row or town house variety. One room wide with a long hall running down one side and three or four rooms deep, houses abutted one another to form a residential block. Gustavus Wulfing was a merchant in Louisville and St. Louis before returning to his native Germany. His wife and several of the Wulfing children prepared a diagram of their Louisville house to send to relatives (Fig. 7-3).[85] The diagram locates every large object in the house and depicts typical family activities. Another family lived in an apartment on the second floor.

Travelers saw the gentry at their best at parties. Fredrika Bremer described in 1850 a typical affair at Cincinnati: "One never sees the gentlemen here all crowding into one room and the ladies into another. People sit on lounges, or on small sofas of all sorts in pairs, conversing together; or the gentleman gives the lady his arm and they take a promenade through the room."[86] Not all viewed "polite society" in the West quite so favorably. "The women invariably herd together at one part of the room and the men at the other. . . . Sometimes a small attempt at music produces a partial reunion," Mrs. Trollope wrote in 1828.[87] She continued: "The gentlemen spit, talk of elections and the price of produce, and spit again. The ladies look at each other's dresses till they know every pin by heart; talk of Parson Somebody's last sermon . . . or Dr. T'otherbody's new pills for dyspepsia, till the 'tea' is announced."[88]

Lexington, Kentucky, had the largest gentry population for its size. Owners of large Blue Grass plantations as often lived in Lexington preferring accessibility to the town's college, its academies, the Athenaeum or library, and the other urban amenities, not the least of which were the crass billiard halls, taverns, and other places of pleasure.

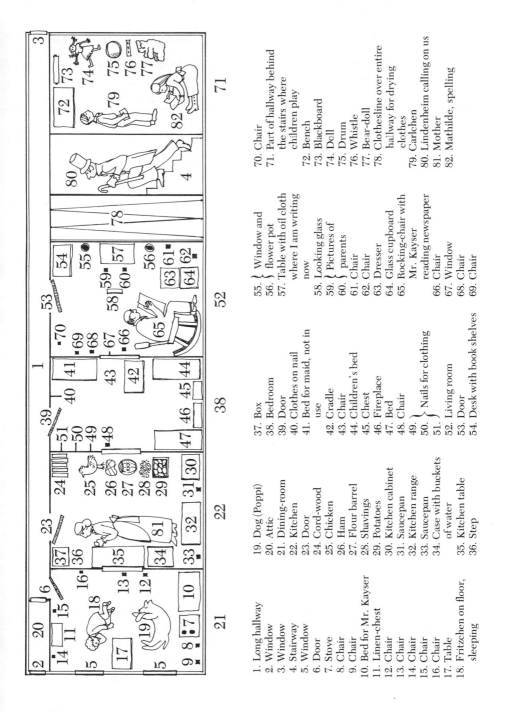

1. Long hallway
2. Window
3. Window
4. Stairway
5. Window
6. Door
7. Stove
8. Chair
9. Chair
10. Bed for Mr. Kayser
11. Linen-chest
12. Chair
13. Chair
14. Chair
15. Chair
16. Chair
17. Table
18. Fritzchen on floor, sleeping
19. Dog (Poppi)
20. Attic
21. Dining-room
22. Kitchen
23. Door
24. Cord-wood
25. Chicken
26. Ham
27. Flour barrel
28. Shavings
29. Potatoes
30. Kitchen cabinet
31. Saucepan
32. Kitchen range
33. Saucepan
34. Case with buckets of water
35. Kitchen table
36. Step
37. Box
38. Bedroom
39. Door
40. Clothes on nail
41. Bed for maid, not in use
42. Cradle
43. Chair
44. Children's bed
45. Chest
46. Fireplace
47. Chair
48. Chair
49. ⎫ Nails for clothing
50. ⎬
51. ⎭
51. Living room
52. Living room
53. Door
54. Desk with book shelves
55. ⎫ Window and
56. ⎬ flower pot
57. Table with oil cloth where I am writing now
58. Looking glass
59. ⎫ Pictures of
60. ⎬ parents
61. Chair
62. Chair
63. Dresser
64. Glass cupboard
65. Rocking-chair with Mr. Kayser reading newspaper
66. Chair
67. Window
68. Chair
69. Chair
70. Chair
71. Part of hallway behind the stairs where children play
72. Bench
73. Blackboard
74. Doll
75. Drum
76. Whistle
77. Bear-doll
78. Clothesline over entire hallway for drying clothes
79. Carlchen
80. Lindenheim calling on us
81. Mother
82. Mathilde, spelling

Figure 7-3.
Diagram of a Louisville House, c. 1840. (Gustavus Wulfing, *The Letters of Gustavus Wulfing,* translated by Carl Hirsch, Fulton, Mo., 1941)

Nonetheless, Lexington called itself the "Athens of the West." Travelers seemed to agree. In 1826 Timothy Flint wrote that the town had "an air of leisure and opulence" which distinguished it from Cincinnati and other towns.[89] "In the circles where I visited," he wrote, "literature was most commonly the topic of conversation. The window-seats presented the blank covers of the new and most interesting publications. Lexington has taken on the tone of a literary place."[90] Another traveler observed, "Living is generally high: besides the comforts of life, which are here abundantly enjoyed, a taste for its elegance and luxuries prevails; and the fashions and manners of polished Europe are found."[91]

Sense of Place

Although the new towns of the West shared many things in common, each sought to be distinctive. Boosters promoted specific images.[92] Pittsburgh was called both the "Smoky City," smoke being a synonym for progress, and the "Iron City," iron being the city's principal product. Wheeling became the "Bridge City" after completion of its suspension bridge. Cincinnati was called "Porkopolis" by some and the "Queen City" by others. Louisville was called the "Falls City," and Indianapolis, a latecomer to urban prominence, was dubbed the "Railroad City."

A town's proper name could, of course, reflect its peculiar situation or, again, its founders' anticipation. Cincinnati, built around Fort Washington in the late 1790s, was named after the society of former officers of the Revolutionary Army. The town had originally been called Losantiville, a Latinate abbreviation of the "city opposite the mouth of the Licking River." Most towns were named for other places, not only real places, but mythical places as well. "The traveler is amused with the singular and various tastes displayed in the names of places," James Hall wrote.[93] "Europe, Asia, and Africa have been ransacked and we have called all the fields of literature, sacred, classic, and profane," he continued.[94] James Buckingham observed, "In this art of 'turning the world upside down,' the Americans excel every other people known."[95] Above Cincinnati on the Ohio River he had passed Delphi, Palestine, and Moscow; below Cincinnati he would pass Aurora, Warsaw, Ghent, Vevay, Hanover, Rome, and Troy.

Some hoped that Indian names would be applied to the land. Josiah Harmar, the first military commander at Marietta, wrote, "The original

Indian names were generally expressive of some peculiar and distin-
guishing quality or circumstance . . . [and] ought to be adopted in
preference to our copying names from England and other parts of Europe."[96] But such was not to be. Hall recognized that "no other nation
has had the opportunity which we enjoy, of forming its own geographical vocabulary," but was reconciled to the "foolish propensity of emigrants for naming the place at which they settle in honour of that
which they have left."[97] "We have now in the U.S. about twenty Sa-
lems; we have Fairfields, Clearfields, and Middletowns without number. The Washingtons, Waynes, and Jeffersons baffle calculation," he
complained.[98]

What made a town distinctive was its physical site, its economy, its
mixture of different peoples, and its landmarks. Each town presented
a slightly different mix to the visitor. Travelers sought to identify a
town's essence, to give themselves a sense of being in a new and different place. One struck out "to see the lions" in the parlance of the nineteenth century. What was it then that travelers saw when they visited
the various towns? What images of place attached to the names? Discussion below focuses on Cincinnati as the Ohio Valley's largest city.

CINCINNATI

Cincinnati was built on two terraces ringed by hills on the east, north,
and west (Fig. 7-4). When viewed from a bluff the site looked like an
amphitheater facing the river. Fort Washington was built in 1789 at the
riverbank, a "most substantial square fortress" of hewn logs two stories
high with four block houses at the angles," General Harmar wrote.[99]
The lower terrace extended back from the river about one-third of a
mile to a steep bank about forty feet high. Beyond ran another plain
which subsided as a marsh at the base of the bluff line. The hills rose
300 to 400 feet above the second terrace. The entire site was heavily
forested.

The town did not grow rapidly until after 1800. In 1808 Fortescue
Cuming found many brick houses with "that air of neatness which is so
conspicuous in Connecticut and Jersey" and even a four-story building
was then under construction, a sure sign of urban prosperity.[100] By
1817 the traveler found a mature town. Morris Birkbeck exclaimed
over "the substantial brick houses, the spacious and busy markets, the
substantial public buildings, the thousands of properous, well-dressed,
industrious inhabitants, the numerous wagons and drays, [and] the

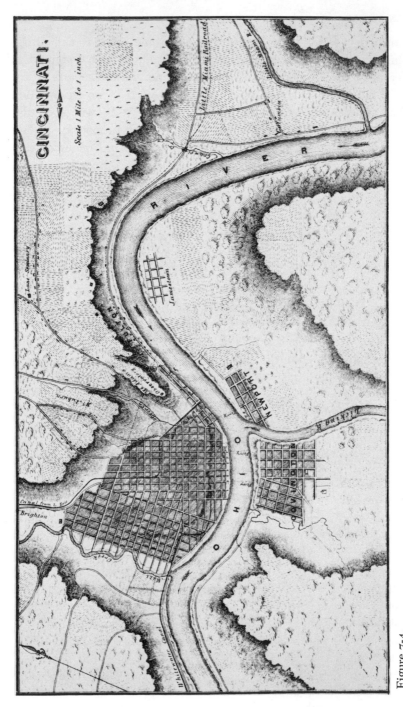

Figure 7-4.
Cincinnati in 1850. (Daniel Drake, *A Systematic Treatise, Historical, Etio-logical, and Practical on the Principal Diseases of the Interior Valley of North America*, Cincinnati, 1849)

gay carriages and elegant females."[101] A "busy stir" prevailed, Morris
Birkbeck observed, with house building, boat building, and the paving
and leveling for streets as well as "the numbers of country people constantly coming and going with the spacious taverns crowded with
travelers."[102]

In 1821 George Ogden, a Quaker merchant from Massachusetts,
summarized Cincinnati as "about 1500 buildings, most of which are
brick" which as one approached by steamboat showed "to great advantage."[103] Prominent at the water's edge was a gristmill of stone some
nine stories high "the walls of which, at their base, are ten feet thick,"
he wrote.[104] Here also were saw mills, cotton and woolen mills, several
glassworks, papermills, several foundries, and to the west, where Mill
Creek joined the Ohio River, a powder mill was located.[105]

Cincinnati was also laid out with a grid street plan in the "manner
of Philadelphia," as many travelers pointed out. "The town is built
. . . in squares, as they call them," Mrs. Trollope observed, "but these
. . . are the reverse of our's, being solid instead of hollow."[106] Streets
which ran east and west were numbered consecutively starting at the
river. "Main Street for a mile in length from north to south," Caleb
Atwater wrote, "presents a scene as busy, as bustling, as crowded, and
if possible more noisy, especially about the intersection of Fourth
Street . . . as can be found in New York."[107] "If the ear is not quite so
much affected with strange cries, as in Philadelphia and Baltimore,
[then] for drumming and organ grinding, I should suppose . . . few
spots . . . would exceed anything of the sort in the world," he continued.[108]

The principal landmarks in 1830 included the courthouse, large
Episcopalian, Roman Catholic, and Presbyterian churches, an academy, and a branch of the United States Bank, all in classical Revival
style. In addition, a hospital and several large hotels caught the travelers' attention.[109] But Mrs. Trollope found the city lacking distinctive
landmarks. It was "by no means a city of striking appearance" for it
lacked "domes, towers, and steeples," she wrote.[110] To this outspoken
critic, Cincinnati was "a little town . . . without even an attempt at
beauty in any of its edifices, and with only just enough of the air of a
city to make it noisy and bustling."[111] Of all the travelers to criticize
the city's appearance, only Mrs. Trollope set out to rectify the circumstance. As part of the business scheme which had brought her to the
city, she built a "bazaar," a four-story building with women's shops

and a public ballroom. The front facade was executed in a different architectural mode on each floor. "A more absurd compound of every species of architecture never entered the head of any architect," the Swede, Karl Arfwedson, wrote, for "the sublime in the Gothic style, the tasteful in the Greek, the ridiculous in the Chinese—have all been grouped together into an unnatural and disfigured whole."[112] The building was dubbed "Trollope's Folly" by local residents.

Most European travelers of the 1830s looked favorably on Cincinnati. Arfwedson wrote:

> Cincinnati has already the appearance of a large city. The first glance leaves an impression of splendour, which the traveller is far from anticipating in these remote western regions. Handsome brick houses, wide streets, and magnificent public buildings, strike the astonished eye of the stranger, who expected to find only wooden houses and narrow lanes. Near the bridges, he sees the same bustle and activity as on the quays of New Orleans and New York. Advancing into the town, he sees at each step brilliant shops, exquisites and dandies lounging about, and ladies attired in the last Parisian fashions. On entering the hotel he finds himself in a five-story building, containing apartments without number and halls almost endless.[113]

Michel Chevalier, who had been sent to the United States by the French Minister of the Interior to inspect American engineering works, observed:

> The architecture of Cincinnati is very nearly the same with that of the new quarters of the English towns. The houses are generally of brick, most commonly three stories high, with the windows shining with cleanliness, calculated each for a single family and regularly placed along well paved and spacious streets, sixty feet in width. Here and there the prevailing uniformity is interrupted by some houses of hewn stone in very good taste, real palaces in miniature, with neat porticoes. . . . In another direction you see a small, plain church . . . without coloured glass or gothic arches. . . . On another side, stands a huge hotel, which from its exterior you would take for a royal residence.[114]

Chevalier went to the top of Mt. Auburn, directly north of the city, to take the view.

> The eye takes in the windings of the Ohio and the course of the Licking which enters the former at right angles, the steamboats that fill the port, the basin of the Miami Canal, with the warehouses that line it and the locks that connect it with the river, the white-washed spinning

works of Newport and Covington with their tall chimnies [*sic*], the Federal arsenal, above which floats the starry banner, and numerous wooden spires that crown the churches.[115]

A year earlier in 1834, Charles Hoffman counted twenty spires "gleaming among gardens and shrubbery . . . as if spread upon a map beneath you."[116] The Scot George Lewis thought the scene "like a chessboard upon which a couple dozen larger and smaller towers represent the chessmen."[117]

The levee at Cincinnati excited considerable interest (Fig. 7-5). The waterfront of the 1850s was a curious blend of flatboats and steamboats which symbolized, as much as anything, the commercial vitality of the city. To travelers more familiar with the eastern port cities, Cincinnati and the other Ohio River towns seemed strange for their lack of "rigged vessels." The levee was a paved area extending along the river for over half a mile east and west from the foot of Main Street. In the 1840s one might see as many as forty-five or fifty steamboats moored at the levee at any one time.[118] The German traveler Moritz Busch provided the best description of Cincinnati's waterfront in the 1850s:

A row of . . . colorfully painted three deck steamboats extended almost beyond the field of vision, most of them giving off smoke from two chimneys, forms the base of the spacious, gently sloping public landing. The landing is covered with all sorts of bales, goods, and barrels and is crowded with carts, porters, sailors, merchants, and departing and arriving travelers. It is, so to speak, the face of the city, and at the same time the entrance to the beehive that it resembles. White or brick-red buildings, with green awnings and tall, narrow warehouses covered to the top story with advertising signs legible at a great distance border [the levee]. From this central point of commerce, into which pours a throng of businessmen from Main Street and two other important streets traveled by hundreds of omnibuses and coaches, two outspread wings extend to the right and left. On the right, factories are giving forth dense clouds of smoke, the trains of the railroad from Xenia are roaring, and an army of carpenters in the shipyards are hammering and sawing on two new steamboats . . . on the left . . . [the] gothic steeple of the . . . Presbyterian church . . . [the] dome of the gigantic Burnet House . . . [and] still farther, the Catholic Cathedral. . . . toward the west it becomes more scattered, frequently interrupted by still-unused building lots and it grows poorer and more wooden until Mill Creek . . . sets a temporary limit to it. To the east it is blocked by Mount Adams, [its] limestone hills . . . covered with gardens, vineyards, and country homes.[119]

Figure 7-5.
The Cincinnati Waterfront in 1848. (Daguerrotypes by W. S. Porter, courtesy of the Cincinnati Public Library)

Street improvement was a sure sign of progress. Travelers, by describing street conditions, symbolized by analogy a town's general character and its prosperity. In 1810 Cincinnati's streets were not paved, only the sidewalks on Main Street had been improved with brick.[120] By 1828 all the city's principal streets had been paved with limestone blocks.[121] The law, Mrs. Trollope observed, forbade the throwing of refuse at the sides of the streets; garbage was to be placed in the middle where the hogs could more easily take it away.[122] Beginning in the 1820s travelers noted the systematic planting of trees along the city's streets. "The streets have a row of trees on each side, near the curbstone; and most of the houses have a small frontage filled with luxuriant flowering shrubs, of which the Althea Frutex [*Hibiscus syriacus* or Rose of Sharon] is the most common," one traveler wrote.[123] Sycamores were also planted throughout the town.

The 1840s and 1850s brought more refinement to the city's streets. In 1842 Charles Dickens, who saw much to criticize in the United States, found "clean houses of red and white brick, its well-paved roads and footways of bright tile."[124] He wrote: "the streets are broad and airy, the shops extremely good, the private residences remarkable for their elegance and neatness. The disposition to ornament these pretty villas and render them attractive, leads to the culture of trees and flowers, and the laying out of well kept gardens."[125] So many roses were planted around the houses in the better neighborhoods that many called Cincinnati the "rose city." But, the hogs still roamed the streets. There was "scarcely a street in which some dozen may not be seen poking their noses into the dirt-heaps, or acting as dams to the gutters in which they repose during the heat of the day," one traveler reported.[126] The favorite amusement of small boys, Charles Lyell observed, was "to ride upon the pigs, and we were shown one sagacious old hog, who was in the habit of lying down as soon as a boy came in sight."[127] During the 1850s the principal streets were lit with gas lamps.[128] Many of the older streets paved with limestone had begun to show their age. One visitor complained of "water-worn stone . . . full of ruts" as he drove through the city by carriage.[129]

The city's business district intrigued many visitors. During the summer hundreds of wagons covered with white canvas tops were backed against the pavements of the several market houses. The surrounding streets likewise were jammed with vehicles, the tailgates down "to form a kind of counter" and the owners sitting "amidst the displayed produce of their farms," one observer wrote.[130] Pork, beef, butter, cheese, corn, flour, fish, and vegetables and other groceries were thus supplied to the city. "The buildings here are all modern," Cyrus Bradley, a college student from New Hampshire visiting the city in 1835, wrote; "they are generally dated, the year of their erection being placed close to the waterspouts near the roof."[131] Most of the buildings he saw seemed to date from 1830 or 1831.[132] Another visitor noted that Cincinnati differed from other large cities for the use of white, gray and yellow brick.[133] By and large, the business district appeared a jumble of architecture. Buildings differed not only by color of brick, but by size and design. Mrs. Houstoun, visiting from England, complained of "a great want of uniformity in the buildings."[134] Others complained of the lack of architectural decoration. "Everywhere that there is a disposition to the beautiful, it is choked by the utilitarian," Moritz Busch wrote.[135]

Nothing was more utilitarian than the signs which covered most commercial buildings (Fig. 7-6). Busch compared Cincinnati's business district of the 1850s to a newspaper page:

> To the yard-long columns of the journals correspond the mile-long streets of the city. The former are up to three quarters advertisements; the latter are six eighths commercial firms. The former are crowded with woodcuts illustrating the announcements; the latter exaggeratingly exhibit the originals of the illustrations in a super abundant confusion of enormous rifles advertising the gun shop, great golden mortars advertising the physician and the apothecary, monstrous boots advertising the footwear artist, and colorfully patterned building walls that advertise the rug manufacturers. Great plows, likewise put up as high as the building permits, greet the farmer as a customer at 3,000 paces. The city is a bazaar; the newspapers are merely maps to help in getting around.[136]

Also strange to the European eye was the sight of advertising pennants and flags strung across streets or hung from buildings.

The business day began at dawn. Visiting Cincinnati during June of 1817, Morris Birkbeck noted, "The stores are open, the markets thronged, and business in full career by five o'clock in the morning."[137] In gentry families, husbands did the shopping in the late morning, bringing the groceries home to be prepared for the family's main meal at noon. Business picked up again in the early afternoon continuing until dusk. There was little activity on the city's streets at night, for,

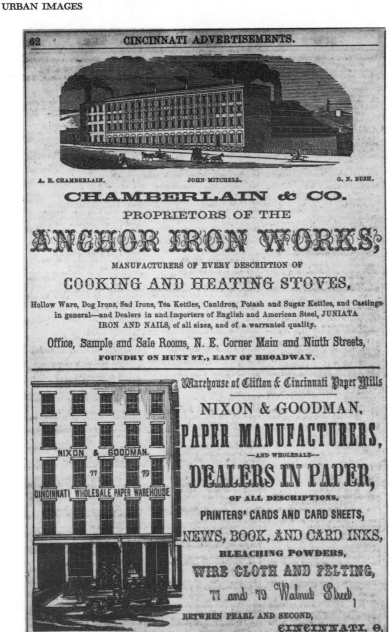

Figure 7-6.
Advertisements illustrating Cincinnati's new industrial and commercial architecture. (C. S. Williams, *Williams' Cincinnati City Guide and Business Mirror for 1858*, Cincinnati, 1858)

as Birkbeck reported, "Nine o'clock is the common hour for retiring to rest."[138]

By 1840 Cincinnati was very much an industrial town. Steamboat passengers approaching the town at night noted the glare of the furnaces and the sparks from the factory chimneys.[139] Factory machinery amazed many visitors to Cincinnati: "I visited establishments where, by the aid of ingenious machinery, 500 dozen chairs were made weekly," one traveler noted.[140] Other factories made bedsteads, baby-rockers, chests of drawers, churns, cupboards, and sundry other furnishings for outfitting the prospering new farms of the region. One factory was owned and operated by a black man who, having invented a new kind of bedstead, sought to mass produce it.[141]

Meat packing attracted the most attention. The slaughterhouses were located in the northwestern section of town along Mill Creek which was nicknamed "Bloody Run" for the color of its water during the late fall and early winter when the slaughtering was done. Slaughterhouses were usually long wooden sheds, the walls containing movable panels which could be opened allowing air to circulate. Hog carcasses were carried hanging on racks in wagons to packing plants throughout the city. "Alive or dead, whole and divided into portions, their outsides and their insides, their grunts and their squeals, meet you at every moment," Mrs. Houstoun wrote.[142] "All Cincinnati is redolent of swine," another visitor wrote.[143] Swine prowled the streets, barrels of pork lined the quays, and cartloads of their carcasses filled the city.

After 1830 over half of the Ohio Valley travelers stopped for extended periods at Cincinnati (Figs. E through H). This gave them time to explore the city and learn something of its social life. Longer layovers left more time to attend church, the museums, and the theater, and inquire as to the quality of schools and libraries. Churches were among the most visible landmarks in the city. By 1832 there were twenty churches and one synagogue, with Presbyterian and Methodist congregations accounting for one-half the total churches.[144] Most travelers agreed that St. Peter's, the large Roman Catholic Cathedral, was the most impressive church in the city. The steeple was over 200 feet high; the portico contained twelve columns, six across the front and three on either side.[145] One visitor paced off the interior of the church, finding it to be sixty paces long and forty paces wide, but the next day when he paced the gentlemen's cabin of his steamboat he found it to be twenty paces longer.[146] Few ministers visiting Cincinnati appreciated St. Peter's, for it dwarfed the Protestant churches. The considerable antagonism which existed between the Roman Catholics and the Protestants was heightened by the massive influx of Catholic Germans into Cincinnati beginning in the 1830s.

The Europeans were very interested in the black congregations. Fredrika Bremer visited an African Methodist church to find "African ardor and African life."[147] She wrote: "The singing ascended and poured forth like a melodious torrent and the heads, feet, and elbows of the congregation moved all in unison with it."[148] Then the preacher sketched a picture of an enslaved people increasing in numbers and improving themselves by purchasing their freedom from slavery. This brought cries of "Yes! Yes!" and "Oh, glory!" throughout the church. He told how they purchased land and bought houses, large houses, larger and still larger houses until the rulers of the land began to be terrified, and to say, "they are becoming too strong for us; let us send them over to Liberia!"[149] Most blacks opposed colonization in Africa, but the movement was strong, fueled primarily by the white Protestant churches in the city. The decorum of the black churches contrasted sharply with that of most white churches. In the typical white congregation Ebenezer Davies, a visiting English minister, noted, "A man marches into his pew . . . sits down, wipes his nose, and stares at the people all about him; and at the close, the moment the 'Amen' is uttered, he is off with as much speed as if the house were on fire."[150]

Many travelers sought out the theaters of Cincinnati. In 1855, Charles Weld visited the National Theater where he found the spectators "more an object of curiosity" than the actors.[151] The theater was crammed except for the back balcony occupied by about a score of blacks. Weld wrote: "The acting was vile, but it gave great satisfaction to the audience, who manifested their approbation by yelling furiously. The great applause emanated from the pittites, who sat in their shirt sleeves chewing and spitting with proper republican liberty."[152] As for the play, it was a military drama representing the capture of Algiers by the French with the help of a small American fleet. "On the announcement that victory was now certain, as the fleet bearing the star-spangled banner was in sight," Weld wrote, "I really thought the audience would have gone into fits, so savagely did they yell their delight."[153]

Museums provided additional entertainment. Run as private businesses they catered in the unique and the spectacular. Most contained, as Michel Chevalier described them, "some mammoth bones . . . an Egyptian mummy, some Indian weapons and dresses, and a half dozen wax-figures, representing, for instance, Washington, General Jackson, and the Indian Chiefs, Black Hawk and Tecumseh . . . stuffed birds, [and] snakes preserved in spirits."[154] The most famous of all Cincinnati museum displays was the "infernal regions" exhibit which Mrs. Trollope helped concoct. She herself described the exhibit as "a pandaemonium" containing such "images of horror" as dwarfs that machinery formed into giants, imps of ebony with eyes of flame, and monstrous reptiles "devouring youths of beauty."[155] The whole was visible through a grate of massive iron bars wired to "an electrical machine." Visitors received a "smart shock" and, the cause being unknown, "the effect is exceedingly comic; terror, astonishment [and] curiosity are all set in motion."[156]

The most travelers noted signs of ethnicity in the landscape. Michel Chevalier called Cincinnati "the rendezvous of all nations."[157] "The Germans and Irish are very numerous, and there are some Alsacians," he observed; "I have often heard the harsh accents of the Rhenish French in the streets."[158] Charles Lyell was told that most Germans came from Bavaria, Baden, Swabia, Wirtemberg, and the Black Forest District. Three German language newspapers were published daily.[159] The Germans, one visitor reported, were "chiefly of the lower class, employed as servants and laborers, but are very frugal, and, so soon as they have saved a little, settle on a small farm of their own, or set up stores."[160] By 1859 the German population had increased to nearly 50,000 or approximately forty-five percent of the city's total.[161]

The northwestern portion of the city between the Miami Canal and the cliffs of Mt. Auburn evolved as the German section. The canal was nicknamed "the Rhine," and the district was called "Über den Rhein." Here almost everyone had German accents. One traveler, Edward Dicey, wrote: "The women, with their squat, stout figures, their dull blue eyes, and fair flaxen hair, sit knitting at their doors, dressed in the stuffed woolen petticoats of German fashion. The men have still the woolen jackets, the blue worsted pantaloons, and the low-crowned hats one knows so well in Bavaria and the Tyrol. There are 'Bier Gartens,' 'Restaurations,' and 'Tanz Saales,' on every side."[162] Dicey visited a beer garden. "Women had brought their babies and knitting with them, the men had their long pipes, and both men and women sat drinking the lager beer and eating the inevitable sausages, and the

. . . 'butterbrod und schicken' sandwiches," he wrote.[163] Most spoke broken English, and among the younger generation Dicey thought "the placid expressions of the German face had already changed for the sharp anxious look so universal to the native-born American."[164]

By 1850 Cincinnati had a well-established black district called "Little Africa" by most whites.[165] It was the poorest section of the city, for its inhabitants were primarily freed slaves who suffered at the bottom of the city's class system. "The streets and the houses have, it is true, the Anglo-American regularity; but broken windows and rags hanging from them, a certain neglected, disorderly aspect, both of houses and streets, testified of Negro management," Fredrika Bremer wrote.[166] Most journalists saw the blacks as victims of social and economic oppression and not as the instigators of their plight. Harriet Martineau wrote bitterly: "They are citizens, yet their houses and schools are pulled down, and they can obtain no remedy at law. They are thrust out of offices, and excluded from the most honourable employments, and stripped of all the best benefits of society by fellow-citizens who, once a year, solemnly lay their hands on their hearts, and declare that all men are born free and equal."[167] Cincinnati was a hotbed for the Abolitionist movement. Nonetheless, the city's reliance on the trade of northern Kentucky produced a strong "southern" sentiment favoring slavery. Even many of the whites who opposed the "peculiar institution" remained biased toward blacks, viewing them as inferior to whites and, as such, unnecessary to the city's economy and society.

Many of the more affluent families of Cincinnati had by the 1840s moved from the city's center to its suburbs. The suburbs included the waterfronts at Covington and Newport on the Kentucky side of the Ohio River and the heights around the city such as Mt. Adams and Mt. Auburn. James Buckingham wrote of wooded hills "studded with villas and country residences . . . [and] delightful drives . . . agreeably shaded with large trees."[168] One traveler, William Bullock, an English businessman returning to England from Mexico, was so taken by Covington that he purchased the large estate of Thomas Carneal, a land speculator and industrialist, intending to make the place his permanent residence. "The house," he wrote, "is situated on a gentle acclivity, about 150 yards from the river, with beautiful pleasure grounds in front, laid out with taste, and decorated with . . . flowers."[169] Bullock planned an elaborate suburban city, called Hygeia, to be built on his land. Although the city never materialized, its plan, ex-

ecuted in England, stood as a model for town planners throughout
the nineteenth century. The suburban houses of Covington were
reached by steam ferry from the foot of Cincinnati's Main Street.

Nicholas Longworth, another land speculator and industrialist and
reputedly Cincinnati's wealthiest citizen, built a large mansion on Mt.
Adams. The surrounding hills were covered with his vineyards. Here
the Catawba grape was perfected. Catawba wine was the delight of
polite society in nineteenth-century America. Henry Wadsworth Longfellow penned:

> For richest and best
> Is the Wine of the West,
> That grows by the beautiful river.[170]

But all was not beautiful on the bluffs behind the city. Several hills had
been excavated for fill in the town below, leaving ugly scars. Industry
competed for land. Mrs. Trollope had rented a country villa only to
discover new construction next door. "Tis to be a slaughterhouse for
hogs," she was told.[171] As there were several gentry houses in the
neighborhood, she asked if the slaughterhouse would not be considered
a nuisance. "A what? No, No!" was the reply. "That may do very well
for your tyrannical country, where a rich man's nose is more thought
of than a poor man's mouth."[172] Thus did Mrs. Trollope conclude, "All
freedom enjoyed in America, beyond what is enjoyed in England, is
enjoyed solely by the disorderly at the expense of the orderly."[173]

Cities as Progress

Towns and cities symbolized progress: progress both as past accomplishment and as future resolve. "Stranger! Stop one moment to con-
template the progress and grandeur of this Western Empire!" one
author exclaimed; "No where else can so entire a transformation, accomplished in so short a time, be found."[174] There thrived at Cincinnati
in 1850 a metropolis where fifty years before there had been nothing
but wilderness. Similar success stories could be told at Pittsburgh,
Louisville, Lexington, Wheeling, Nashville, and all the other towns,
large and small. But more importantly, the town and city were symbols
of the things to come. "The most interesting view of the new towns in
the West," one British traveler wrote, "is to regard them not as they
are but as what they may become."[175] Americans often acted as if the
future had actually arrived. Morris Birkbeck quipped, "There is a

figure of rhetoric adopted by the Americans, and much used in description; it simply consists in the use of the present indicative, instead of the future subjunctive; it is called anticipation."[176] In 1844, Tyrone Power stood above Pittsburgh anticipating the city below:

> As the city grows, it must by necessity climb the steep bluffs by which it is encompassed; and on these it is not too much to imagine, at no far period, the squares, terraces, and crescents of a wealthy and public spirited community; whilst within the crowded triangle beneath, the clang of the noisy steam-engine and the black smoke will lie drowned, and along the narrow strips of level soil skirting the rivers will rise the warehouses and wharves of commerce.[177]

Most travelers were certain that a new urban order would completely obscure the old. "I thought I could discover . . . a burning desire, a strong predilection, for everything new," one visitor in Cincinnati wrote.[178] New towns were popping up all along the rivers, roads, and railroads. A mania for town building seized the speculators. Michel Chevalier described the process: "First rises a huge hotel with a wooden colonnade . . . the landlord being, as a matter of course, a general or, at least, a colonel of the militia. The bar-room is at once the exchange, where hundreds of bargains are made under the influence of a glass of whiskey or gin, and the club-room, which resounds with political debate, and is the theatre of preparations for civil and military elections."[179] A post office and store, dwelling houses, a church, a school, a newspaper, and a bank soon follow "to complete the three-fold representation of religion, learning, and industry," he added.[180] William Oliver observed, "Let not the traveller, when he looks at his map, and sees the name of some city [expect more than] a store and a spirit shop, with a bit of board stuck up, on which some one has scrawled the word HOTEL, apparently with his finger dipt [sic] in ink; with one or two log houses scattered along the river's bank."[181]

Not every traveler saw unbridled progress in the new towns. The larger places thrived on industry. Industry meant the factory and a new way of life for laboring people. Many visitors from Europe had already seen what industry could do to a pastoral landscape. "The smoke and steam of these factories have not yet blackened the town as much as many English ones," one German traveler at Wheeling wrote; "The woods on the mountains enclosing the river banks are not yet destroyed; but they will soon be overtaken by this fate, which must greatly injure the beauty of the surrounding scenery."[182]

8 CONCLUSION

I felt in a new country, for I had been listening all through the drive to stories of the Indian cities and fortifications in Kentucky and to legends about the Devil's Pulpit and Dismal Rock. I had been driving through twelve miles of plantations, cheek by jowl with a thin lean American, suffering from the "ager" [ague], and who carried anxiously on his knees to my great annoyance, an enormous wire-cage, with a frightened mocking-bird inside it. . . . I had been talking to a young dentist from Cincinnati, whose first successful bit of practice had been drawing a lion's tooth for a menagerie keeper; and above all, I had lunched off gumbo soup and wild turkey and here I was just preparing to descend into the Mammoth Cave.

James Booty

Travelers recorded a wide spectrum of images in their journals—the weather, the look of the farms and towns, the customs of the people. Nearly everything that could be seen or experienced was commented upon. Certain places and, more important, certain types of places tended to elicit specific kinds of descriptions both in content and tone. Places were categorized according to the associated people, activities, and supporting structures and objects. In addition, places were appreciated according to prevailing environment values.

Most travelers used a hierarchy of images to describe the region according to its most significant parts. Wilder images, the impressions of a nature relatively unspoiled by human activity, contrasted with the images of the man-made habitat. Most cultural landscapes were stereotyped according to rural or urban conditions. Urban places were easily categorized by size, but rural communities were often nebulous and difficult for travelers to comprehend as distinctive places. Only the towns provided a sense of centrality, through combination of distinctive architecture and streetscape. Urban and rural places were further subdivided into behavioral settings, places defined at microscales. For example, each town consisted of both private and public settings: many public spaces were organized especially for travelers. Streets, levees, taverns, hotels, and depots were the travelers' special habitats.

What travelers saw and understood of a landscape and the society which shaped it depended largely upon their needs. Impressions could be classified either as operational or as inferential. The logistics or mechanics of travel dominated the former. The landscape was interpreted as the traveler decided which route to take, survived his trek from place to place, sought food and lodging and otherwise combatted the hazards of being a stranger in a new location. From inferential statements came an interpretation of the surrounding scene, a reaching out beyond the logistics of travel to find fuller meaning in the passing landscape. At any one point, the travelers' attention might be focused on single objects, patterns of objects, relationships between patterns, or whole systems of interrelationship. A log cabin in a forest clearing might be seen as crude, and a sequence of such clearings as monotonous. Such landscape uniformity might be related to a frontier community's social immaturity; yet the numerous log cabins might also symbolize vigorous pioneering which, when coupled with the notion of unlimited forest, suggested a system of progress unequalled anywhere. Negative conceptions at one level often translated into positive conclusions at another.

Utilitarian value judgments dominated. The landscape was appreciated most for its profit potential. Such appreciations gave travelers a sense of involvement, for they could calculate and compare the prospective opportunities from place to place as readily as any other. Esthetic interests included a search for both the picturesque and the romantic, the former clearly the stronger impulse. A traveler's experiences were largely visual, the geographies of sound and smell vastly inferior to the impact of what he or she saw. The search for a "good view" was constant with most travelers. Such a quest enhanced the exhilaration of being in a different place and often offered inspiration. The appreciation of nature was primitive and restricted largely to those with backgrounds in natural history. For such travelers the discovery of place differences in nature only enhanced the sense of adventure that came from being in unfamiliar places.

In general, certain stereotypes applied to the Ohio Valley as a whole. It was a place of large-scale landscapes in comparison to the eastern seaboard or Europe. As a frontier it was seen as an immature landscape filled with uniformity. Travelers looked carefully from one section of the region to another searching for differences in place. Generally, they found subtle changes from East to West and from North to South. The latter differences became more pronounced after 1830, eventually dissolving the notion of the Ohio Valley as a region in the minds of most Americans: a "Middle West" emerging to the north of the Ohio River in contrast with the "South." The Ohio Valley was considered a region of opportunity and adventure. It was the American nation's first "West." There the pattern of warfare and treaty violation that deprived the Indians of an entire continent first evolved. There the nation's dominant systems of land tenure and farming were perfected. There the first industrial metropolises of the nation were built.

Travelers flocked to the new area both as participants in the saga of westward expansion and as tourists to witness the great experiment in the building of a nation. Before the Civil War the Ohio Valley was a symbol of national progress and promise. Travelers from the older sections of the country and those from Europe saw the image of the nation's future in the region's landscape. Americans bragged not so much about their accomplishments, although they were great, but of what the future would bring. The Ohio Valley offered proof of that future greatness in the new farms and plantations and in the new towns and cities which grew before the travelers' eyes.

Impressions of the Ohio Valley changed through time. The travelers' routes and destinations, as they shifted over the decades, influenced these changes (Figs. A through H). The travelers who left journals emphasized the northeastern section of the Ohio Valley in the early years between 1740 and 1769 (Fig. A). Clearly, the Indian towns of western Pennsylvania and Ohio were their principal destinations. None of the "long hunters" who early crossed the southern Appalachians into Kentucky and Tennessee recorded their experiences. Diaries representative of the period were written primarily by envoys to the northern Indians, military personnel, and surveyors and explorers for various land companies. Primary were the wilder images and the images of conflict, both real and potential. In the eastern and western parts of the region, where the British and French dominated after 1760, travelers' routes led from fort to fort. In the central section, travelers moved primarily from one Indian town to another. The French traveled mainly by canoe and the English by horse.

Between 1770 and 1789 Forbes' Road became the primary route of access to the Ohio Valley (Fig. B). New routes through Cumberland Gap and along the New and Kanawha rivers in western Virginia offered alternative means of access. The new American forts and towns replaced the Indian villages as destinations in the central portion of the region. In southwestern Pennsylvania and the Kentucky Blue Grass the agricultural settlements attracted many travelers. Pittsburgh served to funnel a large proportion of the travelers down the Ohio River. Pastoral and urban images appeared in the travelers' accounts of the Ohio Valley for the first time.

These patterns were reinforced between 1790 and 1809 (Fig. C). Forbes' Road (also called the Pennsylvania Road) remained the most important approach to the region. Travel to Tennessee and northern Alabama and Mississippi marked both the beginning of settlement in these areas and the opening of the Natchez Trace. More travelers left the Ohio Valley by way of the Mississippi River and New Orleans rather than returning East overland. More entered the Ohio Valley by way of Lake Erie. War dominated the northern part of the region during this period, as the chain of American forts north from Cincinnati testified. Wilder and pastoral images dominated the travelers' diaries, although most travelers stayed in urban places for extended periods of time. More than forty percent of the travelers moved by flatboat down the upper Ohio River (Fig. C).

Between 1810 and 1819 areas of frontier settlement in the Old Northwest attracted many travelers, as did the more mature Kentucky Blue Grass (Fig. D). Pittsburgh continued to function as the Ohio Valley's great eastern gateway for people traveling from Philadelphia. Wheeling served a similar function for those traveling on the new Cumberland Road from Baltimore. Many continued west from Wheeling on Zane's Trace to Maysville and on to Lexington, Kentucky. It was clearly the decade of overland transportation. Stagecoaches served most of the travelers in all parts of the Ohio Valley, and all major roads were lined with taverns. The era of safer and more comfortable travel had begun.

The steamboats made a profound impact during the 1820s (Fig. E).

Most travelers continued west from Pittsburgh and Wheeling by steamboat. The Cumberland or National Road replaced the Pennsylvania Road as the most important route between the Upper Ohio River and the eastern seaboard as more travelers visited Washington, D.C., before heading west. Although the Kentucky Blue Grass continued to attract travelers, as many travelers visited the Illinois prairies where settlement was just beginning. Cincinnati had become the region's primary urban attraction. Urban images had begun to dominate the travelers' journals.

The 1830s marked the heyday of travel journalists. Canals and railroads appeared, and when coupled with the traditional forms of travel they provided travelers with a wide spectrum of ways to go. Travelers ranged wider afield than at any other period. The states of Ohio, Indiana, and Illinois received the greatest emphasis. The Erie Canal and Lake Erie served as a significant route of access to the region. Places like White Sulphur Springs and Mammoth Cave, where wilder images were carefully packaged, appeared prominently on the map of travelers' destinations (Fig. F). Tourists had come into their own. Luxury hotels catered to the travelers at the resorts and in the larger towns and cities.

The 1840s stood as the decade of steamboat travel. More than sixty percent of the travelers who left journals traveled by Ohio River steamer (Fig. G). Cincinnati, midway on the river, continued to be the single most important stopping place. The 1840s saw the further extension of the Baltimore and Ohio and Pennsylvania railroads in the East, further reinforcing two traditional routes of access to the Ohio Valley. However, many travelers came by Great Lakes steamer or by Mississippi River steamboat from New Orleans. Indeed, as many travelers now laid over in St. Louis as in Cincinnati. Travelers placed even more emphasis on states north of the Ohio River. Movement between the Ohio and Lake Erie was pronounced and the region's first major railroad connected Cincinnati with Sandusky on Lake Erie (Fig. G).

The decade of the 1850s saw an abrupt abandonment of steamboat travel except on the lower Ohio and Mississippi rivers (Fig. H). The railroads had clearly come to dominate. The Baltimore and Ohio and the Pennsylvania railroads were completed to Wheeling and Pittsburgh, respectively. A web of connecting lines north of the Ohio River stretched as far as the Mississippi River. The mature rail network in the North reflected that area's rapid economic development. It is clear that tourists were diverted from the agrarian slave states. The new railroads of the North sped travelers from city to city, and images of towns and cities clearly dominated.

The period 1740 to 1860 was unique in the history of travel. Geographical mobility was on the increase in the western world, but, except in the United States, traveling was still the privilege of a relative few. In the States, men and women were encouraged to travel. Many recorded their impressions in writing. Many sought to publish their journals, since a large reading public had come to crave descriptions of new and unusual places. A few travelers attracted to the Ohio Valley left descriptions of their travels in journals, diaries, and letters. Their impressions enable us to glimpse past geographies in fuller detail and determine in broad outlines how people defined and occupied places.

The travelers' view of the past also provides us a mirror in which to glimpse ourselves. Few people living in the Ohio Valley today share a sense of identity predicated on the region's past. Middle Westerners look north to the new lake cities and the farms of the corn and dairy belts for a sense of past landscape, and Southerners look more to the coastal cities and plantations of the Deep South. The authentic landscape heritage of the Ohio Valley has been little appreciated. In most river cities and towns the waterfronts have been destroyed by urban renewal, and once exquisite residential neighborhoods, now deteriorated, have not been recognized for their distinctiveness and potential for redevelopment.

Much of the authentic historical character of the Ohio Valley remains imprinted on the contemporary scene. The personality of the area is rooted in the late eighteenth and the early nineteenth century when the towns were founded and agricultural settlements initiated. After 1860 much of the region stagnated economically. Landscape changed less in the Ohio Valley as compared with the more highly industrialized Upper Middle West and Northeast. Many landscape elements seen by the early travelers can still be seen today: from the town houses of Cincinnati's "Uber den Rhine" to the log cabin hidden in residual Appalachian forests. The early travelers' impressions invite us to look around and rediscover the early Ohio Valley in our own time.

APPENDIX

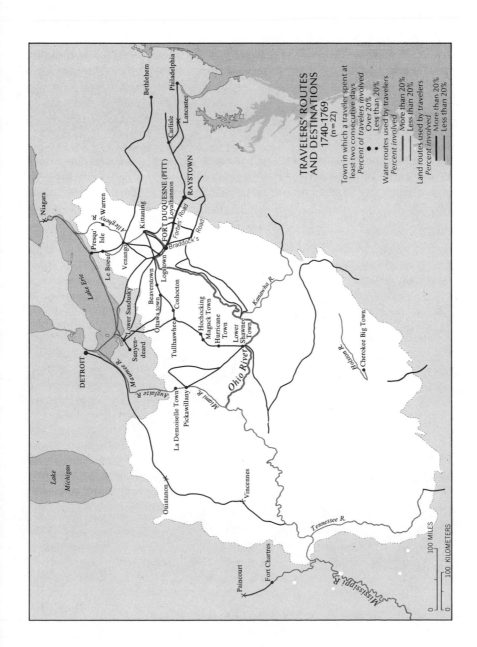

TRAVELERS' ROUTES
AND DESTINATIONS
1740–1769
(n=22)

Town in which a traveler spent at
least two consecutive days
Percent of travelers involved
● Over 20%
● Less than 20%
Water routes used by travelers
Percent involved
More than 20%
Less than 20%
Land routes used by travelers
Percent involved
More than 20%
Less than 20%

100 MILES

100 KILOMETERS

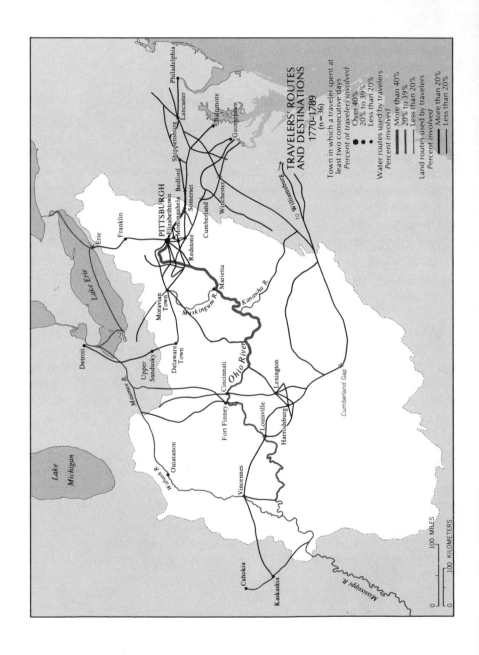

TRAVELERS' ROUTES
AND DESTINATIONS
1770-1789
(n=36)

Town in which a traveler spent at
least two consecutive days
Percent of travelers involved
● ● ●   Over 40%
         20% to 39%
         Less than 20%

Water routes used by travelers
Percent involved
         More than 40%
         20% to 39%
         Less than 20%

Land routes used by travelers
Percent involved
         More than 20%
         Less than 20%

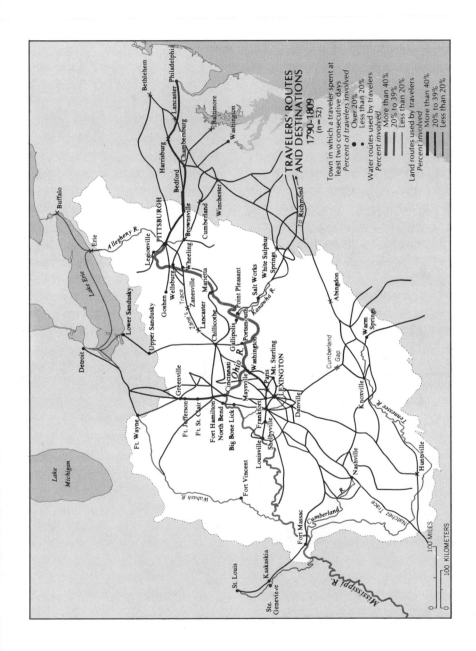

TRAVELERS' ROUTES
AND DESTINATIONS
1790–1809
(n=52)

Town in which a traveler spent at
least two consecutive days
Percent of travelers involved
● Over 20%
• Less than 20%
Water routes used by travelers
Percent involved
More than 40%
20% to 39%
Less than 20%
Land routes used by travelers
Percent involved
More than 40%
20% to 39%
Less than 20%

100 MILES

100 KILOMETERS

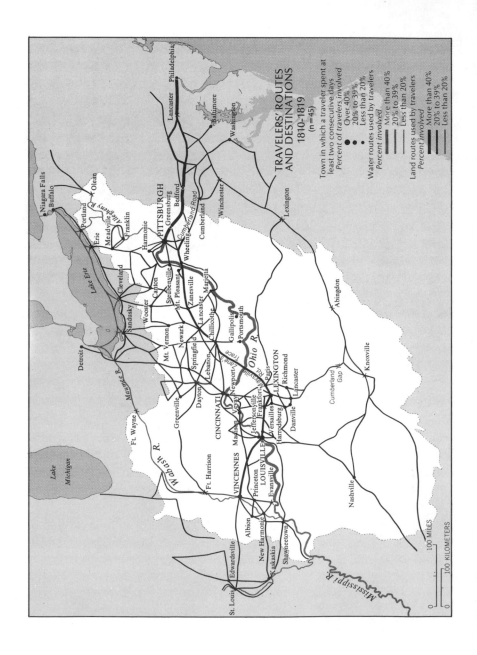

TRAVELERS' ROUTES
AND DESTINATIONS
1810–1819
(n = 45)

Town in which a traveler spent at
least two consecutive days

Percent of travelers involved
● ● ●   Over 40%
● ●   20% to 39%
●   Less than 20%

Water routes used by travelers
Percent involved
         More than 40%
         20% to 39%
         Less than 20%

Land routes used by travelers
Percent involved
         More than 40%
         20% to 39%
         Less than 20%

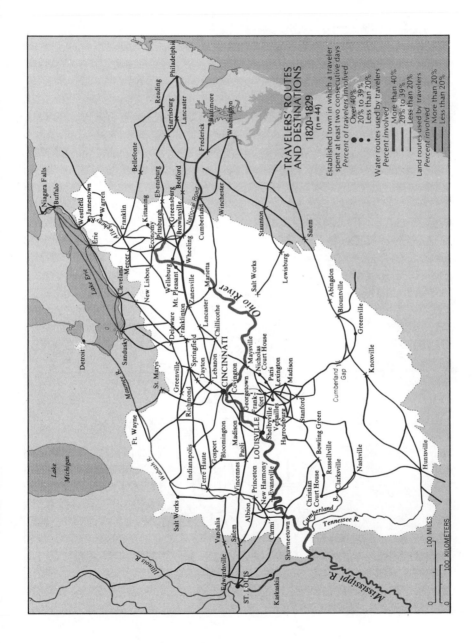

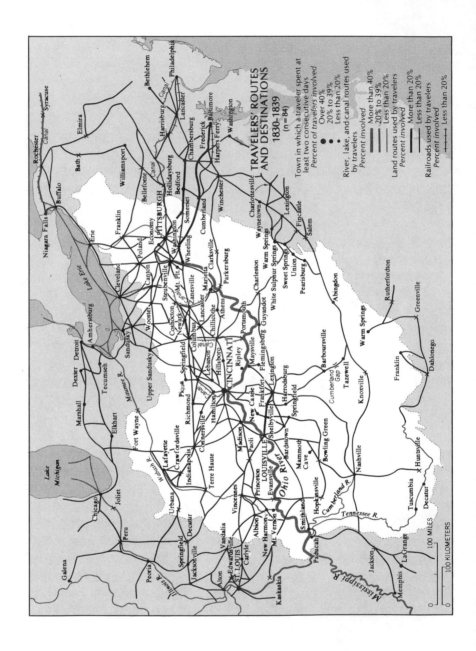

TRAVELERS' ROUTES AND DESTINATIONS 1830-1839 (n = 84)

Town in which a traveler spent at least two consecutive days
Percent of travelers involved
Over 40%
20% to 39%
Less than 20%

River, lake, and canal routes used by travelers
Percent involved
More than 40%
20% to 39%
Less than 20%

Land routes used by travelers
Percent involved
More than 20%
Less than 20%

Railroads used by travelers
Percent involved
Less than 20%

100 MILES

100 KILOMETERS

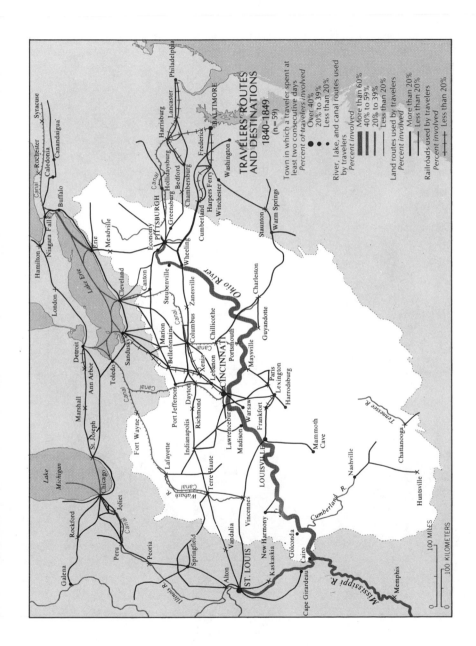

TRAVELERS' ROUTES
AND DESTINATIONS
1840-1849
(n = 59)

Town in which a traveler spent at
least two consecutive days
Percent of travelers involved
  Over 40%
  20% to 39%
  Less than 20%

River, lake, and canal routes used
by travelers
Percent involved
  More than 60%
  40% to 59%
  20% to 39%
  Less than 20%

Land routes used by travelers
Percent involved
  More than 20%
  Less than 20%

Railroads used by travelers
Percent involved
  Less than 20%

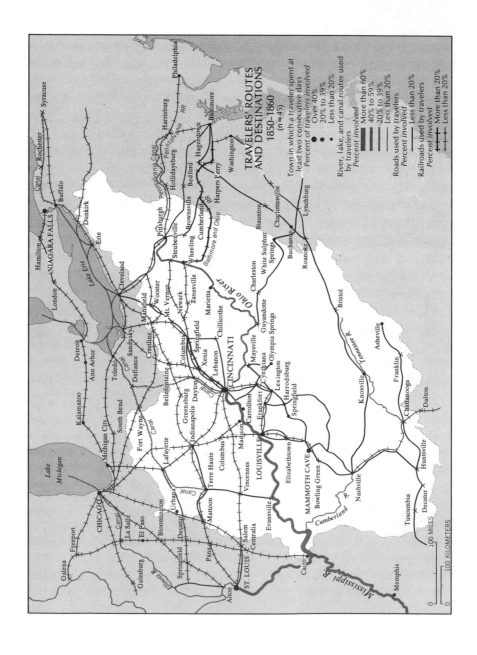

TRAVELERS' ROUTES
AND DESTINATIONS
1850-1860
(n = 45)

Town in which a traveler spent at
least two consecutive days
Percent of travelers involved
Over 40%
20% to 39%
Less than 20%

River, lake, and canal routes used
by travelers
Percent of travelers
More than 60%
40% to 59%
20% to 39%
Less than 20%

Roads used by travelers
Percent involved
More than 20%
Less than 20%

Railroads used by travelers
Percent involved
More than 20%
Less than 20%

NOTES

Chapter 1   Introduction

1. James S. Buckingham, *The Eastern and Western States of America*, 2 vols. (London, 1840), vol. 2, p. 198.

2. Moritz Busch, *Wanderungen zwischen Hudson und Mississippi, 1851 und 1852* (Stuttgart and Tübigen, 1853), vol. 1, p. 150.

3. *Ibid.*

4. James Hall, *Letters from the West; Containing Sketches of Scenery, Manners, and Customs; and Anecdotes Connected with the First Settlements of the Western Section of the United States* (London, 1828), p. 155.

5. *Ibid.*, p. 30.

6. Charles Dickens, *American Notes for General Circulation* (London, 1842), p. 134.

7. Frances Trollope, *Domestic Manners of the Americans*, edited by Donald Smalley (New York, 1949), p. 33.

8. James Dixon, *Methodism in America: With the Personal Narrative of the Author during a Tour through a Part of the United States and Canada* (London, 1849), p. 78.

9. C. F. Hoffman, *A Winter in the Far West* (London, 1835), p. 48.

10. Buckingham, *op. cit.*, vol. 2, p. 266.

11. James H. Rodabaugh (ed.), "From England to Ohio, 1830–1832: The Journal of Thomas K. Wharton," *Ohio Historical Quarterly*, 65 (1956), 131.

12. *Ibid.*

13. [Edmund Flagg], *The Far West: Or a Tour beyond the Mountains* (New York, 1838), p. 47.

14. *Ibid.*

15. Caleb Atwater, *Remarks Made on a Tour to Prairie Du Chien; Thence to Washington City in 1829* (Columbus, Ohio, 1831), p. 230.

16. Gilbert Imlay, *A Topographical Description of the Western Territory of North America* (London, 1793), p. 282.

17. Hall, *op. cit.*, p. 79.

18. Milo M. Quaife (ed.), "The Journals of Captain Meriwether Lewis and Sergeant John Ordway Kept on the Expedition of Western Exploration, 1803–1804," *Wisconsin Historical Society Collections,* 22 (1916), 31.

19. Two bibliographies were used to locate the Ohio Valley travel literature: Thomas D. Clark (ed.), *Travels in the Old South: A Bibliography,* vols. 2 and 3 (Norman, Okla., 1956), and Robert R. Hubach, *Early Midwestern Travel Narratives, An Annotated Bibliography 1634–1850* (Detroit: Wayne State University Press, 1961).

20. C[onstantine] F. Volney, *View of the Climate and Soil of the United States of America* (London, 1804); Basil Hall, *Travels in North America in the Years 1827 and 1828* (Edinburgh, 1830).

21. John S. Wright, *Letters from the West; Or a Caution to Emigrants* (Salem, N.Y., 1819).

22. *Ibid.*

23. Harriet Martineau, *Retrospect of Western Travel* (London, 1838); Anne Royall, *Mrs. Royall's Southern Tour, Or, Second Series of the Black Book,* 3 vols. (Washington, D.C., 1830–31).

24. William W. Brown, *Narrative of William W. Brown, a Fugitive Slave, Written by Himself* (Boston, 1847).

25. W. E. Baxter, *America and the Americans* (London, 1855), p. 9.

26. Elias Fordham, *Personal Narrative of Travels* (Cleveland, 1906), p. 64.

27. *Ibid.*

28. *Ibid.*

29. Daniel Drake, *Discourses on the History, Character, and Prospects of the West* (Cincinnati, 1834), p. 7.

30. *Ibid.*

31. Jay Monaghan (ed.), "From England to Illinois in 1821. The Journal of William Hall," *Journal, Illinois State Historical Society,* 39 (1946), 225.

32. Recommended histories of the Ohio Valley include: Thomas P. Abernethy, *Three Virginia Frontiers* (Baton Rouge, La., 1940); Harriette Arnow, *Flowering of the Cumberland* (New York, 1963); B. W. Bond, *The Civilization of the Old Northwest* (New York, 1934); Randolph C. Downes, *Frontier Ohio, 1788–1803* (Columbus, Ohio, 1935); and Frederic L. Paxson, *History of the American Frontier, 1763–1893* (Boston, 1924).

33. Hector St. Jean de Crèvecoeur, *Letters from an American Farmer* (London, 1872); Alexis de Tocqueville, *Democracy in America* (New York, 1835). For analyses of the traveler's political, economic, and social views see: Max Berger, *The British Traveler in America, 1836–1860* (New York, 1943); Jane Louise Mesick, *The English Traveller in America, 1785–1835* (New York, 1922); Ralph Leslie Rusk, *The Literature of the Middle Western Frontier* (New York, 1926); and Henry T. Tuckerman, *America and*

Her Commentators, with a Critical Sketch of Travel in the United States (New York, 1864).

34. The best description of the Ohio Valley by a historical geographer appears in Ralph H. Brown, *Historical Geography of the United States* (New York, 1948).

Chapter 2   Images of Travel

1. Karl Postl [Charles Sealsfield], *The Americans as They Are: Described in a Tour through the Valley of the Mississippi* (London, 1828), p. 104.

2. John Woods, *Two Years' Residence in the Settlement on the English Prairie in the Illinois Country* (London, 1822), p. 160.

3. *Ibid.*

4. Timothy Flint, *Recollections of the Last Ten Years Passed in Occasional Residences and Journeyings in the Valley of the Mississippi* (Boston, 1826), p. 76.

5. *Ibid.*

6. Simon A. Ferrall, *A Ramble of Six Thousand Miles through the United States of America* (London, 1832), p. 167.

7. Estwick Evans, *A Pedestrian Tour, of Four Thousand Miles, through the Western States and Territories* (Concord, N.H., 1819), p. 3.

8. C. F. Hoffman, *A Winter in the Far West* (New York, 1835), p. 40.

9. Thomas Ashe, *Travels in America Performed in 1806* (London, 1808), p. 23.

10. Hoffman, *op. cit.*, p. 42.

11. John James Audubon, *Ornithological Biography* (Edinburgh, 1831–39), p. 290.

12. Richard Lee Mason, *Narrative of Richard Lee Mason in the Pioneer West, 1819* (New York, 1915), p. 28.

13. Lorenzo Dow, *Perambulations of a Cosmopolite* (Rochester, N.Y., 1842), p. 147.

14. Morris Birkbeck, *Notes on a Journey in America, from the Coast of Virginia to the Territory of Illinois* (Philadelphia, 1817), p. 44.

15. *Ibid.*

16. F[ortescue] Cuming, *Sketches of a Tour to the Western Country* (Pittsburgh, 1810), p. 151.

17. Flint, Timothy, *op. cit.*, p. 276.

18. William Oliver, *Eight Months in Illinois; with Information to Immigrants* (Newcastle Upon Tyne, 1843), p. 104.

19. James S. Buckingham, *The Eastern and Western States of America*, 2 vols. (London, 1840), vol. 1, p. 242.

20. Hoffman, *op. cit.*, p. 43.

21. John Cotton, "From Rhode Island to Ohio in 1815," *Journal of American History*, 16 (1922), 251.

22. John Richard Beste, *The Wabash: Or Adventures of an English Gentleman's Family in the Interior of America* (London, 1855), vol. 2, p. 48.

23. James Dixon, *Methodism in America: With the Personal Narrative of the Author, during a Tour through a Part of the United States and Canada* (London, 1849), p. 79.

24. Emory Holloway (ed.), *The Uncollected Poetry and Prose of Walt Whitman* (New York, 1921), p. 184.

25. Amelia Murray, *Letters from the United States, Cuba, and Canada* (New York, 1856), p. 320.

26. Charles Dickens, *American Notes for General Circulation* (London, 1842), p. 130.

27. Godfrey Vigne, *Six Months in America* (London, 1832), vol. 2, p. 82.

28. Charles Lyell, *Travels in North America* (London, 1845), vol. 2, p. 73.

29. Buckingham, *op. cit.*, vol. 2, p. 160.

30. *Ibid.*, p. 269.

31. William T. Harris, *Remarks Made during a Tour through the United States of America* (London, 1821), p. 123.

32. Cuming, *op. cit.*, p. 72.

33. Flint, Timothy, *op. cit.*, p. 13.

34. James Flint, *Letters from America* (Edinburgh, 1822), p. 73.

35. Elias P. Fordham, *Personal Narrative of Travels in Virginia, Maryland, Pennsylvania, Ohio, Kentucky, and of a Residence in the Illinois Territory* (Cleveland, 1906), p. 79.

36. Zodak Cramer, *The Navigator* (Pittsburgh, 1806).

37. Fordham, *op. cit.*, p. 79.

38. Zodak Cramer, *The Navigator*, 9th ed. (Pittsburgh, 1814), p. 37.

39. Gilbert Imlay, *A Topographical Description of the Western Territory of North America* (London, 1793), p. 81.

40. Flint, Timothy, *op. cit.*, p. 27.

41. Harris, *op. cit.*, p. 98.

42. William Cooper Howells, *Recollections of Life in Ohio, 1813–1840* (Cincinnati, 1895), p. 84.

43. Audubon, *op. cit.*, p. 2.

44. Jay Monaghan (ed.), "From England to Illinois in 1821, the Journal of William Hall," *Journal, Illinois State Historical Society*, 39 (1946), 48.

45. Flint, Timothy, *op. cit.*, p. 24.

46. Samuel S. Forman, *Narrative of a Journey down the Ohio and Mississippi in 1789–90* (Cincinnati, 1888), p. 23.

47. Woods, *op. cit.*, p. 97.

48. James Hall, *Letters from the West; Containing Sketches of Scenery, Manners, and Customs; and Anecdotes Connected with the First Settlement of the Western Sections of the United States* (London, 1828), p. 87.

49. George Combe, *Notes on the United States of North America, during a Phrenological Visit in 1838–39–40* (Philadelphia, 1841), p. 338.

50. *Ibid.*

51. *Ibid.*, p. 339.

52. Dickens, *op. cit.*, p. 102.

53. *Ibid.*, p. 106.

54. Combe, *op. cit.*, p. 378.

55. Beste, *op. cit.*, vol. 1, p. 154.

56. Combe, *op. cit.*, p. 378.

57. Murray, *op. cit.*, p. 141.

58. Dickens, *op. cit.*, p. 106.

59. Cyrus Bradley, "Journal of Cyrus Bradley," *Ohio Archeological and Historical Quarterly*, 15 (1906), 230.

60. Beste, *op. cit.*, vol. 1, p. 196.

61. Joel W. Hiatt (ed.), "Diary of William Owen, From November 10, 1824, to April 20, 1825," *Indiana Historical Society Publications*, 4 (1906), 20.

62. Henry B. Fearon, *Sketches of America* (London, 1819), p. 246.

63. Fredrika Bremer, *The Homes of the New World: Impressions of America* (New York, 1853), p. 40.

64. Bremer, *op. cit.*, p. 172.

65. James Stuart, *Three Years in North America* (Edinburgh, 1833), p. 472.

66. Beste, *op. cit.*, vol. 1, p. 245.

67. Matilda Houstoun, *Hesperos: Or, Travels in the West* (London, 1850), p. 264.

68. Lester B. Shipper (ed.), *Bishop Whipples' Southern Diary, 1843–1844* (Minneapolis, 1937), p. 139.

69. *Ibid.*

70. Holloway, *op. cit.*, p. 187.

71. W. E. Baxter, *America and the Americans* (London, 1855), p. 230.

72. George Pierce, *Incidents of Western Travel: In a Series of Letters* (Nashville, 1857), p. 20.

73. James Robertson, *A Few Months in America Containing Remarks on Some of Its Industrial and Commercial Interests* (London, 1855), p. 107.

74. Edward Dicey, *Six Months in the Federal States* (London, 1863) in Herbert Mitgang (ed.), *Spectator of America* (Chicago, 1971), p. 164.

75. George W. Thornbury, *Criss-cross Journeys* (London, 1873), p. 26.

76. Isabella Trotter, *First Impressions of the New World on Two Travelers from the Old* (London, 1859), p. 163.

77. Charles MacKay, *Life and Liberty in America; Or Sketches of a Tour in the United States and Canada* (London, 1859), p. 122.

78. Henry A. Murray, *Lands of the Slave and the Free: Or, Cuba, the United States, and Canada* (London, 1855), p. 139.

79. Lillian Foster, *Wayside Glimpses, North and South* (New York, 1860), p. 243.

80. *Ibid.*

81. John A. Clark, *Gleanings by the Way* (Philadelphia, 1842), p. 26.

82. *Ibid.*

83. James Fenimore Cooper, "American and European Scenery Compared," in Motley F. Deakin (ed.), *The Home Book of the Picturesque: Or American Scenery, Art, and Literature* (New York, 1852), p. 65.

84. *Ibid.*

85. Dixon, *op. cit.*, p. 104.

86. Frederick Law Olmsted, *A Journey in the Back Country* in Harvey Wish (ed.), *The Slave States before the Civil War* (New York, 1959), p. 220.

87. Archibald Prentice, *A Tour in the United States* (London, 1848), p. 65.

88. Pierce, *op. cit.*, p. 162.

89. Robert Playfair, *Recollections of a Visit to the United States and the British Provinces of North America* (Edinburgh, 1856), p. 197.

90. William Faux, *Memorable Days in America: Being a Journal of a Tour to the United States* (London, 1823), p. 263.

91. Oliver, *op. cit.*, p. 97.

92. Harris, *op. cit.*, p. 103.

93. Johann D. Schoepf, *Travels in the Confederation* (Philadelphia, 1911), p. 240.

94. Hall, *op. cit.*, p. 173.

95. Olmsted, *op. cit.*, p. 211.

96. Birkbeck, *op. cit.*, p. 96.

97. Buckingham, *op. cit.*, 2, p. 293.

98. Faux, *op. cit.*, p. 20.

99. Louise Fogle (ed.), "Journal of Ebenezer Mattoon Chamberlain, 1832–35," *Indiana Magazine of History*, 15 (1919), 243.

100. Mason, *op. cit.*, p. 20.

101. Oliver, *op. cit.*, p. 99.

102. David Jarrett, "Travel Diary," *Montgomery County [Pennsylvania] Historical Society Sketches*, 6 (1929), 121–36.

103. François André Michaux, *Travels to the West of the Alleghany Mountains in the States of Ohio, Kentucky, and Tennessee* (London, 1805) in Reuben G. Thwaites (ed.), *Early Western Travels, 1748–1846*, vol. 3 (New York, 1966), p. 247.

104. *Ibid.*

105. Frederick Hall, *Letters from the East and from the West* (Baltimore, 1840), p. 132.

106. Houstoun, *op. cit.*, p. 252.

107. *Ibid.*

108. Édouard de Montule, *Voyage en Amérique* (Paris, 1821), p. 129.

109. Mason, *op. cit.*, p. 20.

110. John S. Wright, *Letters from the West; Or a Caution to Emigrants* (Salem, N.Y., 1819), p. 22.

111. *Ibid.*, p. 40.

112. Patrick Shirreff, *A Tour through North America; Together with a*

Comprehensive View of the Canadas and United States. As Adopted for Agricultural Emigration (Edinburgh, 1835), p. 288.

113. Sidney Smith, *The Settler's New Home: Or The Emigrants' Location, Being a Guide to Emigrants in the Selection of a Settlement and the Preliminary Details of the Voyage* (London, 1849), p. 103.

114. Marie Grandfort, *The New World* (New Orleans, 1855), p. 113.

115. *Ibid.*

116. Beste, *op. cit.,* p. 175.

117. Playfair, *op. cit.,* p. 197.

118. Beste, *op. cit.,* vol. 2, p. 6.

119. *Ibid.,* vol. 2, p. 68.

120. *Ibid.,* vol. 2, p. 70.

121. *Ibid.,* vol. 2, p. 71.

122. Houstoun, *op. cit.,* p. 216.

123. Moritz Busch, *Wanderungen zwischen Hudson und Mississippi, 1851 und 1852* (Stuttgart and Tübingen, 1854), vol. 2, p. 28.

124. Faux, *op. cit.,* p. 173; Grandfort, *op. cit.,* p. 114.

125. Buckingham, *op. cit.,* p. 196.

126. Nathaniel P. Willis, *Health Trip to the Tropics* (New York, 1853), p. 225.

127. Frederick Marryat, *A Diary In America, with Remarks on Its Institutions* (Philadelphia, 1839), p. 210.

128. *Ibid.*

129. Buckingham, *op. cit.,* p. 336.

130. *Ibid.*

131. Welby, *op. cit.,* p. 149.

132. Daniel Drake, *A Systematic Treatise, Historical, Etiological, and Practical on the Principal Diseases of the Interior Valley of North America* (Cincinnati, 1849), p. 629.

133. Buckingham, *op. cit.,* p. 305.

134. *Ibid.,* vol. 2, p. 259.

135. Shirreff, *op. cit.,* p. 276.

136. Nicholas Cresswell, *The Journal of Nicholas Cresswell, 1774–1777* (New York, 1924), p. 91.

137. *Ibid.,* p. 103.

138. *Ibid.*

139. Charles G. Rosenberg, *Jenny Lind in America* (New York, 1851), p. 190.

140. Friedrich W. von Wrede, *Lebensbilder Aus Den Vereinigten Staaten Von Nordamerika und Texas* (n.p., 1844), p. 163.

141. Edward S. Abdy, *Journal of a Residence and Tour in the United States of North America* (London, 1833), vol. 2, p. 385.

142. *Ibid.*

143. James Logan, *Notes of a Journey through Canada, the United States of America, and the West Indies* (Edinburgh, 1838), p. 120.

144. Anon., *An Immigrant of a Hundred Years Ago: A Story of Some-one's Ancester, Translated and Retold by an Old Hand* (Hattiesburg, Miss., 1941), p. 47.

145. *Ibid.*

146. Thomas L. Nicholas, *Forty-Years of American Life* (London, 1864), p. 1.

147. Edward Dicey, *Six Months in the Federal States* (London, 1863) in Herbert Mitgang (ed.), *Spectator of America* (Chicago, 1971), p. 164.

148. Josiah Espy, *Memorandums of a Tour Made by Josiah Espy in the States of Ohio and Kentucky and Indiana Territory in 1805* (Cincinnati, 1870), p. 20.

Chapter 3   Wilder Images

1. Henry T. Tuckerman, *America and Her Commentators, with a Critical Sketch of Travel in the United States* (New York, 1864), p. 132.

2. John Filson, *The Discovery, Settlement, and Present State of Kentucke* (Wilmington [Del.], 1784), p. 316.

3. C[onstantine] F. Volney, *View of the Climate and Soil of the United States of America* (London, 1804), p. 147.

4. Caleb Atwater, *Remarks Made on a Tour to Prairie Du Chien; Thence to Washington City in 1829* (Columbus, Ohio, 1831), p. 227.

5. Daniel Drake, *A Systematic Treatise, Historical, Etiological, and Practical on the Principal Diseases of the Interior Valley of North America* (Cincinnati, 1849), p. 500.

6. *Ibid.*, p. 465.

7. Mrs. Basil [Margaret] Hall, "Letters of Mrs. Basil Hall, 1827–1828," in Una Pope-Hennessy (ed.), *The Aristocratic Journey* (New York, 1931), p. 268.

8. William Oliver, *Eight Months in Illinois with Information to Immigrants* (Newcastle Upon Tyne, 1843), p. 36.

9. *Ibid.*

10. Volney, *op. cit.*, p. 264.

11. Andrew Reed and James Matheson, *A Narrative of the Visit to the American Churches* (New York, 1835), p. 122.

12. Drake, *op. cit.*, p. 608.

13. Volney, *op. cit.*, p. 147.

14. Drake, *op. cit.*, p. 603.

15. *Ibid.*, p. 591.

16. *Ibid.*

17. Volney, *op. cit.*, p. 25.

18. Gilbert Imlay, *A Topographical Description of the Western Territory of North America* (London, 1792), p. 141.

19. Drake, *op. cit.*, p. 427.

20. Harriet Martineau, *Society in America* (London, 1837), p. 237.

21. Reed and Matheson, *op. cit.*, p. 111.

22. John James Audubon, *Ornithological Biography* (Edinburgh, 1831–39), p. 53.

23. Edward Dicey, *Six Months in the Federal States* (London, 1863) in Herbert Mitgang (ed.), *Spectator of America* (Chicago, 1971), p. 167.

24. C. F. Hoffman, *A Winter in the Far West* (New York, 1835), vol. 1, p. 38.

25. Reed and Matheson, *op. cit.*, p. 148.

26. John Melish, *Travels through the United States* (Belfast, Northern Ireland, 1818), p. 375.

27. Reed and Matheson, *op. cit.*, p. 299.

28. Drake, *op. cit.*, p. 623.

29. George Washington, "Journal, January 1 to December 31, 1770," in John C. Fitzpatrick (ed.), *The Diaries of George Washington, 1748–1799* (Boston, 1925), p. 429.

30. James Flint, *Letters from America Containing Observations on the Climate and Agriculture of the Western States* (Edinburgh, 1822), p. 257.

31. Thaddeus Harris, *Journal of a Tour into the Territory Northwest of the Alleghany Mountains; Made in the Spring of the Year 1803* in Reuben G. Thwaites (ed.), *Early Western Travels*, vol. 3 (New York, 1968), p. 327.

32. Andrew Ellicott, *The Journal of Andrew Ellicott* (Philadelphia, 1803), p. 8.

33. François Michaux, *Travels to the West of the Alleghany Mountains in the States of Ohio, Kentucky, and Tennessee* in Reuben G. Thwaites (ed.), *Early Western Travels*, vol. 3 (New York, 1966), p. 214.

34. Morris Birkbeck, *Notes on a Journey in America from the Coast of Virginia to the Territory of Illinois* (London, 1817), p. 111.

35. S. A. Ferrall, *A Ramble of Six Thousand Miles through the United States of America* (London, 1832), p. 113.

36. Basil Hall, *Travels in North America, in the Years 1827 and 1828* (Edinburgh, 1830), p. 385.

37. Ferrall, *op. cit.*, p. 113.

38. Richard Flower, *Letters from Lexington and the Illinois Containing a Brief Account of the English Settlement in the Latter Territority* (London, 1819) in Reuben G. Thwaites (ed.), *Early Western Travels*, vol. 10 (New York, 1966), p. 204.

39. Jay Monaghan (ed.), "From England to Illinois in 1821, The Journal of William Hall," *Journal, Illinois State Historical Society*, 39 (1946), 64.

40. *Ibid.*

41. George Croghan, "A Selection of George Croghan's Letters and Journals Relating to Tours into the Western Country—November 16, 1750, to November 1765," in Reuben G. Thwaites (ed.), *Early Western Travels*, vol. 1 (New York, 1966), p. 131.

42. Filson, *op. cit.*, p. 30.

43. *Ibid.*, p. 32.

44. Johann D. Schoepf, *Travels in the Confederation* (Philadelphia, 1911), p. 274.

45. Édouard de Montule, *Voyage en Amérique* (Paris, 1821), p. 121.

46. Maximilian, Prince of Wied, *Travels in the Interior of North America* (London, 1843), p. 64.

47. Thomas Hutchins, *A Topographical Description of Virginia, Pennsylvania, Maryland, and North Carolina* (London, 1778); edited by Frederick Hicks (Cleveland, 1904), p. 83.

48. Thomas Hulme, *Hulme's Journal of a Tour in the Western Countries of America* in Reuben G. Thwaites (ed.), *Early Western Travels,* vol. 10 (New York, 1966), p. 69; Cresswell, *op. cit.,* p. 69.

49. Volney, *op. cit.,* p. 16.

50. Richard Lee Mason, *Narrative of Richard Lee Mason in the Pioneer West, 1819* (New York, 1915), p. 17.

51. Henry B. Fearon, *Sketches of America* (London, 1819), p. 196.

52. *Ibid.*

53. Joseph J. Gurney, *A Journey in North America* (Norwich, England, 1841), p. 51.

54. Reed and Matheson, *op. cit.,* p. 140.

55. Elizabeth Willson, *A Journey in 1836 from New Jersey to Ohio* (Morrison, Illinois, 1929), n.p.

56. *Ibid.*

57. Philip Kelland, *Transatlantic Sketches* (Edinburgh, 1858), p. 58.

58. Martineau, *op. cit.,* p. 229.

59. Emmeline Stuart-Wortley, *Travels in the United States* (New York, 1851), p. 96.

60. *Ibid.*

61. Martineau, *op. cit.,* p. 233.

62. *Ibid.*

63. *Ibid.*

64. *Ibid.*

65. W. Williams, *Appleton's New and Complete United States Guide Book for Travellers* (New York, 1853), p. 79.

66. James Booty, *Three Months in Canada and the United States* (London, 1862), p. 33.

67. *Ibid.*

68. George W. Thornbury, *Criss-cross Journeys* (London, 1873), p. 3.

69. Nathaniel P. Willis, *Health Trip to the Tropics* (New York, 1853), p. 146.

70. George W. Featherstonhaugh, *A Canoe Voyage Up the Minnay Sotor* (London, 1847), p. 211.

71. Charles Lyell, *Travels in North America* (London, 1845), vol. 2, p. 224.

72. Volney, *op. cit.,* p. 43.

73. *Ibid.,* p. 23.

74. *Ibid.*

75. Audubon, *op. cit.,* p. 48.

76. *Ibid.*

77. Lydia Bacon, "Mrs. Lydia B. Bacon's Journal 1811–1812," *Indiana Magazine of History*, 40 (1944), 367–86; 41 (1945), 59–79.

78. Frances Trollope, *Domestic Manners of the Americans*, edited by Donald Smalley (New York, 1949), p. 35.

79. Frederick J. Jobson, *America and American Methodism* (London, 1857), p. 291.

80. *Ibid.*

81. James Stirling, *Letters from the Slave States* (London, 1857), p. 41.

82. Trollope, *op. cit.*, p. 88.

83. Dicey, *op. cit.*, p. 205.

84. *Ibid.*

85. Daniel Drake, *Discourses on the History, Character, and Prospects of the West* (Cincinnati, 1834), p. 16.

86. Martineau, *op. cit.*, p. 212.

Chapter 4   Images of Aboriginal Life

1. Thomas Walker, *Journal of an Exploration in the Spring of the Year 1750* (Boston, 1888), p. 49.

2. Nicholas Cresswell, *The Journal of Nicholas Cresswell, 1774–1777* (New York, 1924), p. 71.

3. Milo Quaife (ed.), "The Journals of Captain Meriwether Lewis and Sargeant John Ordway Kept on the Expedition of Western Exploration, 1803–1804," *Wisconsin Historical Society Collections*, 22 (1916), 41.

4. F[ortescue] Cuming, *Sketches of a Tour to the Western Country* (Pittsburgh, 1810), p. 97.

5. William Henry Harrison, *Discourse on the Aborigines of the Valley of the Ohio* (Cincinnati, 1838), p. 1.

6. Beverly W. Bond (ed.), "Two Westward Journeys of John Filson, 1785," *Mississippi Valley Historical Review*, 9 (1923), 323.

7. *Ibid.*

8. Thomas Ashe, *Travels in America Performed in 1806* (London, 1808), p. 207.

9. *Ibid.*

10. James S. Buckingham, *The Slave States of America* (London, 1842), vol. 2, p. 397.

11. James Smith, *An Account of the Remarkable Occurrences in the Life and Travels of Col. James Smith* (Lexington, Ky., 1799), p. 81.

12. James E. Seaver, *A Narrative of the Life of Mrs. Mary Jemison* (Canandaigua, N.Y., 1824), p. 15.

13. Smith, *op. cit.*, p. 86.

14. *Ibid.*

15. Seaver, *op. cit.*, p. 56.

16. John D. Barnhart (ed.), *Journal of Henry Hamilton* (Crawfordsville, Ind., 1951), p. 182.

17. Smith, *op. cit.*, p. 89.

18. Mathew Bunn, *A Journal of the Adventures of Mathew Bunn* (Providence, R.I., 1796), p. 11.

19. David Jones, *A Journal of Two Visits Made to Some Nations of Indians on the West Side of the River Ohio* (New York, 1865), p. 88.

20. *Ibid.*

21. Bunn, *op. cit.*, p. 11.

22. Henry Timberlake, *The Memoirs of Lieut. Henry Timberlake* (London, 1765), p. 29.

23. C[onstantine] F. Volney, *View of the Climate and Soil of the United States of America* (London, 1804), p. 411.

24. *Ibid.*

25. *Ibid.*, p. 396.

26. Gilbert Imlay, *A Topographical Description of the Western Territory of North America* (London, 1793), p. 290.

27. John Jennings, "Journal from Fort Pitt to Fort Chartres in the Illinois Country, March-April, 1766," *Pennsylvania Magazine of History and Biography*, 31 (1907), 145.

28. Christopher Gist, "A Journal of Christopher Gist's Journey, Begun . . . October 31, 1750, Continued Down the Ohio," in Thomas Pownall, *A Topographical Description of . . . North America* (London, 1776), p. 44.

29. *Ibid.*

30. John Filson, *The Discovery, Settlement, and Present State of Kentucke* (Wilmington [Del.], 1784), p. 102.

31. Johann D. Schoepf, *Travels in the Confederation* (Philadelphia, 1911), p. 275.

32. Cresswell, *op. cit.*, p. 106.

33. Filson, *op. cit.*, p. 102.

34. Alan Hodgson, *Remarks during a Journey through North America in the Years 1819, 1820, and 1821* (New York, 1823), p. 240.

35. *Ibid.*

36. *Ibid.*

37. Henry R. Schoolcraft, *Travels in the Central Portion of the Mississippi Valley* (New York, 1825), p. 92.

38. *Ibid.*

39. David Macelner, "An Abstract of the Journal of a Mission to the Delaware Indians, West of the Ohio," in Eleazar Wheelock (ed.), *A Continuation of the Narrative of the Indian Charity-School Begun in Lebanon in Connecticut* (n.p., 1773), p. 57.

Chapter 5   Images of Military Life

1. Milo M. Quaife (ed.), "A Picture of the First United States Army: The Journal of Captain Samuel Newman," *Wisconsin Magazine of History*, 2 (1918), 67.

2. "Daily Journal of Wayne's Campaign," in Samuel L. Metcalf (ed.), *A*

NOTES   187

Collection of Some of the Most Interesting Narratives of Indian Warfare in the West (Lexington, Ky., 1821), p. 120.

3. Ebenezer Denny, *Military Journal of Major Ebenezer Denny* (Philadelphia, 1859), p. 359.

4. Letter from Major James Grant to Col. Henry Bouquet, in Sylvester Stevens and Donald Kent (eds.), *The Expedition of Baron de Longueil* (Harrisburg, 1941), p. 503.

5. George R. Clark, "Memoir," in W. H. English (ed.), *Conquest of the Country Northwest of the River Ohio* (Indianapolis, 1779), p. 522.

6. Thomas Irwin, "Journal," in James McBride (ed.), *Pioneer Biography, Sketches of the Lives of Some of the Early Settlers of Butler County, Ohio* (Cincinnati, 1869), p. 153.

7. *Ibid.*

8. Letter from General Arthur St. Clair to the Secretary of War, November 9, 1791, in Samuel L. Metcalf (ed.), *A Collection of Some of the Most Interesting Narratives of Indian Warfare in the West* (Lexington, Ky., 1821), p. 115.

9. Letter from Col. Henry Bouquet to General Forbes, July 31, 1758, in Stevens and Kent, *op. cit.*, p. 292.

10. *Ibid.*

11. Letter from Col. Henry Bouquet to General Forbes, August 26, 1758, *Ibid.*, p. 424.

12. Metcalf, *op. cit.*, p. 102.

13. Irwin, *op. cit.*, p. 153.

14. St. Clair, *op. cit.*, p. 104.

15. Irwin, *op. cit.*, p. 167.

16. John Reily, "Journal," in McBride, *op. cit.*, p. 33.

17. *Ibid.*

18. John May, *Journal and Letters of Col. John May, of Boston Relative to Two Journeys to the Ohio Country in 1788 and 1789* (Cincinnati, 1873), p. 48.

19. C. F. Hoffman, *A Winter in the Far West* (London, 1835), p. 69.

20. David Thomas, *Travels Through the Western Country in the Summer of 1816* (Auburn, N.Y., 1819), p. 123.

21. John Filson, *The Discovery, Settlement, and Present State of Kentucke* (Wilmington [Del.], 1784).

22. James S. Buckingham, *The Slave States of America* (London, 1842), vol. 2, p. 510.

23. Hoffman, *op. cit.*, p. 79.

24. *Ibid.*

Chapter 6   Pastoral Images

1. J. E. Alexander, *Transatlantic Sketches, Comprising Visits to the Most Interesting Scenes in North and South America* (London, 1833), p. 99.

2. Henry B. Fearon, *Sketches of America* (London, 1819), p. 221.

3. Morris Birkbeck, *Notes on a Journey in America, from the Coast of Virginia to the Territory of Illinois* (London, 1817), p. 39.

4. *Ibid.*

5. Fearon, *op. cit.*, p. 216.

6. *Ibid.*, p. 235.

7. Harry Toulmin, *A Description of Kentucky in North America: To Which Are Prefixed Miscellaneous Observations Respecting the United States* (Lexington, Ky., 1945), p. 99.

8. Andrew Reed and James Matheson, *A Narrative of the Visit to the American Churches* (New York, 1835), p. 104.

9. William Faux, *Memorable Days in America: Being a Journal of a Tour to the United States* (London, 1823), p. 205.

10. William T. Harris, *Remarks Made during a Tour through the United States of America in 1817, 1818, 1819* (London, 1821), p. 107.

11. William Oliver, *Eight Months in Illinois; with Information to Immigrants* (Newcastle Upon Tyne, 1843), p. 132.

12. James S. Buckingham, *The Eastern and Western States of America,* 2 vols. (London, 1840), vol. 2, p. 294.

13. John Woods, *Two Years' Residence in the Settlement on the English Prairie in the Illinois Country* (London, 1822), p. 165.

14. *Ibid.*

15. Oliver, *op. cit.*, p. 141.

16. Faux, *op. cit.*, p. 242.

17. *Ibid.*

18. *Ibid.*, p. 255.

19. Elias P. Fordham, *Personal Narrative of Travels* (Cleveland, 1906), p. 134.

20. François A. Michaux, *Travels to the West of the Alleghany Mountains in the States of Ohio, Kentucky, and Tennessee* in Reuben G. Thwaites (ed.), *Early Western Travels*, vol. 3 (New York, 1966), p. 244.

21. Harry Toulmin, *The Western Country in 1793, Reports on Kentucky and Virginia* (San Marino, Calif., 1948), p. 81.

22. Sidney Smith, *The Settler's New Home: Or the Emigrants' Location, Being a Guide to Emigrants in the Selection of a Settlement and the Preliminary Details of the Voyage* (London, 1849), p. 13.

23. Toulmin, *The Western Country, op. cit.*, p. 131.

24. Gershom Flagg, "Pioneer Letters of Gershom Flagg," *Transaction, Illinois State Historical Society, 1910* (Springfield, Ill.: Illinois State Historical Library, 1912), p. 145.

25. Toulmin, *The Western Country, op. cit.*, p. 135.

26. Thomas Hamilton, *Men and Manners in America* (Philadelphia, 1833), p. 182.

27. James Flint, *Letters from America Containing Observations on the Climate and Agriculture of the Western States* (Edinburgh, 1822), p. 189.

28. James Hall, *Sketches of History, Life, and Manners in the West* (Philadelphia, 1835), p. 14.

29. *Ibid.*, p. 15.

30. Henry T. Tuckerman, *America and Her Commentators, with a Critical Sketch of Travel in the United States* (New York, 1864), p. 131.

31. *Ibid.*

32. Sandford C. Cox, *Recollections of the Early Settlement of the Wabash Valley* (LaFayette, Ind., 1860), p. 30.

33. Tuckerman, *op. cit.*, p. 117.

34. *Ibid.*

35. Frederick J. Turner, "The Significance of the Frontier in American History," *Proceedings of the State Historical Society of Wisconsin*, (vol. 41, 1893); reprinted in *The Frontier in American History* (New York: Holt, Rinehart, and Winston, 1962).

36. Oliver, *op. cit.*, p. 38.

37. Maximilian, Prince of Wied, *Travels in the Interior of North America* (London, 1843), p. 84.

38. Oliver, *op. cit.*, p. 38.

39. *Ibid.*, p. 40.

40. Maximilian, *op. cit.*, p. 84.

41. C. F. Hoffman, *A Winter in the Far West* (New York, 1835), vol. 2, p. 244.

42. Timothy Flint, *Recollections of the Last Ten Years Passed in Occasional Residences and Journeyings in the Valley of the Mississippi* (Boston, 1826), p. 66.

43. Godfrey T. Vigne, *Six Months in America* (London, 1832), vol. 2, p. 42.

44. Jay Monaghan (ed.), "From England to Illinois in 1821. The Journal of William Hall," *Journal, Illinois State Historical Society*, 39 (1946), 44.

45. J. G. Harker, "Report about and from America Given from First-Hand Observation in the Years 1848 and 1849," translated by Richard B. O'Connell (ed.), *Mississippi Valley Collection Bulletin*, 3 (1970), 60.

46. *Ibid.*, p. 71.

47. Maximilian, *op. cit.*, p. 84.

48. Harker, *op. cit.*, p. 71.

49. *Ibid.*

50. F[ortescue] Cuming, *Sketches of a Tour to the Western Country* (Pittsburgh, 1810), p. 134.

51. Faux, *op. cit.*, p. 238.

52. Michaux, *op. cit.*, p. 276.

53. *Ibid.*

54. Cuming, *op. cit.*, p. 134.

55. Toulmin, *The Western Country*, *op. cit.*, p. 81.

56. Faux, *op. cit.*, p. 177.

57. Timothy Flint, *op. cit.*, p. 66.

58. Toulmin, *The Western Country, op. cit.*, p. 84.

59. *Ibid.*

60. *Ibid.*

61. Joseph Gurney, *A Journey in North America, Described in Familiar Letters to Amelia Opie* (Norwich, England, 1841), p. 49.

62. James Dixon, *Methodism in America: With the Personal Narrative of the Author during a Tour through a Part of the United States and Canada* (London, 1849), p. 74.

63. George Combe, *Notes on the United States of North America, during a Phrenological Visit in 1838–39–40* (Philadelphia, 1841), p. 333.

64. Flint, James, *op. cit.*, p. 117.

65. Marshall Hall, *The Two-Fold Slavery of the United States; With a Project of Self-Emancipation* (London, 1854), p. 11.

66. Lillian Foster, *Wayside Glimpses, North and South* (New York, 1860), p. 80.

67. Henry Caswell, *The Western World Revisited* (Oxford, England, 1854), p. 242.

68. John Melish, *Travels through the United States* (Belfast, Northern Ireland, 1818), p. 403.

69. Joel W. Hiatt (ed.), "Diary of William Owen, from November 10, 1824, to April 20, 1825," *Indiana Historical Society Publications*, 4 (1906), 66.

70. Oliver, *op. cit.*, p. 129.

71. Harker, *op. cit.*, p. 60.

72. Oliver, *op. cit.*, p. 133.

73. Harker, *op. cit.*, p. 60.

74. Faux, *op. cit.*, p. 244.

75. Birkbeck, *op. cit.*, p. 102.

76. Thomas Ashe, *Travels in America Performed in 1806* (London, 1808), p. 231.

77. John M. McDermott (ed.), *The Western Journals of Washington Irving* (Norman, Okla., 1944), p. 76.

78. *Ibid.*

79. Woods, *op. cit.*, p. 107.

80. *Ibid.*

81. Simon A. Ferrall, *A Ramble of Six Thousand Miles through the United States of America* (London, 1832), p. 63.

82. Oliver, *op. cit.*, p. 130.

83. C. F. Hoffman, *A Winter in the Far West* (London, 1835), p. 25.

84. Charles Lyell, *Travels in North America* (London, 1845), vol. 2, p. 203.

85. Friedrich von Raumer, *America and the American People* (New York, 1846), p. 44.

86. Gilbert Imlay, *A Topographical Description of the Western Territory of North America* (London, 1793), p. 30.

87. Harker, *op. cit.*, p. 48.

88. Flagg, *op. cit.*, p. 143.

89. Woods, *op. cit.*, p. 177.

90. James Hall, *Letters from the West, Containing Sketches of Scenery, Manners, and Customs; and Anecdotes Connected with the First Settlements of the Western Sections of the United States* (London, 1828), p. 360.

91. *Ibid.*

92. Francis Asbury, *The Journal of the Rev. Francis Asbury* (New York, 1821), p. 257.

93. Flint, James, *op. cit.*, p. 267.

94. Fordham, *op. cit.*, p. 128.

95. Monaghan, *op. cit.*

96. Edward Abdy, *Journal of a Residence and Tour in the United States of North America* (London, 1833), vol. 1, p. 365.

97. *Ibid.*

98. *Ibid.*, vol. 2, p. 39.

99. John S. Wright, *Letters from the West; Or a Caution to Emigrants* (Salem, N.Y., 1819), p. 67.

100. Richard L. Mason, *Narrative of Richard Lee Mason in the Pioneer West, 1819* (New York, 1915), p. 22.

101. George W. Featherstonhaugh, *A Canoe Voyage up the Minnay Sotar* (London, 1847), p. 90.

102. Hoffman, *op. cit.*, p. 24.

103. John Clark, *Gleanings by the Way* (Philadelphia and New York, 1842), p. 54.

104. Fredrika Bremer, *The Homes of the New World; Impressions of America* (New York, 1853), p. 105.

105. *Ibid.*

106. Karl Postl [Charles Sealsfield], *The Americans as They Are: Described in a Tour through the Valley of the Mississippi* (London, 1828), p. 19.

107. Charles Dickens, *American Notes for General Circulation* (London, 1842), p. 92.

108. James Stirling, *Letters From the Slave States* (London, 1854), p. 42.

109. James S. Buckingham, *The Slave States of America* (London, 1842), vol. 2, p. 446.

110. *Ibid.*

111. Caleb Atwater, *Remarks Made on a Tour to Prairie Du Chien; Thence to Washington City in 1829* (Columbus, Ohio, 1831), p. 204.

112. Harris, *op. cit.*, p. 51.

113. Flint, Timothy, *op. cit.*, p. 52.

114. *Ibid.*

Chapter 7   Urban Images

1. *U.S. Census of Population*, 1800.

2. *U.S. Census of Population*, 1850.

3. Daniel Drake, *A Systematic Treatise, Historical, Etiological, and Practical on the Principal Diseases of the Interior Valley of North America* (Cincinnati, 1849), p. 224.

4. Godfrey Vigne, *Six Months in America* (London, 1832), vol. 2, p. 27.

5. F[ortescue] Cuming, *Sketches of a Tour to the Western Country* (Pittsburgh, 1810), p. 194.

6. *Ibid.*, p. 213.

7. Caleb Atwater, *Remarks Made on a Tour to Prairie Du Chien; Thence to Washington City in 1829* (Columbus, Ohio, 1831), p. 12.

8. John Richard Beste, *The Wabash: Or Adventures of an English Gentleman's Family in the Interior of America* (London, 1855), vol. 1, p. 170.

9. Zodak Cramer, *The Navigator* (Pittsburgh, 1804), p. 238.

10. Cuming, *op. cit.*, p. 170.

11. David Thomas, *Travels through the Western Country in the Summer of 1816* (Auburn, N.Y., 1819), p. 74.

12. Robert Heywood, *A Journey to America in 1834* (Cambridge, England, 1919), p. 49.

13. James E. Alexander, *Transatlantic Sketches, Comprising Visits to the Most Interesting Scenes in North and South America* (London, 1833), p. 121.

14. George F. Pierce, *Incidents of Western Travel: In a Series of Letters* (Nashville, 1857), p. 165.

15. Frances Trollope, *Domestic Manners of the Americans* (London, 1832), p. 89.

16. Drake, *op. cit.*, p. 679.

17. *Ibid.*

18. *Ibid.*

19. Cyrus Bradley, "Journal of Cyrus P. Bradley," *Ohio Archeological and Historical Quarterly*, 15 (1906), 232.

20. Cuming, *op. cit.*, p. 194.

21. *Ibid.*

22. François A. Michaux, *Travels to the West of the Alleghany Mountains* in Reuben G. Thwaites (ed.), *Early Western Travels*, vol. 3 (New York, 1966), p. 103.

23. Andrew Reed and James Matheson, *A Narrative of the Visit to the American Churches* (New York, 1835), p. 126.

24. Timothy Flint, *Recollections of the Last Ten Years Passed in Occasional Residences and Journeyings in the Valley of the Mississippi* (Boston, 1826), p. 51.

25. *Ibid.*

26. Henry Baxter, "Rafting on the Alleghany and Ohio, 1844," *Pennsylvania Magazine of History and Biography*, 51 (1927), 143.

27. *Ibid.*

28. James Kimball, "A Journey to the West in 1817," *Essex Institute Historical Collections*, 8 (1866), 231.

29. James S. Buckingham, *The Eastern and Western States of America*, 2 vols. (London, 1840), vol. 1, p. 244.

30. Needham Parry, "The Journal of Needham Parry, 1794," *Kentucky Historical Society Register*, 34 (1936), 383.

31. Lillian Foster, *Wayside Glimpses, North and South* (New York, 1859), p. 135.

32. Alexander, *op. cit.*, p. 100.

33. Henry Caswell, *The Western World Revisited* (Oxford, England, 1854), p. 244.

34. *Ibid.*

35. Joseph Gurney, *A Journey in North America, Described in Familiar Letters to Amelia Opie* (Norwich, England, 1841), p. 36.

36. Isabella Trotter, *First Impressions of the New World on Two Travellers From the Old* (London, 1859), p. 139.

37. *Ibid.*

38. Charles Weld, *A Vacation Tour in the United States and Canada* (London, 1855), p. 223.

39. Buckingham, *op. cit.*, vol. 2, p. 502.

40. [Henry C. Knight], *Letters from the South and West by Arthur Singleton, Esq.* [Pseud.], (Boston, 1824), p. 84.

41. Harry Toulmin, *The Western Country in 1793, Reports on Kentucky and Virginia* (San Marino, Cal., 1948), p. 111.

42. *Ibid.*

43. *Ibid.*, p. 125.

44. Kimball, *op. cit.*, p. 234.

45. John Melish, *Travels through the United States* (Belfast, Northern Ireland, 1818), p. 315.

46. *Ibid.*, p. 316.

47. *Ibid.*, p. 317.

48. James Dixon, *Methodism in America; With the Personal Narrative of the Author during a Tour through a Part of the United States and Canada* (London, 1849), p. 96.

49. William F. Gray, *From Virginia to Texas, 1835* (Houston, 1909), p. 87.

50. Charles Lyell, *A Second Visit to the United States of North America* (New York, 1849), p. 225.

51. John A. Young, "Traveling in the Middle West in 1838," *Annals of Iowa*, 19 (1933), p. 181.

52. Anne Newport Royall, *Sketches of History, Life, and Manners in the United States, by a Traveler* (New Haven, 1826), p. 46.

53. Atwater, *op. cit.*, p. 230.

54. Richard Lee Mason, *Narrative of Richard Lee Mason in the Pioneer West, 1819* (New York, 1915), p. 17.

55. *Ibid.*

56. William Richardson, *Journal from Boston to the West Country and*

Down the Ohio and Mississippi Rivers to New Orleans, 1815–1816 (New York, 1940), p. 7.

57. John S. Wright, *Letters from the West; Or a Caution to Emigrants* (Salem, N.Y., 1819), p. 13.

58. *Ibid.*, p. 15.

59. John Clark, *Gleanings by the Way* (Philadelphia and New York, 1842), p. 43.

60. *Ibid.*

61. George W. Featherstonhaugh, *A Canoe Voyage up the Minnay Sotar* (London, 1847), p. 33.

62. James Hall, *Letters from the West* (London, 1828), p. 30.

63. Mason, *op. cit.*, Footnote 59, p. 17; Clark, *op. cit.*, p. 43.

64. Thomas Hulme, *Hulme's Journal of a Tour in the Western Countries of America* in Reuben Gold Thwaites (ed.), *Early Western Travels, 1748–1846*, vol. 10 (New York, 1966), p. 79.

65. Clark, *op. cit.*, p. 44.

66. Caswell, *op. cit.*, p. 239.

67. Frances Trollope, *Domestic Manners of the Americans* (London, 1832), p. 88.

68. Ele Bowen, *Rambles in the Path of the Steam-Horse* (Philadelphia, 1855), p. 325.

69. *Ibid.*

70. Wright, *op. cit.*, p. 16.

71. James L. Scott, *A Journal of a Missionary Tour* (Providence, R.I., 1843), p. 61.

72. Weld, *op. cit.*, p. 212.

73. Charles Danbeny, *Journal of a Tour through the United States and in Canada* (Oxford, 1843), p. 181.

74. Mason, *op. cit.*, p. 19.

75. James Stuart, *Three Years in North America* (Edinburgh, 1833), p. 392.

76. Gurney, *op. cit.*, p. 30.

77. Scott, *op. cit.*, p. 34.

78. Edward Abdy, *Journal of a Residence and Tour in the United States of North America* (London, 1833), vol. 1, p. 345.

79. Cuming, *op. cit.*, p. 71.

80. *Ibid.*, p. 200.

81. Ferencz and Theresa Pulszky, *White, Red, Black. Sketches of Society in the United States* (London, 1853), vol. 1, p. 294.

82. Buckingham, *op. cit.*, vol. 2, p. 520.

83. Flint, *op. cit.*, p. 192.

84. Trotter, *op. cit.*, p. 190.

85. Gustavus Wulfing, *The Letters of Gustavus Wulfing* (Fulton, Mo., 1941), p. 104.

86. Fredrika Bremer, *The Houses of the New World; Impressions of America* (New York, 1853), p. 117.

87. Trollope, *op. cit.*, p. 58.

88. *Ibid.*

89. Flint, *op. cit.*, p. 65.

90. *Ibid.*

91. William T. Harris, *Remarks Made during a Tour through the United States of America* (London, 1821), p. 145.

92. Amelia Murray, *Letters from the United States, Cuba, and Canada* (New York, 1856), p. 344.

93. Hall, *op. cit.*, p. 193.

94. *Ibid.*

95. Buckingham, *op. cit.*, vol. 2, p. 435.

96. Josiah Harmar, "Letter to Nicholas Way, March 13, 1789," *Memoirs of the Historical Society of Pennsylvania,* 7 (1860), 440.

97. Hall, *op. cit.*, p. 193.

98. *Ibid.*

99. Josiah Harmer, "Letter to General Knox, Secretary of War, January 14, 1790," *Memoirs of the Historical Society of Pennsylvania,* 7 (1861), 448.

100. Cuming, *op. cit.*, p. 232.

101. Morris Birkbeck, *Notes on a Journey in America, from the Coast of Virginia to the Territory of Illinois* (London, 1817), p. 78.

102. *Ibid.*

103. George W. Ogden, *Letters from the West, Comprising a Tour through the Western Country, and a Residence of Two Summers in the States of Ohio and Kentucky* (New Bedford, Mass., 1823), p. 19.

104. *Ibid.*, p. 36.

105. William Bullock, *Sketch of a Journey through the Western States of North America* (Cincinnati, 1827), p. xvi.

106. Trollope, *op. cit.*, p. 36.

107. Atwater, *op. cit.*, p. 6.

108. *Ibid.*

109. Karl Postl [Charles Sealsfield], *The Americans as They Are: Described in a Tour through the Valley of the Mississippi* (London, 1828), p. 1.

110. Trollope, *op. cit.*, p. 36.

111. *Ibid.*, p. 39.

112. Karl Arfwedson, *The United States and Canada* (London, 1834), p. 128.

113. *Ibid.*

114. Michel Chevalier, *Society and Manners in North America* (Boston, 1839), p. 191.

115. *Ibid.*, p. 195.

116. Charles Hoffman, *A Winter in the Far West* (London, 1835), vol. 2, p. 125.

117. G[eorge] Lewis, *Impressions of America and the American Churches* (Edinburgh, 1845), p. 311.

118. Thomas H. James, *Rambles in the United States and Canada* (London, 1846), p. 137.

119. Moritz Busch, *Wanderungen zwischen Hudson und Mississippi* (Stuttgart and Tübingen, 1854), vol. 1, p. 31.

120. Melish, *op. cit.*, p. 361.

121. Trollope, *op. cit.*, p. 40.

122. *Ibid.*, p. 38.

123. Frederick Marryat, *A Diary in America, with Remarks on Its Institutions* (Philadelphia, 1839), p. 259.

124. Charles Dickens, *American Notes for General Circulation* (London, 1855), p. 112.

125. *Ibid.*

126. Weld, *op. cit.*, p. 205.

127. Charles Lyell, *Travels in North America* (London, 1845), vol. 1, p. 72.

128. James Booty, *Three Months in Canada and the United States* (London, 1862), p. 22.

129. Lewis, *op. cit.*, p. 313.

130. Bullock, *op. cit.*, p. xvi.

131. Bradley, *op. cit.*, p. 218.

132. *Ibid.*

133. Hoffman, *op. cit.*, vol. 2, p. 125.

134. Matilda Houstoun, *Hesperos: Or, Travels in the West* (London, 1850), p. 276.

135. Busch, *op. cit.*, p. 45.

136. *Ibid.*, p. 31.

137. Birkbeck, *op. cit.*, p. 81.

138. *Ibid.*

139. Harriet Martineau, *Society in America* (London, 1837), p. 219.

140. Weld, *op. cit.*, p. 201.

141. Marshall Hall, *The Two-Fold Slavery of the United States; With a Project of Self-Emancipation* (London, 1854), p. 133.

142. Houstoun, *op. cit.*, p. 191.

143. Charles MacKay, *Life and Liberty in America; Or Sketches of a Tour in the United States and Canada* (London, 1859), p. 127.

144. Buckingham, *op. cit.*, vol. 2, p. 394; Ebenezer Davies, *American Scenes and Christian Slavery: A Recent Tour of Four Thousand Miles in the United States* (London, 1849), p. 157.

145. Davies, *op. cit.*, p. 157.

146. Caswell, *op. cit.*, p. 231.

147. Bremer, *op. cit.*, p. 157.

148. *Ibid.*

149. *Ibid.*

150. Davies, *op. cit.*, p. 123.

151. Weld, *op. cit.*, p. 209.

152. *Ibid.*

153. *Ibid.*

154. Chevalier, *op. cit.,* p. 192.

155. Trollope, *op. cit.,* p. 62.

156. Arthur Adams and Sarah A. Risley (eds.), "Daniel Lake Collins' Diary," in *A Genealogy of the Lake Family* (Hartford, 1915), p. 285.

157. Chevalier, *op. cit.,* p. 191.

158. *Ibid.*

159. Lyell, *op. cit.,* vol. 2, p. 218.

160. Lewis, *op. cit.,* p. 311.

161. MacKay, *op. cit.,* p. 137.

162. Edward Dicey, *Six Months in the Federal States* (London, 1863) in Herbert Mitgang (ed.), *Spectator of America* (Chicago, 1971), p. 170.

163. *Ibid.*

164. *Ibid.*

165. Trollope, *op. cit.,* p. 39.

166. Bremer, *op. cit.,* p. 152.

167. Martineau, *op. cit.,* p. 196.

168. Buckingham, *op. cit.,* vol. 2, p. 385.

169. Bullock, *op. cit.,* p. xii.

170. Henry Wadsworth Longfellow, quoted in MacKay, *op. cit.,* p. 130.

171. Trollope, *op. cit.,* p. 105.

172. *Ibid.*

173. *Ibid.*

174. *Ohio Railroad Guide; Illustrated, Cincinnati to Erie Via Columbus and Cleveland* (Columbus, 1854), p. 2.

175. Archibald Prentice, *A Tour in the United States* (London, 1848), p. 42.

176. Birkbeck, *op. cit.,* p. 39.

177. Tyrone Power, *Impressions of America* (London, 1836), p. 315.

178. Arfwedson, *op. cit.,* p. 132.

179. Chevalier, *op. cit.,* p. 173.

180. *Ibid.*

181. William Oliver, *Eight Months in Illinois, with Information to Immigrants* (Newcastle Upon Tyne, 1843), p. 13.

182. Friedrich von Raumer, *America and the American People* (New York, 1846), p. 438.

SELECTED BIBLIOGRAPHY

Travel Journals

1740–1769

Barton, Thomas, "Thomas Barton and the Forbes Expedition," *Pennsylvania Magazine of History and Biography*, 95 (1971), 431–83.

Céloron de Blainville [Bienville], Pierre Joseph de, "Céloron's Journal," Andrew A. Lambing (ed.), *Ohio Archaeological and Historical Quarterly* (1920); reprinted in C. B. Galbreath (ed.), *Expedition of Céloron to the Ohio Country in 1749* (Columbus, Ohio: E. J. Herr, 1921).

Gist, Christopher, "A Journal of Christopher Gist's Journey, Begun . . . October 31, 1750, Continued down the Ohio," in Thomas Pownall, *A Topographical Description of . . . North America* (London: Thomas Pownall, 1776).

Croghan, George, "A Selection of George Croghan's Letter and Journals Relating to Tours into the Western Country—November 16, 1750, to November, 1765," in Reuben Gold Thwaites (ed.), *Early Western Travels, 1478–1846*, vol. 1 (New York: A.M.S. Press, 1966), pp. 45–173.

Gordon, Harry, "Journal of Captain Harry Gordon's Journey from Pittsburgh Down the Ohio and Mississippi to New Orleans, Mobile, and Pensacola, 1766," in Thomas Pownall, *Topographical Description of . . . North America* (London: Thomas Pownall, 1776).

Jemison, Mary, *A Narrative of the Life of Mrs. Mary Jemison* (Canandaigua, N.Y.: J. D. Bemis and Co., 1824); reprinted in Harriet S. Caswell (ed.), *Our Life among the Iroquois Indians* (Boston and Chicago: Congregational Sunday-School and Publishing Society, 1892).

Jennings, John, "Journal from Fort Pitt to Fort Chartres in the Illinois Coun-
    try, March-April, 1766," *Pennsylvania Magazine of History and Bi-
    ography*, 31 (1907), 145–56.
Post, Frederick, "Two Journals of Western Tours, By Charles Frederick
    Post: One, to the Neighborhood of Fort DuQuesne (July and Sep-
    tember, 1758); The Other, to the Ohio (October, 1758 to January,
    1759)," in Reuben Gold Thwaites (ed.), *Early Western Travels,
    1748–1846*, vol. 1 (New York: A.M.S. Press, 1966), 185–291.
Smith, James, *An Account of the Remarkable Occurrences in the Life and
    Travels of Col. James Smith, Now a Citizen of Bourbon County, Ken-
    tucky, During His Captivity with the Indians in the Years 1755,
    1756, 1757, 1758, and 1759* . . . (Lexington, Ky.: John Bradford,
    1799); reprinted in Howard H. Peckham (ed.), *Narratives of Colo-
    nial America 1704–1760* (Chicago: R. R. Donnelley and Sons, 1971).
Stuart, Charles, "The Captivity of Charles Stuart, 1755–57," Beverley W.
    Bond, Jr. (ed.), *Mississippi Valley Historical Review*, 13 (1926),
    58–81.
Taylor, G. A., *A Voyage to North America Perform'd by G. Taylor of Shef-
    field, in the Years 1768 and 1769* . . . *Up the River Mississippi to
    the Illinois and Down from Fort Chartres over the Ohio River* (Not-
    tingham: S. Cresswell for the Author, 1771).
Timberlake, Henry, *The Memoirs of Lieut. Henry Timberlake* (London: the
    Author, 1765).
Trent, William, *Journal of Captain William Trent from Logstown to Picka-
    willany A.D. 1752*, Alfred E. Goodman (ed.) (Cincinnati: R. Clarke,
    1871).
Walker, Thomas, *Journal of an Exploration in the Year 1750* (Boston: Little,
    Brown, 1888).
Washington, George, "Journal, October 31, 1753, to January 16, 1754," and
    "Journal, March 31 to June 27, 1754," in John C. Fitzpatrick (ed.),
    The Diaries of George Washington, 1748–1799 (Boston: Houghton
    Mifflin, 1925).
Weiser, Conrad, "Journal of a Tour to the Ohio, August 11 to October 2,
    1748," in Reuben Gold Thwaites (ed.), *Early Western Travels, 1748–
    1846*, vol. 1 (New York: A.M.S. Press, 1966), pp. 21–44.

1770–1789

Clark, George Rogers, "George Rogers Clark Papers, 1771–1781," James A.
    James (ed.), *Illinois Historical Collections*, 8 (1912), 114–54, 164–
    74, 208–302.
Cresswell, Nicholas, *The Journal of Nicholas Cresswell 1774–1777* (New
    York: Dial Press, 1924).
Cutler, Manasseh, "Journal of a Journey from Ipswich, Massachusetts, to the
    Muskingum, in 1788," in William P. and Julia P. Cutler (eds.), *The
    Life, Journals, and Correspondence of Manasseh Cutler, LL.D.* (Cin-
    cinnati: R. Clarke, 1888).

Denny, Ebenezer, *Military Journal of Major Ebenezer Denny* (Philadelphia: J. B. Lippincott, 1859).

Fleming, William, "Journal of Travel in Kentucky, 1779–1780 and 1783," in N. D. Mereness (ed.), *Travels In the American Colonies* (New York: Macmillan, 1916), pp. 615–74.

Forman, Samuel S., *Narrative of a Journey down the Ohio and Mississippi in 1789–1790* (Cincinnati: R. Clarke, 1888).

Hamilton, Henry, *Journal of Henry Hamilton*, John D. Barnhart (ed.) (Crawfordsville, Ind.: R. E. Banta, 1951).

Heckewelder, John Gottlieb, "A Canoe Journey from the Big Beaver to the Tuscarawes in 1773: A Travel Diary of John Heckewelder," August C. Mahr (ed.), *Ohio Archaeological and Historical Quarterly*, 61 (1952), 283–98.

Hutchins, Thomas, *A Topographical Description of Virginia, Pennsylvania, Maryland, and North Carolina* (London: 1778); Frederick Chartes Hicks (ed.) (Cleveland: Arthur H. Clark, 1904).

Jones, David, *A Journal of Two Visits Made to Some Nations of Indians on the West Side of the River Ohio, in the Years 1772 and 1773* (New York: Joseph Sain, 1865).

Knight, John, and John Slover, *Indian Atrocities, Narratives of the Perils and Sufferings of Dr. John Knight and John Slover among the Indians during the Revolutionary War*, reprinted in John B. Linn (ed.), "The Sandusky Expedition," *Pennsylvania Archives*, 2nd Series, 14 (1892), 704–44.

May, John, *Journals and Letters of Col. John May of Boston Relative to Two Journeys to the Ohio Country In 1788 and 1789* (Cincinnati: R. Clarke, 1873).

Montgomery, Samuel, "A Journey through the Indian Country beyond the Ohio, 1785," *Mississippi Valley Historical Review*, 2 (1915), 261–73.

Ridout, Thomas, "An Account of My Capture by the Shawanese Indians Dwelling on the River in North America and of My Residence among Them during the Spring and Part of the Summer of the Year 1788," *Blackwood's Magazine*, 223 (1928), 289–314.

Schoepf, Johann D., *Travels In the Confederation* [1783–1784], Alfred J. Morrison (ed.) (Philadelphia: William J. Campbell, 1911).

Smith, James, "Tours Into Kentucky and the Northwest Territory—1783 [?]—1795–1797," Josiah Morrow (ed.), *Ohio Archaeological and Historical Quarterly*, 16 (1907), 348–401.

1790–1809

Anonymous, "Daily Journal of Wayne's Campaign from Green Ville to Fallen Timbers, 1794, [attributed to Lieutenant John Bowyer (Boyer)]," edited by Dwight L. Smith, *From Green Ville to Fallen Timbers, A Journal of the Wayne Campaign, July 28-September 14, 1794* (Indianapolis: Indiana Historical Society Publications), 16:3 (1952), 237–333.

Ashe, Thomas, *Travels in America Performed in 1806 for the Purpose of Exploring the Rivers Allegheny, Monongahela, Ohio, and Mississippi* (London: Richard Phillips, 1808).

Bacon, David, "An Unsuccessful Mission to the Shawanese, 1802," *Northwest Ohio Quarterly*, 15 (1944), 22–40.

Bunn, Matthew, *A Journal of the Adventures of Matthew Bunn, a Native of Brookfield, Massachusetts, Who Enlisted . . . in the Year 1791 on a Expedition into the Western Country—Was Taken by the Savages and Made His Escape into Detroit the 30th of April, 1792* (Providence, R.I.: Litchfield, 1796); reprinted as "The Life and Adventures of Matthew Bunn," *Buffalo Historical Society Publications*, 7 (1904), 377–436.

Chambers, Charlotte, "Diary," in Lewis H. Garrard (ed.), *Memoir of Charlotte Chambers* (Philadelphia: Printed for the Author, 1856).

Clark, William, "William Clark's Journal of General Wayne's Campaign," *Mississippi Valley Historical Review*, 1 (1914–15), 418–44.

Collot, George Henri, *A Journey in North America* [1796] (Paris: Arthur Bertrand, 1826).

Condict, Lewis, "Journal of a Trip to Kentucky in 1795," *New Jersey Historical Society Proceedings*, New Series, 4 (1919), 103–27.

Cramer, Zodak, *The Navigator; Containing Directions for Navigating the Monongahela, Allegheny, Ohio and Mississippi Rivers* (Pittsburgh: Cramer, Spear, and Eichbaum, 1804).

Cuming, F[ortescue], *Sketches of a Tour to the Western Country, through the States of Ohio and Kentucky* (Pittsburgh: Cramer, Spear, and Eichbaum, 1810), in Reuben Gold Thwaites (ed.), *Early Western Travels, 1748–1846*, vol. 4 (New York: A.M.S. Press, 1966), 25–377.

Espy, Josiah, *Memorandums of a Tour Made by Josiah Espy in the States of Ohio and Kentucky and Indiana Territory in 1805* (Cincannati: R. Clarke, 1870).

Harris, Thaddeus Mason, *Journal of a Tour into the Territory Northwest of the Alleghany Mountains; Made in the Spring of the Year 1803* (Boston: Manning and Loring, 1805); reprinted in Reuben Gold Thwaites (ed.), *Early Western Travels, 1748–1846*, vol. 3 (New York: A.M.S. Press, 1966), 309–82.

Hastings, Sally, *Poems on Different Subjects to which Is Added a Descriptive Account of a Family Tour to the West in the Year 1800, in a Letter to a Lady* (Lancaster, Pa.: William Dickson, 1808).

Imlay, Gilbert, *A Topographical Description of the Western Territory of North America* (London: J. Debrett, 1792).

Johonnot, Jackson, *The Remarkable Adventures of Jackson Johonnot of Massachusetts: Who Served As a Soldier in the Western Army—in the Expedition under General Harmar—Containing an Account of His Captivity, Sufferings, and Escape from the Kickapoo Indians* (Lexington, Mass., and Boston: Samuel Hall, 1793).

Ker, Henry, *Travels through the Western Interior of the United States from the Year 1808 up to the Year 1816* (Elizabethtown, N.J.: Author, 1816).

Kluge, John Peter, "Diary from Goshen on the Muskingum to White River, March 24 to May 25, 1801," Lawrence Gipson (ed.), *Indiana Historical Collections*, 23 (1938), 67–101.

Lewis, Meriwether, and Sergeant John Ordway, "The Journals of Captain Meriwether Lewis and Sergeant John Ordway Kept on the Expedition of Western Exploration, 1803–1804," Milo M. Quaife (ed.), *Wisconsin Historical Society Collections*, 22 (1916), 31–402.

Michaux, André, "Journal of Travels into Kentucky, July 15, 1793, to April 11, 1796," in Reuben Gold Thwaites (ed.), *Early Western Travels, 1748–1846*, vol. 3 (New York: A.M.S. Press, 1966), 25–104.

Michaux, François A., *Travels to the West of the Alleghany Mountains in the States of Ohio, Kentucky, and Tennessee* (London: 1805), in Reuben Gold Thwaites (ed.), *Early Western Travels, 1748–1846*, vol. 3 (New York: A.M.S. Press, 1966), 109–306.

Newman, Samuel, "A Picture of the First United States Army: The Journal of Captain Samuel Newman," Milo M. Quaife (ed.), *Wisconsin Magazine of History*, 2 (1918), 40–73.

Parry, Needham, "The Journal Of Needham Parry, 1794," *Kentucky Historical Society Register*, 34 (1936), 379–91.

Schultz, Christian, *Travels on an Inland Voyage through the States of New York, Pennsylvania, Ohio, Virginia, Kentucky and Tennessee and through the Territories of Indiana, Louisiana, Mississippi, and New Orleans; Performed in the Years 1807 and 1808* (New York: Isaac Riley, 1810).

Stuart, John C., "A Journal Remarks Or Observations in a Voyage down the Kentucky, Ohio, Mississippi Rivers Etc.," *Kentucky Historical Society Register*, 50 (1952), 5–25.

Volney, C[onstantine] F., *View of the Climate and Soil of the United States of America* (London: J. Johnson, 1804).

1810–1819

Bacon, Lydia B., "Mrs. Lydia B. Bacon's Journal, 1811–1812," Mary M. Crawford (ed.), *Indiana Magazine of History*, 40 (1944), 367–86; 41 (1945), 59–79.

Birkbeck, Morris, *Notes on a Journey in America from the Coast of Virginia to the Territory of Illinois*, 4th ed. (London: James Ridgway, 1818).

Buttrick, Tilly, Jr., *Voyages, Travels and Discoveries* (Boston: 1831), in Reuben Gold Thwaites (ed.), *Early Western Travels, 1748–1846*, 8 (New York: A.M.S. Press, 1966), 17–89.

Cotton, John, "From Rhode Island to Ohio In 1815," *Journal of American History*, 16 (1922), 36–49, 249–60.

Dean, Thomas, "Journal of Thomas Dean, A Voyage to Indiana in 1817,"

John C. Dean (ed.), *Indiana Historical Society Publications*, 6 (1918), 273–345.

Dwight, Margaret Van Horn, *A Journey to Ohio in 1810 As Recorded in the Journal of Margaret Van Horn Dwight*, Max Farrand (ed.) (New Haven: Yale University Press, 1914).

Evans, Estwick, *A Pedestrian Tour of Four Thousand Miles, through the Western States and Territories during the Winter and Spring of 1818* (Concord, N.H.: Joseph C. Spear, 1819), in Reuben Gold Thwaites (ed.), *Early Western Travels, 1748–1846*, vol. 8 (New York: A.M.S. Press, 1966), 101–364.

Faux, William, *Memorable Days in America: Being a Journal of a Tour to the United States* (London: W. Simpkin and R. Marshall, 1823), in Reuben Gold Thwaites (ed.), *Early Western Travels, 1748–1846*, vol. 11 (New York: A.M.S. Press, 1966), 16–305; 12, 11–138.

Fearon, Henry Bradshaw, *Sketches of America, A Narrative of a Journey of Five Thousand Miles through the Eastern and Western States of America* (London: Longman, Hurst, Rees, Orme, and Brown, 1819).

Flint, James, *Letters from America Containing Observations on the Climatic and Agriculture of the Western States* (Edinburgh: W. and C. Tait, 1822).

Flower, Richard, *Letters from Lexington and the Illinois Containing a Brief Account of the English Settlement in the Latter Territory* (London: J. Ridgway, 1819), in Reuben Gold Thwaites (ed.), *Early Western Travels, 1748–1846*, vol. 10 (New York: A.M.S. Press, 1966), 85–169.

Fordham, Elias Pym, *Personal Narrative of Travels in Virginia, Maryland, Pennsylvania, Ohio, Kentucky, and of a Residence in the Indiana Territory, 1817–1818*, Frederic A. Ogg (ed.) (Cleveland: Arthur H. Clarke, 1906).

Harris, William Tell, *Remarks Made during a Tour through the United States of America In 1817, 1818, and 1819* (London: Sherwood, Neely, and Jones, 1821).

Hulmes, Thomas, *Hulmes' Journal of a Tour in the Western Countries of America, September 30, 1818 to August 8, 1819*, extracted and reprinted from William Cobbett's *A Year's Residence in the United States of America* (London, 1828) in Reuben Gold Thwaites (ed.), *Early Western Travels, 1748–1846*, vol. 10 (New York: A.M.S. Press, 1966), 16–84.

Mason, Richard Lee, *Narrative of Richard Lee Mason in the Pioneer West, 1819* (New York: Chas. and Fred. Heartman, 1915).

Melish, John, *Travels through the United States of America in the Years 1806 and 1807, and 1809, 1810, and 1811 . . . With Corrections and Improvements till 1815* (Belfast: Reprinted by J. Smyth, 1818).

Montule, Édouard de, *Voyage en Amérique* (Paris: De Ianney, *et al.*, 1821); translated in part into English by Edward D. Seeber (Bloomington, Ind.: Indiana University Press, 1951).

Schermerhorn, John F., and Samuel J. Mills, *A Correct View of that Part of the United States Which Lies West of the Allegheny Mountains, with Regard to Religion and Morals* (Hartford, Conn.: Peter B. Gleason, 1814).

Thomas, David, *Travels Through the Western Country in the Summer of 1816, Including Notices of the Natural History, Antiquities, Topography, Agriculture, Commerce and Manufactures* (Auburn, N.Y.: David Rumsey, 1819).

Watson, John J., Jr., "The Journey of a Pennsylvania Quaker to Pioneer Ohio," *Bulletin, Cincinnati Historical Society*, 26 (1968), 3–40.

Welby, Adlard, *A Visit to North America and the English Settlements in Illinois* (London: J. Drury, 1821), in Reuben Gold Thwaites (ed.), *Early Western Travels, 1748–1846*, vol. 12 (New York: A.M.S. Press, 1966), 139–341.

Wright, John S., *Letters from the West; Or a Caution to Emigrants: Being Facts and Observations Respecting the States of Ohio, Indiana, Illinois, and Some Parts of New-York, Pennsylvania and Kentucky* (Salem, N.Y.: Dodd & Stevenson, 1819).

1820–1829

Atwater, Caleb, *Remarks Made on a Tour to Prairie Du Chien; Thence To Washington City In 1829* (Columbus: Isaac N. Whiting, 1831).

Bullock, William, *Sketch of a Journey through the Western States of North America from New Orleans, By the Mississippi, Ohio, City of Cincinnati and Falls of the Niagara to New York in 1827* (Cincinnati: B. Drake and E. D. Mansfield, 1827).

Brown, Paul, *Twelve Months in New Harmony; Presenting a Faithful Account of the Principal Occurrences Which Have Taken Place There within that Period* (Cincinnati: William Hill Woodward, 1827).

[Evarts, Jeremiah], *Through the South and West . . . In 1826*, J[ames] Orin Oliphant (ed.) (Lewisburg, Pa.: Bucknell University Press, 1956).

Flint, Timothy, *Recollections of the Last Ten Years Passed in Occasional Residences and Journeyings in the Valley of the Mississippi* (Boston: Cummings, Hilliard, 1826).

Hall, Basil, *Travels in North America, in the Years 1827 and 1828* (Edinburgh: Robert Cadell, 1830).

Hall, Mrs. Basil [Margaret], "Letters of Mrs. Basil Hall, 1827–1828," in Una Pope-Hennessy (ed.), *The Aristocratic Journey* (New York: G. P. Putnam's Sons, 1931).

Hall, James, *Letters from the West; Containing Sketches of Scenery, Manners, and Customs; and Anecdotes Connected with the First Settlements of the Western Sections of the United States* (London: Henry Colburn, 1828).

Hall, William, "From England to Illinois in 1821. The Journal of William

Hall," Jay Monaghan (ed.), *Journal, Illinois State Historical Society,* 39 (1946), 21–67, 208–53.

Ogden, George W., *Letters from the West, Comprising a Tour Through the Western Country, And a Residence of Two Summers in the States of Ohio and Kentucky* (New Bedford, Mass.: Melcher and Rogers, 1823), in Reuben Gold Thwaites (ed.), *Early Western Travels, 1748–1846,* vol. 19 (New York: A.M.S. Press, 1966), 20–112.

Owen, William, "Diary of William Owen, from November 10, 1824, to April 20, 1825," Joel W. Hiatt (ed.), *Indiana Historical Society Publications,* 4 (1906), 1–134.

Owen, Robert Dale, "Travel Journal, 1825–1826," in Joseph M. Elliott (ed.), *To Holland and to New Harmony, Robert Dale Owen's Travel Journal, 1825–1826* (Indianapolis: Indiana Historical Society Publication, vol. 23, part 4, 1969).

Postl, Karl [Charles Sealsfield, pseud.], *The Americans As They Are: Described in a Tour through the Valley of the Mississippi* (London: Hurst, Chance, 1828).

Reed, Isaac, *The Christian Traveller in Five Parts including Nine Years and Eighteen Thousand Miles* (New York: J. and J. Harper, 1828).

Schoolcraft, Henry R., *Travels in the Central Portion of the Mississippi Valley* (New York: Collins and Hannay, 1825).

Suchard, Philippe, *Meine Besuch Amerika's Im Sommer 1824* (Neuchatel: La Baconnière, Boudry, 1947).

The Rambler, Or a Tour through Virginia, Tennessee, Alabama, Mississippi and Louisiana; Describing the Climate, the Manners, Customs and Religion of the Inhabitants . . . By a Citizen of Maryland (Annapolis: J. Green, 1828).

Trollope, Frances, *Domestic Manners of the Americans* (London: Whittaker, Treacher, 1832).

Woods, John, *Two Years' Residence in the Settlement on the English Prairie in the Illinois Country* (London: Longman, Hurst, Rees, Orme, and Brown, 1822); reprinted in Paul M. Angle (ed.), *Two Year's Residence on the English Prairie in Illinois* (Chicago: R. R. Donnelly, 1968).

1830–1839

Abdy, Edward Strutt, *Journal of a Residence and Tour in the United States of North America, from April, 1833 to October, 1834* (London: J. Murray, 1833).

Audubon, John James, *Ornithological Biography, Or an Account of the Habits of the Birds of the United States of America . . . Interspersed with Delineations of American Scenery and Manners,* 5 vols. (Edinburgh: Adams Black, *et al.* [vol. 1] and Adam and Charles Black, *et al.* [vols. 2–5], 1831–39); reprinted as *Delineations of American Scenery and Character* (New York: Arno and The New York Times, 1970).

Bradley, Cyrus P., "Journal of Cyrus P. Bradley," *Ohio Archaeological and Historical Quarterly*, 15 (1906), 207–70.

Buckingham, James Silk, *The Slave States of America* (London and Paris: Fisher, Son & Co. [1842]).

Chevalier, Michel, *Lettres sur l'Amérique du Nord* (Paris: Charles Gosselin and Co., 1836; translated and reprinted as *Society, Manners, and Politics in the United States; Being a Series of Letters in North America*, Thomas G. Bradford (ed.) (Boston: Weeks, Jordan, 1839).

Clark, John Alonso, *Gleanings by the Way* (Philadelphia: W. J. and J. K. Simon; New York: R. Carter, 1842).

Davidson, Robert, *An Excursion to the Mammoth Cave and the Barrens of Kentucky, with Some Notices of the Early Settlement of the State* (Philadelphia: Thomas Cowperthwait, 1840).

Featherstonhaugh, George William, *A Canoe Voyage Up the Minnay Sotor; With an Account of the Lead and Copper Deposits in Wisconsin; Of the Gold Region in the Cherokee Country; and Sketches of Popular Manners* (London: R. Bentley, 1847).

Ferrall, S. A. [O'Ferrall, Simon Ansley], *A Ramble of Six Thousand Miles through the United States of America* (London: Effingham Wilson, 1832).

[Flagg, Edmond], *The Far West: Or a Tour Beyond the Mountains* (New York: Harper and Brothers, 1838), in Reuben Gold Thwaites (ed.), *Early Western Travels, 1748–1846* (New York: A.M.S. Press, 1966), vol. 26, 21–370; vol. 27, 13–121.

Hall, Frederick, *Letters from the East and from the West* (Baltimore: F. Taylor and William M. Morrison, 1840).

Henshaw, Hiram, "A Diary Written By Captain Hiram Henshaw Describing His Journey To Kentucky January 4, 1830, to May 15, 1830," in Mabel Henshaw Gardiner and Ann Henshaw Gardiner, *Chronicles of Old Berkeley, A Narrative History of a Virginia County from Its Beginning to 1926* (Durham, N.C.: The Seeman Press, 1938).

Higbee, Lucy Ann, *The Diary of Lucy Ann Hisbee* (Cleveland: privately printed, 1924).

Hoby, James, and F. A. Cox, *The Baptists in America; A Narrative of the Deputation from the Baptist Union in England to the United States and Canada* (London: Ward, 1836).

Hoffman, C[harles] F., *A Winter in the Far West* (London: Richard Bentley, 1835).

Irving, Washington, *The Western Journals of Washington Irving*, John F. McDermott (ed.) (Norman: University of Oklahoma Press, 1944).

Lillybridge, Dr. C., "Journey of a Party of Cherokee Emigrants [1837]," Grant Foreman (ed.), *Mississippi Valley Historical Review*, 18 (1931–32), 232–45.

Martineau, Harriet, *Retrospect of Western Travel* (London: Saunders and Otley, 1838).

———, *Society in America* (London: Saunders and Otley, 1837).

Marryat, Frederick, *Diary in America, with Remarks on Its Inhabitants* (Philadelphia: Carey and Hart, 1839); reprinted as *Diary in America*, Jules Zanger (ed.) (Bloomington: Indiana University Press, 1960).

Power, Tyrone, *Impressions of America, During the Years 1833, 1834, and 1835* (London: Richard Bentley, 1836).

Rafinesque, C[onstantine] S., *A Life of Travels and Researches in North America and South Europe Or Outlines of the Life, Travels, and Researches of C. S. Rafinesque* (Philadelphia: F. Turner, 1836).

Reed, Andrew and James Matheson, *A Narrative of the Visit to the American Churches by the Deputation from the Congregational Union of England and Wales* (New York: Harper and Brothers, 1835).

Royall, Anne Newport, *Mrs. Royall's Southern Tour, or, Second Series of the Black Book*, 3 vols. (Washington, D.C.: Author, 1830–31).

Stuart, James, *Three Years in North America* (Edinburgh: Robert Cadell, 1833).

Vigne, Godfrey Thomas, *Six Months in America* (London: Whittaker, Treacher, 1832).

Wied-Neuwied, Maximilian Alexander Philipp, Prinz von, *Travels in the Interior of North America* (London: Ackermann, 1843); in Reuben Gold Thwaites (ed.), *Early Western Travels, 1748–1846*, vol. 22 (New York: A.M.S. Press, 1966).

Willson, Elizabeth Lundy, *A Journey in 1836 from New Jersey to Ohio, Being the Diary of* [Mrs.] *Elizabeth Lundy Willson*, William C. Armstrong (ed.) (Morrison, Ill.: Shawver Pub., 1929).

Wulfing, Gustavus, *The Letters of Gustavus Wulfing, Collected by his Grandson*, Carl Hirsch (ed.) (St. Louis and Fulton, Mo.: Ovid Bell Press, 1941).

1840–1849

Baxter, Henry, "Rafting on the Alleghany and Ohio, 1844," *Pennsylvania Magazine of History and Biography*, 51 (1927), 27–78, 143–71, 207–43.

Bremer, Fredrika, *The Homes of the New World; Impressions of America* (New York: Harper and Brothers, 1853).

Buckingham, J[ames] S., *The Eastern and Western States of America*, 2 vols. (London: Fisher, Son, [1840]).

Bullitt, Alexander Clark, *Rambles in the Mammoth Cave during the Year 1844 by a Visitor* (Louisville: Mouton and Griswold, 1845).

Chase, Philander, *Bishop Chase's Reminiscenses; An Autobiography; Second Edition; Comprising a History of the Principal Events in the Author's Life to A.D. 1847* (Boston: Dow, 1848).

Dickens, Charles, *American Notes for General Circulation* (London: Chapman and Hall, 1842).

Dixon, James, *Methodism in America; With the Personal Narrative of the Author during a Tour through a Part of the United States and Canada* (London: John Mason, 1849).

Dole, William P., "William P. Dole: Wabash Valley Merchant and Flatboat-man," *Indiana Magazine of History*, 67 (1971), 335–63.

Fawcett, Jos. W., *Journal of Jos. W. Fawcett (Diary of his Trip down the Ohio and Mississippi Rivers to the Gulf of Mexico and up the Atlantic Coast to Boston)*, Eugene Rigney (ed.) (Chillicothe, Ohio: David K. Webb, 1944).

Harker, J. G., *Report about and from America Given from First-Hand Observation in the Years 1848 and 1849* (Leipzig, 1849); translated from the original German by Richard B. O'Connell (ed.) in *Mississippi Valley Collection Bulletin*, 3 (1970), 1–74.

Hone, Philip, *The Diary of Philip Hone, 1828–1851*, Bayard Tuckerman (ed.) (New York: Dodd, Mead, 1889); reprinted by Allan Nevins (ed.) (New York: Dodd, Mead, 1927).

Lewis, G[eorge], *Impressions of America and the American Churches* (Edinburgh: W. P. Kennedy, 1845).

Lyell, Charles, *A Second Visit to the United States of North America* (New York: Harper and Brothers, 1849).

————, *Travels in North America; with Geological Observations on the United States, Canada, and Nova Scotia* (London: J. Murray, 1846).

Oliver, William, *Eight Months in Illinois with Information to Emigrants* (Newcastle Upon Tyne: William Andrew Mitchell, 1843).

Raumer, Friedrich Ludwig Georg von, *America and the American People*, William W. Turner (ed.) (New York: J. & H. G. Langley, 1846).

Sarmiento, Domingo F[austino], *Travels in the United States in 1847*, Michael Aaron Rockland (ed.), *Sarmiento's Travels in the United States in 1847* (Princeton: Princeton University Press, 1970).

Scott, James Leander, *A Journal of a Missionary Tour through Pennsylvania, Ohio, Indiana, Illinois, Iowa, Wiskonsin, and Michigan* (Providence: the Author, 1843).

Steele, Eliza R., *A Summer Journey in the West* (New York: J. S. Taylor, 1841).

Whipple, Henry Benjamin, *Bishop Whipple's Southern Diary, 1843–1844*, Lester B. Shipper (ed.) (Minneapolis: University of Minnesota Press, 1937).

Whitman, Walt, "Excerpts from a Traveller's Note Book—Nos. 1, 2, and 3," in Emory Holloway (ed.), *The Uncollected Poetry and Prose of Walt Whitman* (New York: Doubleday Page, 1921), vol. I, 181–90; Vol. II, 77–78.

Wortley, Emmeline Stuart, *Travels in the United States, Etc., during 1849 and 1850* (New York: Harper and Brothers, 1851).

1850–1860

Beste, John Richard, *The Wabash: Or Adventures of an English Gentleman's Family in the Interior of America* (London: Hurst and Blackett, 1855).

Bowen, Ele, *Rambles in the Path of the Steam-Horse* (Philadelphia: Wm. Bromwell and Wm. Smith, 1855).

Busch, Moritz, *Wanderungen zwischen Hudson und Mississippi, 1851 und 1852* (Stuttgart und Tübingen: J. G. Cotta'scher, 1854).

Foster, Lillian, *Wayside Glimpses, North and South* (New York: Rudd and Carleton, 1859).

Grandfort, Marie Fontenay, Mme. Manöel, *The New World*, E. C. Wharton (ed.) (New Orleans: Sherman, Wharton, 1855).

Houstoun, Matilda Charlotte (Jesse) Fraser, *Hesperos: Or, Travels in the West* (London: John W. Parker, 1850).

Jobson, Frederick James, *America and American Methodism* (London: J. S. Virtue, 1857).

LaKier, Alexander, "A View of Cincinnati in 1857," *Bulletin, Cincinnati Historical Society*, 29 (1971), 28–51.

Murray, Amelia Matilda, *Letters from the United States, Cuba, and Canada* (New York: G. P. Putnam, 1856).

Murray, Henry A., *Lands of the Slave and the Free: Or, Cuba, the United States, and Canada* (London: John W. Parker and Son, 1855).

Ohio Railroad Guide, Illustrated, Cincinnati to Erie Via Columbus and Cleveland (Columbus: Ohio State Journal Co., 1854).

Olmsted, Frederick Law, *A Journey in the Back Country in the Winter of 1853–54* (New York: Mason Brothers, 1860).

Parsons, Charles Grandison, *Inside View of Slavery: Or, A Tour among the Planters* (Boston: J. P. Jewett; Cleveland: O. Jewett, Proctor, and Worthington, 1855).

Pulszky, Ferencz A. and Theresa Pulszky, *White, Red, Black. Sketches of Society in the United States* (London: Trübner and Co., 1853).

Stirling, James, *Letters from the Slave States* (London: John W. Parker & Son, 1857).

Thornbury, George Walter, *Criss-cross Journeys* (London: Hurst and Blackett, 1873).

Tower, Philo, *Slavery Unmasked: Being a Truthful Narrative of Three Years' Residence and Journeying in Eleven Southern States* (Rochester: E. Darrow and Brother, 1856).

Trotter, Isabella (Strange), *First Impressions of the New World on Two Travellers from the Old in the Autumn of 1858* (London: Longman, Brown, Green, Longmans, and Roberts, 1859).

Weld, Charles Richard, *A Vacation Tour in the United States and Canada* (London: Longman, Brown, Green, and Longmans, 1855).

Willis, Nathaniel Parker, *Health Trip to the Tropics* (New York: C. Scribner, 1853).

SECONDARY SOURCES

Abernethy, Thomas P., *Three Virginia Frontiers* (Baton Rouge: Louisiana University Press, 1940).

Arnow, Harriette S., *Flowering of the Cumberland* (New York: Macmillan, 1963).

Berger, Max, *The British Traveler in America, 1836–1860* (New York: Columbia University Press, 1943).

Bond, B. W., *The Civilization of the Old Northwest* (New York: Macmillan, 1934).

Buley, R. Carlyle, *The Old Northwest, Pioneer Period, 1815–1840* (Bloomington: Indiana University Press, 1950).

Caruso, John, *The Southern Frontier* (Indianapolis: Bobbs-Merrill, 1963).

Clark, Thomas D. (ed.), *Travels in the Old South: A Bibliography*, 3 vols. (Norman: University of Oklahoma Press, 1956).

Deakin, Motley F., *The Home Book of the Picturesque: Or American Scenery, Art, and Literature* (New York: G. P. Putnam, 1852).

Downes, Randolph C., *Frontier Ohio, 1788–1803* (Columbus: Ohio State Archaeological and Historical Society, 1935).

Drake, Daniel, *Pioneer Life in Kentucky* (Cincinnati: R. Clarke, 1870).

Dunbar, Seymour, *A History of Travel in America* (Indianapolis: Bobbs-Merrill, 1915).

Esarey, Logan, *The Indiana Home* (Crawfordsville, Ind.: R. E. Banta, 1943).

Filson, John, *Discovery, Settlement, and Present State of Kentucke* (Wilmington [Del.]: James Adams, 1784).

Hildreth, S. P., *Pioneer History* (Cincinnati: H. W. Derby, 1848).

Hubach, Robert R., *Early Midwestern Travel Narratives: An Annotated Bibliography 1634–1850* (Detroit: Wayne State University Press, 1961).

Jacobs, Wilbur R., *Diplomacy and Indian Gifts; Anglo-French Rivalry along the Ohio and Northwest Frontiers, 1748–1763* (Stanford: Stanford University Press, 1950).

Jordan, Philip D., *The National Road* (Indianapolis: Bobbs-Merrill, 1948).

Mesick, Jane Louise, *The English Traveller in America, 1785–1835* (New York: Columbia University Press, 1922).

Metcalfe, Samuel L., *A Collection of Some of the Most Interesting Narratives of Indian Warfare in the West . . .* (Lexington, Ky.: William G. Hunt, 1821).

Miller, James, *The Genesis of Western Culture: The Upper Ohio Valley, 1800–1825* (Columbus: Ohio State Archaeological and Historical Society, 1938).

Moorman, John J., *The Virginia Springs* (Richmond, Va.: J. W. Randolph, 1854).

Owsley, Frank L., *Plain Folk of the Old South* (Baton Rouge: Louisiana State University Press, 1951).

Paxson, Frederic L., *History of the American Frontier, 1763–1893* (Boston: Houghton Mifflin, 1924).

Rapson, Richard L., *Britons View America, Travel Commentary, 1860–1935* (Seattle: University of Washington Press, 1971).

Rusk, Ralph Leslie, *The Literature of the Middle Western Frontier* (New York: Columbia University Press, 1925).

Silverberg, Robert, *Mound Builders of Ancient America: The Archaeology of a Myth* (Greenwich, Conn.: New York Graphic Society, 1968).

Speed, Thomas, *The Wilderness Road: A Description of the Routes of Travel* (Louisville: The Filson Club, 1886), pp. 34–38.

Toulmin, Henry, *A Description of Kentucky in North America: To Which Are Prefixed Miscellaneous Observations Respecting the United States*, Thomas D. Clark (ed.) (Lexington: University of Kentucky Press, 1945).

————, *The Western Country in 1793: Reports on Kentucky and Virginia by Harry Toulmin*, Marion Tinling and Godfrey Davies (eds.) (San Marino, Calif.: Henry E. Huntington Library and Art Gallery, 1948).

Tuckerman, Henry T., *America and Her Commentators, with a Critical Sketch of Travel in the United States* (New York: Charles Scribner, 1864).

Turner, Frederick, J., *The Frontier in American History* (New York: Holt, 1920).

Vanderbeels, Richard (ed.), *Held Captive by the Indians: Selected Narratives, 1642 to 1836* (Knoxville: University of Tennessee Press, 1973).

Van Every, Dale, *Men of the Western Waters; A Second Look at the First Americans* (Boston: Houghton Mifflin, 1956).

Wade, Richard C., *The Urban Frontier: The Rise of Western Cities, 1790–1830* (Cambridge: Harvard University Press, 1959).

Wright, Louis B., *Culture on the Moving Frontier* (Bloomington: Indiana University Press, 1955).

INDEX